Why Catholics Stay Catholic

Some thoughts from a former priest

By Allan F. Kosack, MA

Dedication

Religions help us deal with sinfulness. People want life lived on a higher level, a level beyond meeting the boss's deadlines and changing diapers. Getting that job done – making real living into the quasi-magical – is religion's task. Believers apply its interpretation to trees, clouds, sunsets and of course church bells.

For that we pay a price. Religions add another element: they treat us as sinners. Everybody. Everyone a sinner. Not very flattering. It's a put-down and degrading. St. Paul says this is basic to his brand of Christianity. Which begs the question: Why do people accept that? Why do they feel it fits our condition?

This book is dedicated to stimulating your enthusiasm for uncovering the answers. It examines St. Paul's ideas about redemption and what makes them attractive. And why he wants women to hide their hair at services. And why the Church won't let women be priests. And why married couples taking their vows first wanted to kneel before their priest. It cites thinkers among the ancient Greeks and the New York Times. Your expositor is worth regarding. He was a priest trained in psychoanalysis.

Contents

Flexing His Muscle

Archbishop Vigeron, the chief Catholic churchman in Michigan, made the open-and-shut case for homosexuals of any religion, or even of no religion at all, when he stated recently that they are somehow flawed human beings if they pursue same-sex partnerships. Their marriages will not be validated, he declared. This dash of heavy-handed authority followed another a couple months ago. That's when he forbade anyone access to the Church's Communion railings if he/she offered any support to the legalization of same-sex marriages. It's about as heavy a hand as he could muster. Listening to or reading his language leaves one with the impression that he'd lead a "new addition of the Spanish Inquisition" if he could. He shows no empathy for the frustration of lovers who are denied their basic rights. He acts like a man who is accustomed to obedience even if he comes off as an unthinking dictator. Those of us brought up under Catholic tutelage have gotten used to it. We've gotten used to some rather ridiculous stuff. Getting unused to it requires actually listening closely to what's being said. Here is a case in point: Catholicism had for centuries disallowed ANY orgasms for ANYBODY unless they occur between a man and a woman by way of their commitment in marriage.

That's harsh. Venereal sensations occur regularly among all post-pubic people. Adjusting to them, learning to live with them, normally occurs in the family setting. Caring parents expect and have a right to expect the community's support, much of it tax-supported. It takes years. Come adulthood the results of patient self-honesty and self-respect return to the community citizens imbued with respect for one's fellows. This highly desirable outcome is not fostered by top–ranked religious authorities condemning all sexual expression they have not "blessed."

Considering the length and depth of the world's problems with all of their complexity the Archbishop is a scandal. What should we do about China's muscling into the South China Sea? Is Israel's policy against statehood for Palestine the best we can hope for? Should the Wall Street executives who sold over-valued mortgages be prosecuted? Millions of Americans don't have health insurance; are there moral factors arising here? Is the Church by-passing its moral responsibility? The Church's authority in the moral realm might broaden society's design for solutions to what troubles it. Confining its focus to matters sexual is a waste of its heft, like swatting flies with a hammer.

A Memoir?

A fine friend* in whom I confided concluded after a lot of listening that I was a conflicted fellow who had looked to the Church for all the answers and found it coming up short. He put this to me: Look what you're doing!   You're grabbing onto another hoped-for absolute. You're putting your hopes on psychoanalytic theory. You're making of it what you failed to find in religion.   He'd heard me say more than once that everyone wants what's truly worthy of one's total giving. Happiness would result if he could invest himself all the way and forever and never have to look back to discover it hadn't been worth it.

I hope to educate my reader on the insights psychoanalytic thinking provides. S/he'll find a lot about that.   But alongside these assertions I will toss its lumens at the Church.   Every human institution - educational, medical, industrial, scientific – I think could profit from such a focus.   I select the Roman Church from among many because I was entwined in its teachings and endeavors. I can speak from experience. What I saw happening to it was not healthy or good. At least that's how I saw it. I hope we can learn from its pitfalls as a guide to what could (and shouldn't) be allowed to happen elsewhere.

I will shine the psychoanalytic light on the currently functioning Church. Additionally I will say some things about what happened to me. Peeling away my normal reserve became easier when I saw doing so would do more than make some interesting reading. Reviewing the modes and manners I took to make sense of what happened to me probably can help lead to another's self-understanding.

*He set up my meeting the woman I married.

As I write this Roy Moore is running for the Senate to replace Jeff Sessions who has become the Attorney General. Moore had already gotten into hot water for ordering his underlings not to obey the Supreme Court's decision to issue marriage licenses to gays. Prior to that when he was an Alabama Supreme Court judge he was rebuked twice for planting monuments of the Ten Commandments on the capitol lawn. What's currently disconcerting is believable testimony that he had unseemly sexual contacts with teenage girls when he was in his early 30s.

He's since become rigid. **Time** magazine (10/30/17) quotes him saying: It is the fallen nature of man that the Constitution meant to restrain. **Time** continues. He's a "...judge who recites anti-abortion poetry, rejects the theory of evolution, doesn't think Muslims should be allowed to serve in Congress, fought to keep antiquated wording in the Alabama constitution requiring school segregation and suggested that the Sept. 11th terrorist attacks were God's punishment for America's sins." Several weeks ago I heard almost those exact words from the lips of a rabbi. I cite him to show that what I'll explain later on as Oedipal consequences don't show up only among Christians. Everyone born of woman picked up distortions about love and sex in their earliest developmental years.

Maybe his dalliances with young girls convinced him that his maleness was sin-prone. About 1600 years earlier St. Augustine (354 – 430) came to similar conclusions. His earlier sexual promptings were of such a volume that he felt helpless when they summoned him. Later on he was to write that they robbed him of choice, of freedom. His intellectual brilliance put together a theology, including a theory Roy Moore would think rings true: all humanity is stained with Original Sin. It holds that the fallout from the disobedience (or independence or free-thinking or just plain curiosity or whatever) of our "first parents", Adam and Eve, means everyone since inherits a "fallen" nature. It was a grim picture Augustine painted. Christianity since has accepted that dour view. Roy Moore and St. Augustine though separated by some 16 centuries have this in common. They both figured if they personally felt sin-prone, then everybody else must also.

It's assuredly our experience that we are born with a hyper responsiveness to violence and sex. But we reject the idea that there's something fundamentally gone wrong with our minds and hearts. Depth psychotherapy uncovers that people feel something's wrong about love and sex, not because love and sex are wrong – our life experience shows them to be good – but our baby experiences got us feeling they were wrong. They lead us into conflicts for which as toddlers we were ill-prepared. They terrorized us to such an extent that we in our first years drove them into unconsciousness. That didn't mean they didn't leave their marks on our developing psyches. Henceforth love-choices and sex were to seem wrong-headed and improper, even unwholesome, compromising our higher nature. They are what Roy Moore and St. Augustine made overly-quick conclusions about. They might have wondered why human love-partnering from which flows all that we hold dear like family and children got to be coated with something evil as if the Creator invented love and sex and then smeared them with a bad odor. Their personal sexual promptings lead them to self-centered conclusions. They didn't look beyond them for other possible meanings.

This book is an attempt to give you a look beyond them.

It's Smart Policy........

Our world has problems galore. The Middle East. The Far East. North Korea. East Africa with an ungovernable Somalia and West Africa plagued with Ebola. Simply pronouncing those titles instantly troubles us; a wide range of nearly unsolvable conflicts faces us. Can we blame the Archbishop for declining to make pronouncements about them if he can get away with it? Answers are hard to come by. Attempting to speak about solutions to big problems will assure a public display of his limitations. He'll wind up looking as fallible a human being as are our leaders who're trying to design answers to complicated questions. He couldn't come off as sure-footedly as he does about sexual matters. He's got to look as infallible as the deity he says he represents. Detroit's Archbishop looks like and talks like the Roman Church has looked and talked since ancient times. Throughout its history it's made a lot of mistakes; it's never been mistaken appealing to mankind's discomfort with sex. Why?   It makes him sound important and pious because we're already predisposed to feel sex is a less than a praiseworthy function. The Archbishop doesn't really make a good feel bad. For all of the goodness sex brings to our lives, we are inclined to feel it's bad. He simply uses that inclination.

You'll notice that he doesn't speak much to the many good things about sex. Not that there's not a lot of good to be said but that would not play to his authority. He's to be the finger-wager as though he's as convinced of sex's evil as you *feel* it to be. He wouldn't sound quite right to be positive about sex.   He sounds appropriate when he advises caution, even abstinence in many cases. A popular Detroit radio host, about whom we'll talk later, made the point without realizing it. We'll see he was over-cautious about sex like the rest of us. That's what gives the Archbishop his power. No one has to inform the Church leader how to comport himself as he takes on the Church's self-appointed task of requiring us what to do to keep our sexual natures in line.   That's because he bears the results from the same kinds of early conflicts regarding love and sex that influenced you and I and the rest of mankind.

Those conflicts make a good thing like sex come off as suspect, wrong-headed and even in some environments as an evil. There is a scene in the 1970s version of the TV adaptation of Alex Haley's book *Roots*. In it a young black couple is walking hand in hand through a large field. They are in love. They are talking about various things, things cheerfully spoken that contrast with the grim lives ahead of them as slaves. Haley wants us to like them and we do.   He accomplishes that with one of them saying what's jarringly out of context: "We haven't as yet made love." Haley dragged that in there because in wanting us to like them he can count on his viewers' inclination to prefer young people who don't have sex.

In ***Fiddler On The Roof*** the writer has a similar challenge. He wants viewers to like the Jews he's presenting in his story and Jews are frequently suspect or even despised; it's much like Haley's purpose of rendering us sympathetic to blacks who also are frequently despised. One scene centers on several young women who are age-appropriate for marriage. Their village's mate-selecting matchmaker is busying herself finding marriage partners for these girls who are untypical in that they sing (***Fiddler*** is a musical) about the problems marital life can occasion and not the optimism young people generally hold toward their marital futures. The writer has to back off on enthusiasm for sex in his subjects if they are to be admired.

There's a pivotal fact about the first months and years of an infant's growth: its love for its mother gets combined with hate.

What happened?

The answer is as complex and as old as humanity. Some masterful thinking got Sophocles to fashion his famous story **Oedipus Rex.** He wrote during ancient Greece's Golden Age. That's when the basics of our Western civilization got set in place, the principles behind mathematics, physics, literature and drama, philosophy and music. Marvelous are the truths they put together early in our history, i.e., some 5-600 years b. c. e.

Sophocles wrote a drama about Oedipus. As a young man he heard some god-sent oracle that 1) he would murder his father and 2) marry his mother. It was an engrossing story even as it was a strange one because it dealt with some scary impressions that occur to all us males when we're mere infants. It told the why and wherefore for the kinds of feelings we had as newborns and what those feelings were about until we got to our fifth and sixth years. (Female infant histories also entangle their opposite-sex parent.) Oedipus took the oracle's message seriously. The very idea repelled him. (It's repugnant to every man.) He spent the following years attempting to prove the oracle's foretelling false. He failed. The years unfolded. When as an old man he realized that he had unknowingly murdered a man who was his father and married the man's wife who was also his mother, he was so stunned - and then guilt-stricken - that he plunged his wife's (mother's) golden broaches into the sockets of his eyes. He punished himself with total blindness. That he killed his father unknowingly and married his mother innocently mattered not at all. No punishment equaled the size of his guilt which he bore even to his death.

Guilt? Why? Sadness, that we understand. But why have guilt? That he had it in abundance we have no doubt. Juries trying murder cases don't condemn respondents who turn out to have accidently and innocently caused someone's death. But who wants to kill his father and marry his mother? The very thought repels. However deep down inside, unconsciously, is the repugnant answer: every one of us; we felt it before we got rational. The Sophocles drama illustrates this with this difference: Oedipus actually kills his father and marries his mother. He actually did both…innocently! Oddly an overwhelming guilt ensued which dis-allowed him to embrace innocence. The murder and marriage felt genuine, like outcomes he somehow wanted. That guilt he could have spared himself if he'd realized that murderous and sexual desires are standard to us all. These two co-exist side by side with a totally consuming love for the "nipple", "breast", "mother". The newborn's organism luxuriates in its total satisfaction. When the breast comes to include a "person" and later the person's lover (daddy), a most discomforting competition – a life and death conflict - follows. It's with baby's opposite sex parent who's seems like a giant. A deeply felt terror of being crushed in the competition had to become unavoidable. More on this later. For now keep the notion that baby comes to feel the love it seeks is wanting what is totally evil. The "crushing" is what it feels is what it's got coming.

These dynamics happen during those earliest months and years of life. And they don't go away.

Sophocles' insight, startling as it is, is basic to understanding human dynamics. His seemingly preposterous story has endured for two and a half millennia. Every person born of woman had conflicts with his/her opposite-sex parent. They occur shortly after birth lasting until we attain the ability to start thinking. That's around age's five to seven. Up until that time what we learn, indeed all we learn, is by way of what we feel.

So far I suppose I've made a skeptic of the reader. I would ask however of her/him to notice one feature about Oedipus' life: he never stopped trying to side-step the Oracle–god's prediction. Because if it became truth he could never forgive himself. Humankind lives life fleeing the same revulsion.

Scary Feelings That Stay

Mother's nurturing breast. It brings absolute contentment. Arnold De Loof, an evolutionist at the Zoological Institute in Leuven, Belgium, writes, "…organisms don't understand…they pursue"…feeling good", i.e. contentment. Baby gets totally distressed should its lips fall from the nipple. Watch it desperately putting all it has into reconnecting. With its lips once again securely around the nipple the absolute comfort comes back. Some psychologists wonder why baby ever advances beyond that supremely all-providing breast.

However trouble is just around the corner. Baby starts to feel he's not all there is. There's a person that comes with the breast. She becomes most dear. No surprise. Baby attaches the person for all she's got with all he's got. Somewhat later another personage's presence gets experienced, an "other" who's looking more and more like a competitor. It's an all or nothing world baby lives in. No greater or lesser, no subtleties, 100% in the one direction or all the way in the other. Baby feels that "other" that's come on the scene. It's total hatred for "that thing" that will turn out to be 1) his father and 2) the "breast's" lover. Another terrifying element: as time goes on its intruder (father) looks to be getting so, so much bigger. The one whom baby hates senses he'll be hated back. To the same degree. He will be crushed.

Side By Side

Two opposing feelings come to exist side by side, loving and hating. Loving a parent and competing with and hating a parent are way, way too much to come to terms with. We've heard a baby's screams. They are intense. Baby really means it. Infants feel! It's deep and thorough from head to toe. This morning I went for a swim in a pool where a part was sectioned off for some young mothers gently introducing their infants to the water. The little ones looked to be ten to eighteen months old. Several babies were calm, held comfortably in their mothers' arms. Others however were screaming their lungs out. The new experience was frightening and they were totally given over to the terror they felt. Their gasping and choking left no room for doubt, babies have deep feelings. No one should be surprised that they get scared easily. Nothing else exists but what they feel sentiently; it's all-absorbing. It will just be a matter of time until they feel hate as a replacement for love – and then the reverse, over and over. Assuredly those leave lasting impressions directly into adulthood.

Here's what's too much for the little mite to feel: his love for his mother against his father's love for the same woman. Vestiges of it get buried in baby's unawareness because the goings-on are so scary that this tiny creature can't bear it. The only outcome will be being crushed by the huge other. That area of the mind where the burying happens psychologists call the **unconscious**. We all have one and don't know it; we are surprised when its contents spill over. Parents of teenagers know the tussle that goes on with their adolescent who just a year ago was so nice to have around. With puberty adolescents become sexually-aware. The sexual conflicts that were buried in the unconscious for some five or so years now try to break through. Teenage boys get scared all over again with competitive feelings for their fathers. They don't know why they're happening. Murderous anxieties inch upward seemingly coming from nowhere. In the same manner they get stunned with how quickly they love. We say they "fall in love" and it's close to what really happens. These feelings give no warning. They happen with overwhelming intensity.

Shakespeare's **Romeo and Juliet** illustrates this. These star-crossed lovers seek out Friar Tuck to marry them immediately. He arranges to hear their vows the following morning. That delay seems unbearable; their "parting" until then "...such sweet sorrow."

Love and hate start co-existing. Kids alarm their parents and scare themselves. It's an important growth stretch. The early grade school years get by with simplistic experiences; then the hormones happen but this time around, unlike during babyhood, they've attained thought and reason and reflection. These assist the kid and the parents and everyone concerned to get to some common sense conclusions.

This is when male (and female) high-schoolers huddle together in groups. They seek each other's support. Boys talk about girls and sex and try to get a grasp for who they are. Adolescence is full of surprises. Teenagers get confused, startled, angry and depressed with what occurs in their hearts. Mom and dad can hardly recognize these newly emerging energies but it's important that they realize that their teenager also doesn't understand what's turning him upside down. He doesn't recognize himself. He needs parent love as much as ever but closeness is also too frightening. He keeps his parents at a distance, the very ones he wants and needs the most. Love and hate flow together but hate is easier. He wants to hate them at the same time that he loves them. He'll need time to work things out. If his experience with mom and dad says that his parents will "take it" and stay loving even when they get bombarded with his rejection and distancing and hate-talk, he'll write another happier chapter to those baby days. It's for mom and dad to hang in there. Newborns are picking up clues constantly. They are amazingly accurate, a fact about their development we easily overlook. Their feelings are their only touchstones with what years ago wrapped up their tiny psyches from top to bottom, thoroughly.

There are important differences in what male babies feel compared to those of females. But they are not essential. Both start centering their reflexes for the opposite-sex parent. I've chosen with some regret to follow those eventuating from the male baby, first of all because I'm a male and can speak from personal experience of male dynamics and the eventual insight my development afforded me. Secondly this is not a text on psychodynamics. Uncovering early male experiences is quite enough for my purposes here. There're close enough to a female's to be instructive.

Doubters over what I'm asserting about our earliest years say I'm speaking absurdity. I talk about an innocent baby's development in ways the reader finds unbelievable. Then I have the gall to say: it's true but you just don't know it because it's in your unconscious. How convenient for me! Sounds like I'm selling snake-oil. To which I respond: we see the results of the unconscious's workings. Let me try to show that it exists.

Fresh Thinking
Sigmund Freud (1856 – 1939) was his era's intellectual force. He formed his studies along with those preceding them into the science of psychology. Remarkably his research included a deep, very profound treatment for neuroses which applied his theory and

confirmed its validity. A huge source of the resistance he was dealt with was his discovery that infants have sexual experiences.   People are bent on thinking that infants and children are innocent, meaning they are sexless. They wish to believe what they want to believe and they feel sex is an evil, that there's something wrong about it, not to be associated with "innocent" little people. However popular notions about our feelings and motivation and anxieties have been permeated with Freudian ideas even as they continue to elicit rejection.

He recognized that Sophocles' **Oedipus** reacted the way his patients had been pre-arranged to react. It happened over and over. Sophocles really had been on to something.

Staff-Sargent Robert Bales was serving his third tour in Afghanistan when he went berserk. He'd had problems going on back home. Bills had mounted and adjusting to married life had become too bland compared to the perpetual tension of war. On March 11, 2012 a buddy in his unit had his leg blown off. Within hours in a drunken rampage he stalked into two villages during the night and murdered 16 Afghans at point blank range.

Back home at Fort Hood the military families who thought they knew him well, as a fine soldier and father of two, were asking, How could he have done it? What they were really questioning was something else, a more personal one: We can't imagine any one of us committing mass murder. What they failed to recognize swirling around within – how could they any more than Oedipus could? – were the repugnant leftovers of our earliest development, sons ardently wishing to murder fathers as competitors for mother's love.   A contradictory mix results: love and hate co-existing. Those inner conflicts are an important part of becoming human. They overwhelm the tiny entities that we are as infants who bury such scary desires from their awareness (unconscious). Each and every one of us goes through it. Each and every one of us has wanted to murder.

Hot To Handle

This stuff is real. It's hard to accept as fact but we see its results. We start believing it when we observe what it does to the likes of S/Sgt. Bales. Shortly we'll see J. P. McCarthy feeling like a "sinner" regarding something sexual that happened to him. He'd not have felt guilty if he'd made equally virtuous choices about opportunities to deceive or steal. When it comes to sexual matters however, he felt he should seek out his priest confessor.   Similarly the Detroit Free Press editors offer stories on scores of issues every day. They strive most of all to get their facts straight. But reporting about rape cases and/or prostitution rings that were busted or similar stories involving sex requires special handling.   Readers give those reports a certain excessive watchfulness exactly because they center on sex.   Sorry experience has the editors holding back even commonplace personal information like the names of the victims of sex crimes because the popular mind attaches them to the offense almost as much as the perpetrator.

Detroit's Archbishop is on record declaring that Roman Catholic priests will continue to be males and males only now and until the end of time. The Twelve Christ chose as his closest compatriots were male, all of them, setting a pattern he sees as immutable. Not so consistent with Church mandate for many centuries were the wives some had, St. Peter being one of them and he was personally chosen by Christ.   History notwithstanding he believes proper theology requires clerical celibacy, an appeal with a long reach into ancient times. The Vestal Virgins of ancient Rome were to remain celibates for thirty years, chosen from the upper classes, assigned to keep the vestal fires burning which assured (?) military successes. They were greatly esteemed. Murderers on their way to execution, if they had the luck to be simply looked upon by any one of them, were freed. It occurred on the spot. Chastity had associations with divine influence. It still does. Roman Catholic priests practice it. It's a boast the Archbishop maintains. Pope Pius XII said priestly celibacy was the single flower of the Roman clergy.

My Catholic parents held to that feeling. They didn't realize that was their reflex until a young minister moved into our neighborhood with his pretty wife. They spontaneously scoffed. He was having sex. He can't be a mediator with God like our priests can. Mom and dad didn't speak it, it was implied. Similarly Christ's mother was said to be virginal. It came to be more than indicating His divinity.   It spun around the notion that she was too good to have sex. Especially among the Irish but by no means exclusively so, that she would be party to sexual intercourse was abhorrent. Catholic lore was ubiquitous with pictures and statues of the Virgin Mother. Nuns were her imitators appropriately dressed from head to toe with special covering hiding their bodies and hair. The Church is an especially anti-sexual organization. However it presents itself as the protector of marriage, as in its indissolubility. Within the marriage bond Catholics feel they can justly give themselves over to mutually induced orgasms because their Church (i.e., God) gives them divine purpose for sexual intercourse, i.e., the procreation of life to populate the Church and eventually Heaven.

For Example...

The popular radio host I mentioned earlier was J.P. McCarthy. He loved our town and the town loved him back. The producers of his show couldn't find enough hours to satisfy his fans; he had early morning assignments and late-afternoon ones too, lengthy exposure that never wore out. His commentary held insights that were entertaining, often droll or humorous. Sadly he was only 62 when he died in 1995 of acute hepatitis. Like so many of us at times he showed himself to be sexually overwrought and didn't realize it. Uptightness seemed like virtue. He fielded a question from a call-in listener with this response: I'd tell her I'm flattered but your offer is one that I must refuse and refuse quickly. Then I'd go to my priest and ask him to hear my confession. The question was: What would you do if a woman whom you found attractive asked you to have sex with her? It's important to notice that he would refuse the woman's offer and he would do so promptly and successfully. It didn't matter. He'd have felt he must seek out a priest who could hear his confession.

Confession is for "forgiving sin". It's not a place primarily for advice and counsel. The radio host would feel sinful though he would be hard pressed to show how he sinned. He said he would find the offer sexually attractive. He could very well consider the offer as yielding an exquisite experience. He might have felt an erection. Most would say he would have acted virtuously, even with courage. In almost any other context, if he'd have sought out his priest at all, it would have been to share a story of victory. If he had driven a neighbor to an emergency ward in the middle of the night, if he had helped an alcoholic fend off a compulsion to drink, if he'd pointed out a conflict of interest in a stock trade, if he'd refused to be part of a deceitful ad campaign, if he'd set aside collusion in some shady land purchase, he might have asked some priest friend to share a whisky in a meeting to celebrate a victory. But sex? Sex has its sticky residuals. For having been forced to give consideration to an adulterous encounter, he would have felt unclean.

A Good Becomes Bad

St. Augustine (354 – 430) as an emerging adolescent first experiencing pubescence was scandalized at his penis's independence, meaning that it rigidified whenever, unpredictably. Those erotic feelings gave him no peace. He considered them sin-prone, therefore evil. Later as one of the Church's most influential theologians he taught that such undisciplined feelings were illustrations, proofs actually, of mankind's fall from grace after Adam "ate the apple" in the Garden of Eden. His other body parts like his arms and legs, head and torso, would follow his choices. But not his penis. It stiffened or relaxed in any way and manner it's reflexes required. It took away his freedom and he hated it. For my purposes his resentment pictured his responses to his Oedipal Complex. In reality a man's stiffening penis says nothing about his goodness or badness. A young adolescent is to accept it as one more aspect of growing up. He is to learn use it in a mature manner, hopefully to accept, enjoy and employ it appropriately. But whatever he may conclude about it he is certainly not to condemn himself for it. Having a functioning penis does not make a man a sinner any more than a developing vagina or clitoris makes a woman sinful.

An ancient Roman writer weighed in on our subject. We'll cite him shortly but for the moment comparing him with Augustine gives me the chance to point out the problem if religion is allowed to lend its weight to a conversation or argument. The one quoting a god can claim the higher ground. The other thinkers have to depend for your belief on their mere logic. How can a mere man stand up to God?

As I write this Roy Moore is running for the Senate to replace Jeff Sessions who has become the Attorney General. Moore had already gotten into hot water for ordering his underlings not to obey the Supreme Court's decision to issue marriage licenses to gays. Prior to that when he was an Alabama Supreme Court judge he was rebuked twice for planting huge monuments of the Ten Commandments on the capitol lawn. What's currently disconcerting is believable testimony that he had unseemly sexual contacts with teenage girls when he was in his early 30s.

He's since become rigid. **Time** magazine (10/30/17) quotes him saying, "It is the fallen nature of man that the Constitution meant to restrain." **Time** continues: He's a "...judge who recites anti-abortion poetry, rejects the theory of evolution, doesn't think Muslims should be allowed to serve in Congress, fought to keep antiquated wording in the Alabama constitution requiring school segregation and suggested that the Sept. 11 terrorist attacks were God's punishment for America's sins."

Maybe his dalliances with young girls convinced him that his manhood was sin prone. St. Augustine came to similar conclusions. His earlier sexual aberrations were such that he felt helpless when they summoned him. Later on he was to write that they robbed him of choice, of freedom. His intellectual brilliance put together a theology, including a theory Roy Moore would think rings true, which included the notion: Original Sin. It's said to be the fallout from the disobedience of our first parents, Adam and Eve, following which everyone inherits a "fallen" nature. It was a grim picture Augustine painted. Christianity has since accepted that view. Roy Moore and St. Augustine though separated by some 15 centuries have this in common. They both figured if they personally felt sin prone, then everybody else must also.

It's certainly our experience that we are born with a leaning to inappropriate violence and sex. But we reject the idea that there's something fundamentally wrong with our minds and hearts. Depth psychotherapy uncovers that people feel something's wrong about love and sex, not because love and sex are wrong – our life experiences show them to be good – but because of the results of the conflicts we ran into as infants for which we were ill-prepared. They left their marks on our developing psyches which made love-choices and sex seem wrong-headed and improper. The conflicts that swirled around them left us feeling love and sex are unwholesome. They are what Roy Moore and St. Augustine made overly quick conclusions about. They might have wondered why human love-partnering from which flow all that we hold hear like family and children got to be coated with evil as if the Creator invented love and sex and then smeared it with a bad odor. Their personal sexual promptings lead them to self-centered conclusions. They didn't look beyond them for other possible meaning.

This book is an attempt to give you a look beyond them.

Marcus Tullius Cicero (106 b.c.e. to 43 b.c.e.) is the ancient who had something to say about sensual pleasures. You will notice how much more level-headed he is compared to the distressed Augustine convinced that orgasms arise from mankind's fallen, sin-prone nature. Cicero is writing about piling on the years when he writes: **What a splendid service does old age render if it takes from us the greatest blot of youth! No more deadly curse than sensual pleasure has been inflicted on mankind by nature....It is the fruitful source of treasons, revolutions....For when appetite is our master there is no place for self-control; nor where pleasure reigns supreme can virtue hold its ground.** (The Harvard Classics, P. F. Collier & Son, New York) Cicero seems to hold to the notion that our natures are worth the effort to set them right, that it's something we can accomplish. Augustine and Moore concluded we're permanently flawed.

An Easy Power Grab

Would that JP's discomfort with his sexuality was unusual. We all have our personal versions – shall we say aversions? - of it. Of such are the sources of the Archbishop's power. He could choose to use his lofty position to deal with complex moral issues, like Wall Street cheating and fashioning a two-state solution with Israel and Palestine. His power is more easily established – by way of matters sexual. Ordinary Catholics "know" or feel instinctively, that puts him on the side of what's holy. It's their consciences prodding them to embrace his regulations. Regarding his restrictions on homosexuals obedience comes easily. Many Catholics don't much like them anyway so the Archbishop isn't taking any big risks in damning them.

A local newspaper pundit's caption for his column read: **Accusation: The Shame That Lingers**. What was he talking about? Simply the shame that attaches to anyone found in a sexual encounter. The pundit is saying the shame clings. The sexual occurrence need not have been sought after. It made little or no difference. The publicity it occasions leaves a special, a unique stickiness. Newspapers have to deal with this. They've set up a standard of special anonymity for the victims of sexual assault. For the victims! Being accosted by another's sexual aggression is "...intrinsically more humiliating than being mugged for one's money, beaten up for one's unpopular political views or being bludgeoned to death for no reason whatsoever..." (cf. **Detroit Free Press**, Brian Dickerson, January 5, 2012).

Single Mindedness

Stanley Kubrick's film **A Clockwork Orange** (1971) fixes on the point Aristotle made long ago when he said virtuous acts have no merit unless they are freely chosen. It presented to us Alex, a violence-prone, teenage gangster prison authorities had declared incapable of reform. Some behaviorists took over. The result: sexual desire made him deathly sick. After a demonstration in which he writhed in agony trying to rape a voluptuous woman, the behaviorists declared success. But a Christian priest in attendance cried foul. Taking away a person's freedom even that of such a despicable person as Alex is to dehumanize him. That's immoral, he declared. Behaviorism abandons him as human. It cares only that he's no longer a menace. Our society is to care for individual personhood or society could get used to taking the path to dehumanize anyone it feels we'd choose not to bother about.

That notion was lost on a pastor of a nearby Catholic church. He overlooked a splendid chance to educate his congregation on the slightly subtle principles which undergird our human dignity. Kubrick was handing him a gift. A responsible community moral leader would have thought through the issues Kubrick's movie was presenting. Instead he failed to see past the nubile limbs of the actress in the demonstration and publicly condemned the film. Asking why is to peel away the thin layer that gives the Church its all-to-easily-acquired authority. It's sex. The pastor focused only on the footage of a beautiful, almost nude, female body. More important that his parishioners not see too much skin rather than accepting guidance in contemplating Aristotle's moral sensitivity which is devoutly to be wished. Some may have applauded him. The same way they applaud the Archbishop: Just keep us from sexual stimulation because we know in our hearts it's bad. We seek out his sexually-abstaining priests to bless our orgasms within marriage. We're happy to be on this sexually-fixated road to Heaven without having to bother gaining an appreciation of Aristotle and those other ancient Greeks who put in place the foundation stones of Western civilization.

St. Augustine recognized the problem. He gladly accepted the authors' interpretation of the Genesis story of Adam and Eve. Simply put they freely chose to disobey their Creator so they deserved to take on – and pass on to us – their "fallen" natures as punishment for "sinning." He saw in our wish for fulfillment through love and sex something perverse. In other words he couldn't see beyond the experiences he'd had as a developing infant. Neither did his mother Monica. (She had her own reasons for seeing them as perverse which we will examine later.) Augustine's sexual compulsions never seemed correct, even after they were part of a devoted relationship he formed with a woman he loved exclusively for fourteen years.

Costing Too Much

JP's feeling the need to cleanse himself would have occurred to many of us. Sex is good. We know that. It's the platform on which we fashion the best life has to offer, things like love and family and purpose in life. At the same time somehow it sticks us with emotions we experience as not quite right. We tend to feel everything God made is good but He lowered His standards when He invented sex. Oedipal interferences exact large costs like that.

For example: Consider the many capable leaders, whose talents we needed urgently, but whom we've forsook, dismissed, even scorned, over their sexual missteps. Indeed we insisted that the directors of our nation's fate keep their pants zipped. We were not all wrong. Misguided sexual practices can partner with untrustworthy characters. But not always. Gary Hart and General Petraeus were deep thinkers, inventive and imaginative. But they were drummed out of office because newspapers made a lot out of publicizing their extra-marital affairs. Few seemed willing to make a public case for retaining their valuable services. Pointing out the adulterer's experience, education, and long records of dedicated service make for strong logic. They wilt however before a torrent of popular outrage over orgasms that occur beyond certain rigid boundaries. White collar criminals do great harm. They shake public confidence in our free economy. Getting them inside prison walls however is plodding work, decidedly dull. People yawn. But how and when and where people get their orgasms grabs public interest.

The popular mind sees sex like candy, it eats it up. It means pleasure and indulgence – and it comes across as something "unworthy", a danger we're too eager to overdo. We want to view harshly those who dare do what we'd like to do. It helps keep us in line.

So I was pleased to read in today's paper, ***Johnson's Controls keeps CEO…after affair***. Its board calculated that the executive's private sex-life hadn't interfered with his splendid management of JC so "the company considers the matter to be closed." A compromise? Sure. But in this case, apparently a prudent one.

Once again a competent executive just about lost his job over this single factor, sexual aberration. Society needs these leaders. Dismissing them becomes everybody's loss. Sometimes it's important to do so; these offenses can bedevil everything that comes close by. Then again often they scuff only the individuals close by, like members of the family. Judge each case separately; there may be things worth saving. Sexual mishaps can skewer good judgment.

Bulldozed!

It can overwhelm our best intentions as well. There's not a woman alive who doesn't fear the unwanted pregnancy. Erotic compulsion can seize control and leave us with results we didn't want and are unprepared for, like responsibility for a baby. A completely dependent infant gets born to a couple, bewildered over its unintended presence in their lives. From then on they may or may not do their best to provide a home. The baby, then toddler then adolescent and adult, will pick up the negative vibes should its parents not have worked out adjusting to home-making routines. We had a bridge partner who exuded insecurity, as in maintaining a less skilled player-partner whom she called out lustily when she erred. Some years ago she confided to us that her father would shout scorn at her mother, then turn to her with: You're why we had to get married!!!!

Some Personal History

I've received training as a psychoanalyst. What I've written so far is an analyst's view of the Roman Catholic Church's source of influence. Previously I had accepted ordination as a priest for the Roman Catholic Archdiocese of Detroit. Much of what I will write from this point on dips into my experiences and observations about those experiences with the conditioning and background of a priest and the insights of a psychoanalyst.

It was April, 1973. I'd finished my appointment at the bishop's mansion and walked into a new world. The click of his massive door closing behind me was the simple, single summary of my resolve to opt out. I was leaving 17 years of service to the Archdiocese of Detroit. That followed 12 years of concentrated preparation for the Roman Catholic priesthood. "Your Excellency, I can't bring myself to believe it anymore!" I explained with quiet confidence. I am telling our spiritual leader, the Most Reverend Joseph Schoenherr, that I felt phony standing at the altar, that it would be hypocritical of me to stay on.

Celebrating Mass, distributing Communion, instructing converts, representing the Roman Church with the wearing of the black suit and "collar" marking me as its servant, once gave me purpose and worth. Not anymore. I'd become edgy, a bit of a crab. Within the Catholic community it could be said, I'd "lost" my faith.

I knew what I didn't want. I didn't know what I did want. I was starting from scratch. No job, no home, no family. No place to stay either, although it was easy enough to rent some place to hang my hat. I'd shucked off my moorings and plunged into what felt like an ocean, all horizons, as yet no land within my purview.

What got me to that point in life is what I write about here. I'd applied some rigorous thinking to where Catholicism had put me; it had become decidedly insufficient, unrealistic. Being a priest had put me in deeper than those Catholics who've decided to show up no longer on Sundays. But my forsaking years of faith-practice had broad similarities. My choice paralleled ones like it on the part of millions of ex-Catholics in America. They too braved that empty feeling that comes from abandoning the special warmth and familiarity of a lifetime.

Our son gave me a push or two: "You've made a radical shift in your life," he said. Telling your story could make interesting reading.   I started writing and I didn't like some of what evolved. Part of it turned out to be scrutiny of my parents. They were looking less than sterling. They desired having children. Whether their wish was prompted by personal, deep-felt promptings or whether they were heeding their Church's guidance I was never able to discern. Somewhere around the early 1940s Mom got a hysterectomy. In referring to Mom's being away at the hospital and why, Dad said, "We were wondering why we weren't having more kids…" That meant one way or another they sought children as desirable.   As I look back on those earlier years I feel they as parents felt they were doing the best they could. I think so too.

Self-Interest

As a youngster the Roman Catholic priesthood had come to look pretty good. I couldn't have foreseen the compromises that came with it. My Mom and Dad were regular Sunday Mass attendees and my sister and I along with them. Everybody dressed up, it was something special. The ambiance inside the church and around the front steps had a generally happy-looking group. The sun seemed to shine a lot. Becoming an altar boy offered closeness to pleasantness. We lived at a distance so "serving" for weekday Masses wouldn't work out.   But it was something I strived for.   I memorized the altar boys' Latin responses and got on the waiting list. So when Dad's wartime job moved us to the city with a church just four blocks away I was all set for promotion to serve on the other side, the "altar" side, the "sacred" side of the Communion Rail where the celibates gathered for liturgical functions properly separated from ordinary people.

I reveled in the distinction. I became the most reliable member. The other kids would forget to show up for their assigned Masses. I was ever available and got called on to fill in. My personal goal was becoming the Master of Ceremonies for the Solemn Masses on the special days of the Church year like Christmas and Easter. He'd stand with the three priests on the altar and direct them with ceremonious bows and gestures when and where to stand and when to sit while waiting for the completion of longer choir passages. It meant I'd ascended as high as a grade school kid could go. Father Thompson promised that the job was to be mine and then forgot.   (He couldn't have had other responsibilities on his mind, could he?) I arrived for the next altar boys' meeting and heard Father announce that Pat Boylan was to be the Master of Ceremonies. I gulped, speechless. But the next day Father handed me the M of C notes. He was angry. I protested, "...but Boylan???" "You called the Rectory last night!," he shot back. "I did not!," I retorted. It turned out that Mom called. She spoke to the pastor, the head man, Father Bertram, who assured her that I would be the M of C. Then added, "You've got a fine boy, Mrs. Kosack." I know this because Mom told me all this in detail.

My Mom

My mother's guidance had been central. She was looking ahead. Calling Fr. Bertram which resulted in the ousting of Pat Boylan and installing me in the top spot meant keeping me on the way toward becoming a celibate.   It spared her from giving up what every mother surrenders when sons choose their life partners. To friends and family she took great pride in God's "calling" one of her offspring into His Church's select circle. But shortly after my ordination I was set back on my heels when I realized that she didn't especially like priests. She liked MY being a priest because it kept me womanless.   She saw my marrying as my rejection of her. That turned out to be unfortunate and strife-ridden for the one who was to become my wife. In the months before her death she came to an acceptance and a measure of peace.

This is not the sort of thing I like to write about because it involves revealing some intimacies about my mother that take a lot of explaining. She was the last of thirteen children born to her alcoholic father. She carried throughout life a lot of sexual conflicts. My father was taciturn for the most part but sometimes said things that were quite sharing. "I like to enjoy my married life," he said on one occasion, "You know what I mean. But not her! She should have been a nun!" Mom did not respect her sexual nature probably because her father's drinking rendered him unpredictable. When she'd cozy up to him for love as all little females do he may have been numbed and rejecting. Or he might have become too free with his hands and frightened his daughter. Who knows what impairment alcohol imposes on one's judgment? Mom as a toddler may have concluded that she had too much influence on her dad, that her need for love would take them too far and she might wind up successful with her desire to replace her mother. We will never know. What we do know is that she disliked sex and would be doing both of us a favor in eschewing it from a place in either of our lives. They fit hand-in-glove with the Roman Church's hold over much of mankind, having found in sex a reliable sphere of influence.

There were times when Mom would caress my face. "You'll make some woman very happy…", words like those she spoke on at least a couple occasions. I'm guessing they made me conflictual, certainly uncomfortably confused and non-plussed. We know the woman she was talking about. Thinking back on them now, I'm embarrassed. She didn't know her place; mothers are to offer parent-love, not the romantic sort. Catholic boys frequently talk about being priests "when I grow up"; priests are respected models of what's lofty and good in Catholic communities. Priesthood is among their choices. My mother probably saw her opportunity when I spoke of my interest. It may have been minimal, initially saying things that every thinking kid says. "The priest that's going to give our Lenten series teaches at the seminary; we could go talk to him," she enthused. We came to the church's sacristy and sought him out. He was most welcoming. Years later he told me how taken he had been with my mother hand-in-hand with her bright smiling kid. That meeting started a two decades long relationship. He began immediately sending postcards of support and friendship. I was a mere Seventh grader and was immensely flattered.

My Dad

Preparing for the priesthood includes adjusting to sexlessness. For me that meant eschewing orgiastic indulgences. As far as I can remember, forswearing the sharing of my life with a woman appeared to be a minimal loss. "Sex is strong in a man," were the words Mom had spoken to me. Helping me get used to living without sexual expression became her mission. I started getting seminal discharges, characteristic occurrences for seventh and eighth grade males. Probably my curious fingers on my stiffening penis set it up. I got scared, really scared. Now what have I gone and done!! I felt I'd done evil. No one had to tell me it was wrong, I felt its wrongness completely. Something in me told me my orgasms were evil. I wish I'd come to Dad about this. Later on in my teenage years when I had been rummaging around in my room upstairs he called up from reading the newspaper with a "knowing" smile in his voice, "What are you doing up there?" He'd never been keen on priesthood. Later on he'd say, "My father liked the Church but...Oh, well...I don't know..." Once when my sister Joan invited a girl-friend for a sleep-over, Dad said, "I think you like her!" He was right, of course. I'd caught a quick glance of her in Joan's bed. One of her (to me) beautiful thighs rewarded my furtive glimpses and I was deeply impressed. I forbade my indulging in it; I was doing my own version of self-preparation for a priest's life. Dad may have been hoping that my attraction to girls might squelch priestly ambitions. "It's not good," he said a couple times; it's "bucking nature." During my senior year in high school he said, "C'mon, let's go for a ride."   We stopped curbside a few blocks away. He said, "Do you really want to be a priest?" I said I did. He was clearly disappointed but not surprised. "Well OK. But if you change your mind, I'll buy you a new Chevrolet convertible." He was playing his trump card. He was certain his son was making a big mistake. Actually he was playing against my adolescent idealism. The sort of thing some Imams hunt for in recruits for ISIS. I told him no, sure that God and His Church would be proud of my heroism. As I look back on it, I think I was scared of the big world. I didn't think I was up to it. As a priest all would be provided, I wouldn't have to work hard in an unhappy world. I always loved cars and I may have had in the back of my head how impressed I was with the pastor's big black Buick I had seen once sitting in the Rectory driveway.   Dad never tried to dissuade me again.

Consolidating Her Gains

That gave Mom the open road. She'd won. After I'd panicked over my first orgiastic discharge, I went to her for help to keep me pure. She eagerly complied, suggesting that we meet bedside every night; she'd encourage me to resist my sexual promptings. She advised prayer and I took that seriously. Her plan and nightly advice had the appearance of success. I don't remember masturbating more than a couple times in the years that followed. Those lapses may have helped keep me alert to my sin-prone nature. Actually in recommending prayer she reached for the same tools the Church utilizes. They were quite amateurish and largely ineffective.   I remained as interested in integrating sex into my life as any other male, however degrading I felt it to be.   My Oedipally-induced conclusions about sex had already been firmly established. They gave the real force behind Mom's counsel and prayer-advice.

During the final years of seminary preparation we were to wear the Roman collar with a black suit. I did so with pride and was garbed as a priest when I went into town and got a haircut. When Mom asked about it afterwards she became startled because a woman turned out to have been the barber. She stormed at me, "No woman is to dare to touch you!"

Mom was dutiful. There was the time when she called my sister and me to an upstairs bedroom – I think she was seeking privacy – and read to us from a small volume about human sexual intercourse. It took all the resolve she could muster; sheer courage pushed her to get through this. Males and females combine their bodies and produce babies, was the point she barely managed to express. I asked, "Do you mean you and daddy…??" Immediately she cut me off with, "Don't talk about me and daddy!" I picked up on her pained words sticking in her throat so I volunteered some relief: "That's beautiful!" I hastened to add to her strained reading. Someone must have told her she had a parent duty to explain to her kids the mechanics of sex and she doggedly got us through it. That was about it. Never again did she broach the subject. Was it helpful? It might have been had she been able to exchange her anxiety for a sincere feeling for the worth of sex in her and my father's life. Her stress had so permeated that upper bedroom that my sister and I were left with no doubt that we were not to bring up the subject again.

Some five years earlier Mom had to have been in a reflective mood when she shared some musings with my sister and me. We were five or six at the time. She had to have been talking in some manner about having babies because I remember asking her, "But why would someone do that?" To which she answered, "Because you fall in love…" It was a splendid answer. We were to take away that "love" shaped our home, our lives, indeed shaped us. In many ways she did a good job.

Ours was a reasonably comfortable household. General Motors employed Dad's engineering skills throughout the Depression years which nevertheless left their mark on my folk's over-valuing money for the rest of their lives together. Worry about money never quite escaped their concerns even as their actual family fortune increased. This circumscribed the good times we might have shared together. Weekends at home were pretty dull. Their soporific backdrop was the radio's baseball play-by-play from an announcer who had a voice like a dial-tone. My folks did see value in the arts. Both my sister and I were provided piano lessons. I recall the few trips downtown to attend a couple plays. Some less than edifying choices our neighbors made included the fellow across the street taking up with a sweet young thing living next door. During World War II women were hired into factories grinding out war production. I complimented Mrs. Waters (she lived two doors away) on her patriotism because she took one of those jobs to which she said, "I'm happy to help my country, Allan." My Dad's spontaneous comment when I told him about this was, "She just wants the almighty dollar." He'd been declared to be an 'essential worker" for the war effort. Some stressful hours at the plant followed.   I took his complaining to heart, comparing his life to those of the priests at our church just four blocks away. Some of the attraction I held for the priesthood had to have been their happy and unhurried demeanor.

Dad Gets Deleted

City living meant I could take a bus and streetcar to the seminary throughout the high school years. That convenience got pulled when the seminary rector, Msgr. Henry Donnelly, got wind of Dad's lack of enchantment for priesthood. We've got to get you out of that environment, he insisted. Donnelly projected goodness and propriety and later was named a bishop. That's when he was assigned a pastorate on the East Side, an exposure that caused his mental breakdown. He'd been shielded amidst the gothic arches of the seminary. He had no real world or real life experience. He'd no idea about all the sex that goes on, at least as he saw it. To illustrate: when a student transferred from another college into the seminary, he ventured onto its tennis courts in shorts. That was normal garb on his former campus. But Donnelly pounced; candidates for the priesthood are not to show that much skin. He made the transfer student put on long pants. Similarly when visiting basketball teams from surrounding Catholic schools played the seminary team (competing teams had to come to the seminary gym, our players were not allowed to travel to theirs), their players wore regular shirts when they competed. Donnelly insisted that seminary students slip on a T-shirt first, then pull over it the normal basketball uniform top, the one he figured was too skimpy for men pursuing celibacy.

The seminary provided for its residents a world unto itself. Classes were required on Saturdays, half-days. Sundays were distinct in that Mass was to be attended twice. Times for smoking followed meals for fifteen minutes. No newspapers or magazines in the library. There was a big emphasis on sports, touch football and basketball. Time for study was sufficient if not ample. Prayers before sleep were mandated; we were to add them to those we had just spoken together previously in the Prayer Hall. Nine-thirty to bed, wake-up at 6:30 (Sundays we slept until Seven). A scant 20 minutes allotted from the morning's wake-up alarm to assembling in the Prayer Hall meant mornings got off to a fast start. There was great camaraderie. The authorities forbade what they cautiously worded as "particular friendships", meaning we were to socialize in groups. Time spent alone with a friend was forbidden. I suspect they were looking for homosexuals whom they were quick to expel. It never occurred to me that was what these rules were about, in large part because it was never verbalized openly. I cooperated fully in keeping the ordinary elements around sexuality at a distance. I never dated or mixed with females at parties. I think I was glad to make a virtue of my confusion and fascination about girls. It was a good deal. I could skirt the conflicts normal adolescents have to work through and get rewarded for my cowardice with God's approval.

Betrayal

The priest Mom and I met during our parish Lenten series turned out to be what's loosely called a pedophile. I didn't realize, probably I didn't want to, what was going on. As I see it now he was a lonely man. Often he'd take me to his cottage on Wednesday afternoons (Wednesday and Saturday afternoons were off days). In the summers we'd swim. I'd feel him coming from behind and rubbing his erect penis against me. At the seminary he'd invite me to watch TV with him after lights-out. I'd creep downstairs and enter his unlocked door. It was fun. I was flattered with all the attention. His orgasms I somehow dismissed. I refused to see a wrong; he was a priest and a respected faculty authority. Should his choices for me be evil, all my plans (and my mother's) for a worthwhile and God-blessed future become suspect.   I couldn't let that happen. He asked me to lie on his bed on one occasion and he began tying my hands and feet to the bedposts. I hated it but I felt impeded from protesting. It was unimaginable that I could stand up to a man so important. In any case he was a priest, a holy man, and a friend.   Evil, especially a big one, simply could not have any part in our relationship. Almost as soon as he had me tied in place he untied me. I was free and figured I had gotten past that one while still preserving this friendship. Some days later I put on my bathrobe and went to the Rec Room. Sitting next to a fellow seminarian during our exchange of pleasantries I began scratching off some white stuff that had dried on my bathrobe. It dawned on me, it was dried sperm! My priest-friend had gotten some of his discharge onto my clothes during that brief bedroom tie-down. I was very embarrassed. As soon as I discreetly could, I said not a word about it, got up from my chair and hurried back to my room.   I think that student I'd sat with figured I'd masturbated while I was wearing the bathrobe. He said not a word.

Tamping Down Sex

That brings forward my conclusions about the aim around so much of seminary life. The quick darting out of bed in the morning, the piling on of prayers at nighttime, the accent on vigorous sports participation, the denial of contact with girls and women, the absence of magazines and newspapers and modern music, the filling up of our free time with daily fifteen-minute visits to the chapel (in the summer to our local church), the lack of novels and secular reading, a regimen of rosaries and prayers we were to spend our time involved with during summers spent back home, these were designed to de-condition us sexually.

Yesterday I stood in line at a water fountain holding a Styrofoam cup waiting for a lady to finish providing cups of water for her three kids. I began returning smiles from her littlest one. She was really a cute kid. I told her mother what a delight she was, to which she volunteered, They are so innocent. To one trained in psychoanalysis innocence is not the first attribute that leaps to my mind when I think about two year olds. Those pre-rational years are loaded with love/hate conflicts. But as I looked at the lovely face of this child what did occur to me was her trust. It was with total trust that she was given over to when she smiled back at me. Clearly her adult world had offered her no reason to feel otherwise. It was a beautiful moment.

Now consider the perversity that would descend upon her tiny world if that trust were to be betrayed. My mother had been betrayed. She was the youngest of a family of twelve with an alcoholic father, and grew up convinced that females were deficient. When our daughter, Kate, expressed interest in violin lessons, Mom told us it was a waste to spend money on her. When Kate in her bouncy cuddly child-manner said, "I love you, grandma," warm words of response stuck in her throat. More than once she decried, "Why did God so curse women?" Somehow, somewhere along the line her worth as a woman got compromised and it left its mark on my sister and me. It permitted her self-serving interpretation of Catholicism. It was not from a page taken from Catholic theology that she saw in its priesthood the chance to keep her son away from other women. That was built out of her neurotic distortion. Unreality was ruling her life, dredged up from her unconscious which in turn was formed through her

Oedipal experiences. Had she gained somehow an awareness of her woman's worth vis-a-vis males, i.e., that one gender is not better than the other, maintaining her grip on me by way of my celibacy would have had no appeal. My selecting another woman to love and make love to would have been an ordinary, unencumbered personal choice, from which she would maintain a proper distance and about which she would feel no personal loss.

Her neurotic distortions utilized the Roman Church. Obviously its disdain for human sexuality is neurotic in itself. It accepts as reality-based the feelings we all develop early on from our infant experiences over love, hate and sex. We hasten to assert that the Church can hardly be expected to offer appropriate regulations, or even practical advice, about a subject it knows nothing about. Love and sex belong in our lives. They deserve a place of honor, not the over-caution and often disdain the Church promulgates. What we concluded about them while infants doesn't fit with adult life and adult experience. Our inclination toward irreverence about them, connecting them to strife and guilt instead of love and creativity, feeds those feelings that our nature is "fallen" and needs "redemption", as St. Paul would have it. He says we're not to be trusted with making our own decisions about when sex belongs in our lives and when it doesn't. The Church is no wiser than he regarding our sexual potential. But the public at large submits to its ill-fitting, rigid strictures about it because they feel right and proper. And they feel right and proper because our unconscious Oedipal conclusions tell us they are right and proper. More about this later.

Misplaced Trust

Neurotic thinking does no one good. It bears a resemblance to a betrayal, although unintended. It calls to mind that barbers used to cut into a customer's vein to drain some blood. A customer, who complained of some symptom or other, might have his barber saying, Maybe your blood is too rich, and he proceeds to cut. It did harm, sometimes seriously, but the intent was well-meaning. Mom trusted the Church promoting celibacy as lofty, God-pleasing practice. She saw its policy as supportive of her own recoiling over sexual intercourse. At the very least she found nothing in her family nurturance to counter her early Oedipal impressions. Everybody thought they were doing good. Looking into those shining eyes and smiling face of that little girl at the water fountain got me earnestly hoping no betrayal enters upon her future. Every bit as earnest is my wish that she never find support for the Oedipal impressions she may be forming at this point in her life. As for that priest-professor at the seminary, his manipulating me was truly a betrayal. Regretfully I was only one of thousands of Catholic youths priest-pedophiles victimized in America. (The precise term for the sexual compulsion of the sexual aggressor who victimized me is ephebophilia, i.e., sexual attraction toward adolescents.)

I wish the entire population could undergo psychoanalysis. That could undergird the emergence of the reality-based thinking our society deserves to live by. That's not going to happen anytime soon. In thinking and then re-thinking about the Church thing, I've come up with what I'm guessing may offer an understanding and maybe an appreciation of the misshapen road I've taken toward the degree of self-acceptance and happiness I enjoy today. Regarding the purpose of this book I expect my experiences will give some shape, some reasonableness, some fuller identification to where a lot of Catholics with doubts as well as ex-Catholics are finding themselves.

Forsaken leadership

In the 1960s Cardinal Dearden was sure bussing suburban kids to inner-city schools and city kids to suburban schools would lift the quality of public education. He was probably correct. But most Catholics were stunned when he recommended they follow plans to actually do it. They dug in their heels. Tackling real injustices was far too demanding, even repulsive. Building nice churches which they could share for weddings and funerals, for that they were willing.   But sending their youngsters into town to prompt better education for Black children, that's not what earning a Heavenly reward was to be about.

I was greeting people after Mass in the vestibule of St. Alfred's Parish in Taylor. I had just explained the Cardinal's bussing plans during Mass. A tall fellow leaned into me and said, "You don't really believe that stuff you were saying up there, do you, Father?"

For the first 30 years of my life I thought the Catholic Church had all the answers. I was grateful to have been ordained as one of its representatives. I wore my collar with pride. People respected it. I concluded that practically everyone held the same general notions about the Church as I did. We were on the same page, or so it appeared. By virtue of my priesthood, I was ipso facto a community leader. I was in for a shock. It was becoming clear that I was to do and say what my parishioners expected me to do and say. They were the leaders. I was to fulfill *their* expectations. That meant that in exchange for Sunday Mass attendance and financial support they could expect a happy eternity. They had been guaranteed the worth of a sacramental approach toward holiness. Nowhere was it written that Catholic virtue meant active concern for matters of social justice. For me to speak of bussing at Mass was like a defilement of the sacred pulpit on which I was standing.

Father Finnegan the pastor of Presentation Church in Detroit had asked me to help out with hearing confessions. I said I would, Finnegan's request coming after my initial six months of clinical psych training. During those months I hadn't given absolution to any kneeling penitents seeking forgiveness.   So when a man with a heavy Italian accent said he had beaten his wife I asked a clinical question, How are you going to stop this? That stopped him in his tracks. Whata you do? Giva mea da what you do! He was disgusted with me, as to one who didn't know how to do his job. He was giving no thought to how he'd quit doing his sinning. He'd spoken his confession; now was for me to deliver for him the familiar Latin formula of absolution. I figured he'd come to hear the formulaic cleaning; I was in no position to deny the assurances his religion had been unquestioningly providing for him. His insistence forced me into a compromising position. He'd come to get magic. I detested playing that part.

The bussing plan was poorly thought through. Were that its only failing, then a better one could be fashioned.   Implementing it would require a sense of justice on the part of many people. They were not to be found among the general Catholic population. Catholics wanted the easy guarantee of Heaven they had been used to. Like that Italian sounding wife-beater who felt he was due magical forgiveness through no effort on his part.   Many of them fashioned as reaction to a heightened social conscience the matter of defilement inside the church walls. When Pope Francis says we're to stop polluting the environment they said he should stick to religion. A friend of mine puts it this way. He attends Mass every day. Sometimes the priest-celebrant sermonizes about the nation's war policies. That unnerves him. I come to Mass to seek peace and not to be challenged, he says earnestly. Peace indeed? Could it be Oedipal relief, i.e., forgiveness at the ready?

Not Walking the Talk

Is it Christ-like to trample on the civil rights of same sex couples? Some Christian theses can't find it conscionable. For centuries they justified rounding up Africans, chaining them into crowded ships and selling them into slavery. Catholics welcome their bishops' support for the revulsion they feel when they watch two males strolling affectionately hand in hand. When Episcopalian bishops required support for same-sex civil rights, not just a few of their churches seceded. I hear a lot of brave talk when gun control, tax reform for the working class, expanding workplace protections for homosexuals, extra funding for inner-city schools, laws tolerant of labor unions and their strike armamentarium, etc., gets mentioned for our consideration. But when we go to mark our secret ballot we get self-protective and politicians know that. So do our bishops.

Some twenty years ago a sister-in-law exclaimed how she gets regurgitative at the very notion of homosexuality. This was before civil rights for same-sex marriages were becoming generally acceptable so she felt free to say they were threatening, disgusting and to be exterminated. Today she'd surely forswear that contemptuous language because society has shifted. She has adapted her language to fit what her neighbors were speaking. Words for her are magical. If she sounds tolerant she figures she is. She's not realized however that her words have not converted her internally. She just thinks they have. An analogy is the priest pouring the baptismal water and saying the baptismal words over baby's head thereby making it a "child of God". Are words really that magically productive? Does my sister-in-law's spoken tolerance of homosexuality really bespeak her tolerance? Revulsion doesn't melt away so simply. Her steady religious practices and visits to the Holy Land merely serve to paper it over.

Oedipal feelings support our inferiority feelings. They have us looking for someone to feel better about. Homosexuals and African-Americans are convenient discoveries rewarding that search.

What's the Attraction?

Some have wondered out loud why we can't tell the Christians from the other people. Preaching that we're to love our fellows doesn't work. Christians aren't better. They're not any worse either. They are just people.

We paste on labels, American, Christian, Caucasian, sportsman, that are skin deep. They are mere designations. Our similarities to the other citizens of earth lie just past our surfaces. Catholicism, pointing to its armamentarium of Mass and sacraments, claims it will make you better, better than the others. In fairness other creeds make like promises. Sometimes their adherents act virtuously but most of their adherents stay quite mediocre. Still people hang on. Priest pedophilia should have destroyed the Church. People keep creeping back. Something else accounts for the discomfort they feel without Church prescription rituals. Some Catholics extend themselves to better humanity's lot. A few of its bishops do too and for that the Church applauds them. But it can get along quite well without their heroism. The Church is for and about what St. Paul was for and about. Not outreach but "in" reach. He will offer you something personal, a personal savior. It became what we call Christianity. First admit you can do nothing of worth so you can become a forgiven sinner. Washed in the blood of the Lamb, is how many put it. You're never however quite clean enough. It resembles a treatment for alcoholism: abstain and keep on abstaining – because you remain an alcoholic.

Sophocles speaks **to** the horror Oedipus experienced when he finally realized he'd married his mother. He also speaks **about** it. 1) Oedipus *knew; he just didn't know he knew.* That's why the Oracle's prediction stunned him: ordinarily a collusion of the two events of loving and murdering are so preposterous that they can be brushed aside. But he gave belief to this absurdity because it didn't seem so absurd; it resonated as real. "Way back when" he had really wanted to marry mom and kill dad, wishes he pushed into his unawareness because they so rattled him. He took it most seriously, dedicating the rest of his life to making certain the preposterous could never occur. 2) Sophocles selected as the protagonist for his drama a soldier, a king, a personage to be admired. Those attending would recognize the social worth of a dedicated and virtuous leader. Indeed viewers of the play have come to it already aware of how things will turn out. But come they do. And have for centuries. The final events rivet the audience with scenes of horror, of unbearable defeat, of the citizenry subdued while witnessing unrelenting remorse. Importantly it was not physical torment but mental anguish that elicited popular sympathy. 3) The mental torment was Sophocles' emphasis, which becomes his singular contribution to our understanding neuroses. The final events in the play are exciting, including the king's plunging out his eyes, an appalling try at appeasement against unyielding guilt. But the initial scenes are the most arresting. Marrying mother and murdering father are laughable - except that they resonate as real, eliciting some genuinely-felt personal history in what's presented on stage. Sophocles made sure we realized Oedipus didn't slough off the oracle's prediction. He took it most in earnest. So do today's viewers; what's played out on the stage, as unbelievable as it would seem, has the ring of what's believable – because it's actually happened to everyone. Therein is the worth of the play. The hero's self-inflicted crippling punishment feels justified because it replays what had already been established as horrifying in infancy. Oedipus recognized a beguiling genuineness about the prediction. Sophocles was not offering evidence of the unconscious mind. But he was getting close. He was illustrating that men are stuck with the results of their babyhood's love and hate, what adult society would declare to be incestuous desire. The Oracle pointed it out and Oedipus "understood", meaning he felt its truth. It determined his life course. Sophocles would have us know that Oedipus was ruled by real, albeit infantile, desires which he despised but which he wanted. He'd hidden his despicable wish in the inner recesses of his mind. It remained however just as influential. From there on in it would determine all his life choices. 4) The play enables us to watch his life progress confirming what the Oracle foretold. His resistance to it, his determination to nullify the prediction, came about consciously. He made it his life-long motivation. Those attending the play know Oedipus's fate is sealed. It

centers on Oedipus's abhorrence to what he felt was sex of the most repugnant kind. He lived out that abhorrence all his life. The oracle guaranteed his edginess because a) its reputation for imparting truth was sterling and unimpeachable, and b) he spent his life fleeing from it. He invested his life energies to proving the Oracle false. 5) The over-arching lesson: we all spend our lives resisting our Oedipal strivings. We'd buried them as babies before we attained the ability to think, reason and examine. The original emotions that adhere to those earliest parent-to-infant encounters center on love and hate, the basics of human psychic energies. They are too fearsome for little psyches to handle. They bury them in the unconscious so they need not accept them as real. The purpose of this book is to point out that the same fearsome dynamics enter upon our adult choices. They encroach on them. They don't let go because we don't know they exist even as they perpetually guide our choices. This book is an effort to do for its readers what the trusted Oracle made clear to Oedipus. A mere reading of this or any book does not cure neuroses. It can illustrate however how neurotic conclusions appear as breakthroughs,
disrupting mature thinking.

Serving the Oedipal

The reader is to arrive at wonderment over humanity's irreversible bent toward distortions of good sense. S/he may come to suspect that those basic hidden, unconscious energies are at work. Freud recognized his patients' likenesses to the insightful drama **Oedipus Rex** written by Sophocles twenty-five centuries ago. He saw in them the results of the Oedipal Conflict.

Does the Oedipal Conflict have much influence? Take a look. I'd been a freshly-minted priest for about six months when a mother of eight children came to my confessional on a Saturday evening: My doctor tells me that I dare not get pregnant again. My uterus may rupture and I might not live through it, were the approximate words that came at me through the screen. She was very nervous. She'd quite likely given endless thought to her dilemma. She could have concluded I'd turn out to be a sympathetic confessor.

What she got back amazes me as I think on it and certainly profoundly disappointed the woman. I parroted to her the conservative line. Something like: My dear lady, Can you imagine God abandoning you? He loves you and wouldn't allow such harm for you and your family, etc. I blanche with wonderment at my surety with this penitent. I know I slept comfortably that night. She lived in the real world in which she found herself. For that I offered her magic. Amazingly I felt I was doing good. God's work. I don't know what the lady decided or what happened to her. I never followed up on her fate; perhaps I could have kept my ear close to the ground, maybe by searching the obituaries. I did nothing. I had no responsibility; I felt none. I was God's lackey.

I was innocent…perhaps
There's an important factor at play. I didn't force the lady to come to my confessional, or anyone else. She had not been comfortable simply making love and having sex with her husband. Orgasms simply to make love were impermissible. I suspect her mate had similar inhibitions. Taking on the rearing of eight children is huge, heroic. Something had been pushing them. It was some conviction, a strong one, that they couldn't

simply make love. Making it permissible was to find a way to make the bad thing good. The Church's blessing fortunately was at their disposal. They would no longer have to share an evil; it had been blessed!

Doing so meant sex must do something good, like making babies to populate God's Church. But so many babies? Apparently it was a price they were willing to pay. The fly in the ointment was her probable death, her and her husband's willingness to continue propagating notwithstanding.

Somewhere along the way they besmirched their feelings about sexual intercourse. The fervently religious often find themselves drifting in that direction. Not just with Catholics. Our daughter's girlfriend since her high school days is Greek Orthodox. Married four years ago, she has borne four children thus far. They'd used rhythm, considered natural, as a contraceptive method, notoriously unreliable. As I see it the only experience common to us all that's sufficiently intense to explain these choices is the Oedipal Conflict. Some prostitutes have told me some clients cannot achieve erections with their wives. They love them and so respect them too much to thrust their penises into them. They've become convinced sex is degrading, requiring a degraded partner.

My mother-in-law had five children, all born three years apart. She and her husband practiced rhythm as a contraceptive method. It made sense. Introducing sheaths, oils and compounds to obviate pregnancy is admitting that sex has merit all on its own. Sex which had become suspect as something evil requires cleansing before God's sinful people, needing and seeking Redemption, dare choose to experience orgasm. Oedipal feelings are strong. They make people jump through religious hoops before they will allow themselves sexual indulgence. They seek to spare themselves the pain of guilt. It's the same kind of guilt that pushed Oedipus to slice into his eyes. If there weren't God's Church conveniently at their Oedipal feelings' beck and call, they couldn't enjoy shared orgasm. Having been blessed to procreate for God's Church they diminish or may even eliminate their discomfort about accepting sex into their love-life.

A Double Standard – Again!

Peggy Orenstein in her book ***Girls and Sex*** talks about a teenager who talked about her confusion over being attractive. Most often when you speak a positive, she says, it's opposite is a negative – and vice versa: Good has ***bad*** as its opposite, so also does sin have ***virtue***. But when referring to girls the opposite for "slut" is "prude". They're both negatives! She complained to Peggy that the unfairness of it all irked her.

She has a point. A young man can flirt and it's accepted. Our culture expects, or at least tolerates, male sexual aggression. It's OK that he reacts person-to-person to a girl's beauty. But it's different for a young woman. Should she send a smile to some male she finds interesting, she can't be sure how he'll receive it. Maybe she's signaled to a lad whose father and mother had helped him form a high regard for the human potential in sex. He will respond with a hope that this girl asserts herself from a basis of self-respect. However he may turn out to be one of those who feel degraded by the sensations a beautiful female body sets up for him. She occasions for him a wrong for which he feels she is responsible. Someone is to require her to cover up her lovely skin, restrain her flowing hair. St. Paul follows the spirit of the fellow who blames the beautiful woman for his "evil" responses. In one of his epistles (1Cor. 11, 2 –

11) he requires that women should cover their hair in church.

We've got a cat that sometimes delights in jumping on our laps. Sometimes he hoists himself by digging into my trousers to hoist him to where I'm sitting. All delightful! But not when we neglect to trim his nails. They feel like needles digging into my thighs and I let out a little shriek. I think that confuses him. We act like we love him but when he wishes to enjoy being close to me I jerk away. Girls get double signals. We love our women. Men generally think ours are more beautiful than those of other countries. However when they fix themselves up with make-up and flattering clothes we don't act consistently with respect for their gorgeousness. I don't like hats generally speaking but I'm grateful when I'm goaded into wearing one by cold weather for one particular reason; I can tip my hat to women when they pass by. That simple gesture lets a woman know that I notice her womanness and instantly offer her respect. Often she will return a quick and lovely smile. It's important that women get support for looking beautiful, that they mean something good and wondrous. That their smooth-flowing figures inspire men who become thankful for the chance to be males who can relate to females.

Women would like to have reinforcement for their desire to be admired. It's hurtful that they must acknowledge that their beauty doesn't always evoke respect and admiration. Not every male thinks the feelings their loveliness evoke is admirable. Many think sexual feelings are wrong, even evil and offensive to their god. What a happier world for everyone involved if women could allow themselves the freedom to be and act and dress themselves uninhibitedly, beautifully. That would be a world wherein those love/sex/hate experiences of infancy would be 1) seen as neurotic; i.e., casting sexual intercourse as compromising human worth and 2) allowing those neurotic feelings to dissolve over time like sores dissolve in sunlight. The result is a mature male feeling about love and sex. This permits a man to put love and sex together in his embrace of a women's love.

It got worse!

My second assignment placed me in the Visitation Parish on the near West side just a few blocks from the Clairmount and Joy Roads, near the "blind pig" police raid that sparked the 1967 Detroit race insurrections. "Visi" had both a grade and high school. Parents paid tuition beyond public school taxes so that their kids could get a Catholic influence on their development. That the school day began at 8:00 am with a celebration of Mass was an attractive bonus. The distribution of Communion took place about 8:22. That's when the congregation advances to the Communion Railing. The priests on staff took turns hearing confessions during Mass; our task was to hear as many confessions in 22 minutes as possible because Communion (the Holy Eucharist) had to be taken in a sinless state. When I took my turn at the confessional there was inevitably a cluster of teen-age boys waiting to be "heard and absolved". There were always a few that didn't make it within that twenty-two minute allotment. Seldom were any girls in the line-up. Their confessions were invariable; masturbation was the chief offense named, declared to be (and felt to be) mortal sins. If they didn't get "heard" in time they must not approach the Railing for Communion because they remained in a "state of serious sin".

It was enormously embarrassing. Any observer would understand why some boys didn't advance to the Communion Rail. These lads were forced into a public display of a very private phase of their developmental life which they felt (and which their religion confirmed) was sinful. For this their parents were paying tuition. I'm betting that many of them felt squeamish about talking to their kids about sexual matters. Paying priests and nuns to do something about their offspring's' hot-bloodedness was money well spent.

All the players – moms and dads, priests and nuns, teachers and confessors and the "Visi" students were dancing to the same rhythm. I am asserting that they all felt prompted by their infantile, Oedipal experiences which trump reasonable thinking. Oedipal conviction is powerful and to the best of my knowledge universal.

A Smart Kid

I was an active part of this expose. I hadn't given it much thought.   I did feel the tension around the confessional screen at which I sat opposite the young kneeling penitents. Then one morning a young man leveled with me, not as an automaton dispensing turnstile absolutions. He talked to me as another male who should understand his predicament. Father, I can't sleep unless I touch myself and get some relief so I can rest. He was utterly sincere. He made a lot of sense. How was he to become alert enough to pass, say, a test in trigonometry the next morning if he hadn't gotten a good night's sleep? Teeners require a lot of rest. However even if his touching his penis did effect a relaxing seminal discharge he'd remain compromised. He'd be sure he'd sinned.   He hadn't required the Church to tell him so. Internally he felt the Church was telling him truth. Truth was what rang true with those first primitive, infant impressions ("conclusions?") which were feeding his future hang-ups, viz. neuroses. He sensed his provoking orgasm was wrong. That it went along with proper male growth was mere observation, no match for the wrongness of his stiffening penis. The Church hadn't built within him this certainty; it was already present within his bones. Oedipal conflicts were determining these decisions, his, his parents', his teachers', and mine as well. None of us realized this: Oedipal consequences remain hidden, unconscious– and all the more influential for being unconscious.

Nevertheless could I not have felt the inner neurotic life Catholic practice was building on? These young men were developing adolescent sensitivity and sexual potential. They were inferring from me and the rest of us that sinful desires are clinging to their growing bodies. Dealing with them as their promptings required caused a dilemma: I can't understand and learn from (and hopefully welcome) these steps I'm taking toward manhood without being sinful. That's a terrible thing to do to a kid. Growing up brings complexities to be felt through with hope and confidence. I was branding them with the dreaded label of sin. All the while thinking I was being appropriate! The Oedipal Conflict is powerful indeed!

Promoting Lust?

Striving to understand the low status we give sex is precarious. Some movie from some time ago showed a distinguished gentleman spitting at Sigmund Freud who was standing at some university's lectern. His offense: he'd dared to speak of infant sexuality. Our touchiness about sex is as ubiquitous as the Toyota Camry. This writer risks such opprobrium. To which I counter, I'm fostering respect and reverence, not unrestricted sex-play. Moms and dads find worth, joy and purpose in the offspring they create. Sex made that possible. It's reckless use hurts, distorts, deprives us of worth. I won't say it shames, which it can, because shame and guilt drive people to the very institutions like the Church which disparages our sexual capability. It's laws build on our suspicions.   Rather I hope this book will promote the worth of sex, the place for sex. I wish to promote freedom and personal choice based on human value. That leaves more space for growth, growth of all kinds, physical, social, intellectual, aesthetic. I'm saying that Oedipal fixations intrude way, way too much. They're wild. They require patience, an awareness of what went wrong way back when. And why. I'll suggest some practical approaches.

Helping

The world at large knew him as *Prince*. He was Prince Rogers Nelson the immensely talented musician and composer. He died at age 57 on April 21, 2016. He addressed for a friend about what I should have wanted to speak for the boys at Visitation High School. Perhaps his friend was going through the same conflicts Prince was. He chose to speak like an observer who's finding his way through tough times but we realize he's writing of conflicts he had borne up with personally. Here are his words:

"If you were a kid growing up in the "80s – maybe let's say you're gay too – this is what you first learned about sex: It will kill you. You don't have sex yet; you don't even really know what it is, but you know that it is lethal. That somehow it leads to the men with the skeletal bodies and the blotchy marks on their skin that you see on the

television, the men who don't look at the camera and are alone.

From this certainty, a whole way of being unfolds. The body, especially the naked body, is gross. Penises are gross; tits are gross; lips are kind of gross too. Ewwwww! Clothing becomes a kind of hallowed armor (except lingerie, which is also gross) and should never be removed, especially in the locker room. Whatever curiosity you have about what adults do behind closed doors, on the cable stations your parents don't subscribe to, is squashed by the notion that sex = death. You stop asking questions. You leave doors closed.

But then, one day on the radio, a song blows those doors open. You don't know who sings it. Or even how many people are singing it, or whether they are boys or girls, or white or black. But the guitar hooks and squeals and pops like nothing else, and a lyric worms its way into your brain and stays there for the next 30 years:

Yeah, everybody's got a bomb
We could all die any day
But before I'll let that happen
I'll dance my life away

Later, you'll learn that the singer is a wholly improbable creature – made of sinew and lace and leather and hair – and that he has a lot of friends, including his band, The Revolution. You'll learn more explicit lyrics to songs like "Darling Nikki" and "Head". But "1999" will always be what turns you inside out, even when it is played ad nauseam at bars in the year 1999. On one side of your childhood, there is Reagan and AIDS and nuclear war and the yelling Christians. And on the other side, there is Prince."

I feel bad about the harm my priesthood did to many of those I serviced. It took a while for me to apply real life solutions to the realities people were dealing with. Not everyone wanted realism. I would have been drummed out of the parishes I had been assigned to had I applied the implications to be discerned from what I saw as Oedipal realism.   No one is spontaneously willing to admit his religious life in conjunction with his sexual life is neurotic. However many find comfort in using religion in this way. It's how they fit unconscious Oedipal influences formed in infancy and babyhood into their adulthood but they don't fit easily. Babies' impressions were the only feelings they could manage at the time with no brain development to bring to bear on them. They were understandable at the time; jamming them into their unawareness is equally understandable. But they have no place in adult life. Baby's reactions are immature. Sometimes they meld with responsible adult choices. Not often however. Most of the time they make a mess of things

Not All Bad

One opportunity came my way. I could try to incorporate Oedipal awareness into lectures to people planning marriage.   They were looking for God's blessing on their orgiastic future.   They generally thought they were on the right track socially and economically. I could do them a service if I could help them be a bit more at ease when they copulated.

I used to give pre-marriage talks for the Archdiocese of Detroit.   I based them on some assumptions: 1) that they had enthusiasm for sexual intercourse generally speaking but most enthusiastically with their loved one; and 2) that running side by side with what their feelings were telling them was unworthy was that "good" people are to be restrained in its performance, that it was fundamentally "dirty". Somewhat daringly I suggested that the male sex organ when erect, stiffened in eager anticipation of insertion between a lover's vaginal walls, symbolizes what a man should be to his partner. The engorged penis, its shaft, bespeaks strength, confidence and commitment as it ecstatically discharges its semen into his partner's beautiful and enthusiastically receiving body. My service was to confront the infantile Oedipal residuals I could safely assume all my listeners had. Necessarily it confronted the Church's accommodations to these neuroses which it nurtures without realizing it. It intends no malice. It is no more aware of the infant's sexuality as it develops than most of the rest of the world population.

Love Making as Poetry
The glans is at the tip of the penis. When it fills with blood it becomes soft and spongy. When the male organ thrusts into the receiving vagina he can do so with energy, with forceful thrusts because his glans assures gentleness accompanies all that aggression. That energy, enthusiasm and indeed aggression is almost a contradiction but in sexual intercourse they combine exquisitely. He is truly possessing the woman's body. Indeed so does she vaginally. "Now I am all around you," is how one loving spouse expressed it. Both are winners, neither is dominant. Most girls grow into womanhood aware of their body's fascination for men. Yet they often share some doubts that they are carrying off its beauty properly. That they don't have the curves and proportions of a starlet hardly matters. The truth is every woman is beautiful. Their love for their partner

vivifies their bodies with magnificence. Physically our bodies are like everyone else's. It's the love commitment the couple brings to their love-making that exceeds their physical ordinariness. Their married life promises over the years to build a unique union; nothing like it will have existed before, nothing like it will eventuate thereafter. There is no aphrodisiac greater than that of a loving, enthusiastic partner.

Straight forward truth-talk about sex begets resistance. Sex is rewarding, highly motivating and has the potential to elicit the most generous aspects within our nature. We know that. All the same we know talking about it gives us not a little discomfort. I'm sure the couples I addressed were grateful listeners. That it was spoken by someone wearing a Roman collar gave it special impetus because the Roman church is famously bent into Oedipally-inspired legalisms. Rome acts like it owns our sexual capacities. It is theirs to parcel out sparingly. It daringly talks that way when it circumscribes it with laws. For example a professor of moral theology instructed us that only one sex position is sinless, that being the "missionary position", the male astride the female. Every other is wrong, sinful. He didn't explain why. Typically these authorities feel they don't have to.

Comparing my notes for the talks I gave on sex for those planning marriage with conclusions I hold today, I don't see much difference between the real-life issues I tried to address in the 1960s and 70s and those extant today. Some incidentals I'd change are like the Tom Jones' recording "Wives and Lovers" I'd put over the loud speakers during the half-time break: "…don't send him off with your hair still in curlers…" what is shamelessly anachronistic. Wives don't stay home on workdays much anymore. And there's small chance she'd wear curlers to the office.

Is it too idealistic to think we can instill these ideas as norms to be ingested by our post-pubic offspring? Perhaps. But perhaps not. If an adolescent has grown up from infancy into puberty in a home where his/her Mom and Dad really love each other and experience in sex the realities we've reviewed here, they have a better than even chance of imparting a reverence for sex. Maybe it falls to Dad to talk to their sons about this. For Mom to do the same for their daughters. Kids bring more trust than embarrassment under these circumstances. Dad can speak of his gratitude for sex, for his penis, and their consequences in his and his wife's lives.

Many More Like It

The big problem concerns the negativity about sexual matters that feeds our discomfort. Masturbation could be seen to serve our best interests, especially for adolescent development. The Church decries any orgasm at all outside sexual intercourse within a marriage bond, and only the one it's bound.   It gets away with this sort of thing over and over again. Nor does the Church stand alone in this regard. It's the accepted belief among all religious stripes whether among Muslims, Methodists, Taoists, not to exclude the irreligious. The Catholic Church didn't invent these feelings in people. They were already there, the result of everyone's first encounters with love and hate during the first months and earliest years we begin our existence. I'm sure the young men attending Visitation High School found confirmation for the evil of their feelings in the priests they confessed to. They knew (i.e., **felt**) they needed cleaning up.   These confessions repeated over and over in their high school years guarantee stress. They can also lead to self-condemnation and later on toward poor life choices. I ran across a revealing conversation with a fellow priest some years ago who was unnerved by the almost universality of masturbation among our youths. His lament: "What are we to do about this?" My answer would have been, should I have thought it would make sense to him, that the very universality of masturbation ought to allow questions about our assertions that it has no place in young lives. Beyond that it can be seen as an acceptable relief to sexual insistence as it is experienced in adolescents. Going further it can offer a choice when sexual compulsion threatens to take over good judgment and someone else could be drawn in. Priests who've wielded their authority over such personal matters, and who've been supported and admired for doing so, will find it hard to consider alternatives. The alternatives psychoanalysts come up with are boldly contrary to Catholicism's restrictions.

Maggie Smith, the lauded performer in the movie *The Second Best Exotic Marigold Hotel*, said in an interview she'd been curious for a long time how it comes about that so often we fear what we love and love what we fear. It's more unconscious angst going on, the effect of which we feel all the while realizing that it makes no sense in our lives. Religious advisors acknowledge that loving God includes fearing Him. It's a combination that cannot be separated. He is the supreme rewarder; fidelity to Him is said to merit eternal happiness. Necessarily however His position vis-à-vis humanity demands that He punish the errant with eternal pain so love of God must include fear of Him as well. There's no escaping that, suggesting that the template for our relating to a divinity is our parents. It's based on our childhood experience with mom and dad. They loved us mightily with rewards that mixed in what we needed which they provided and which they exceeded because their love called for everything they could provide. They did it with love. They also brought down punishment on our heads and that scared us. Love and fear combined. They combine the same way as we approach God, calling forth the same parent-feelings we experienced as babies, as infants and toddlers. We love what we fear and we fear what we love.

As we grow into adulthood love for mom and dad become tenderer; elements of fear diminish or even vanish. But our God keeps on getting the love-fear notions we returned to mom and dad before we could think. Human love is another thing altogether. It can eliminate fear. If the couple is adult, i.e., mature, capable of self-surrender for love of the other, and seeking the rewards of a love commitment, love without the element of fear is the likely result. When it starts it may contain fear of loss and rejection and the pain that may follow. My speculation is that human love for a deity has to contain some fear, being largely based on our earliest life experiences. Some saints may dispute this, their devotion having eliminated any potential punishment. Human love that has endured the rigors that can come its way over the years can become total. No fearing what we love and loving what we fear in that instance. Maggie Smith's contemplation applies to less advanced love, like loving a deity which is suffused with those earliest love experiences with one's parents. Here's evidence about how Maggie spends free time, resulting in profound insight, which may be telling us something about her reliable interpretations on film of our human situation.

Leftovers

That's what we call neurosis: when the left-overs from infancy crowd in on what mature judgment tells us is right and good. This introduces the central theme of this book: Oedipal conflicts rule!

Because our unconscious rules us. No one easily accepts this. We don't want to think we're not free, that our choices are influenced outside of our awareness. That means we don't see what's happening within. We can however see its workings **INDIRECTLY**. We see its results on our lives, stuff that doesn't fit good judgment. We've already elucidated them operating in several quite sad events, events that admit of no other explanation. We're disbelieving like the friends and neighbors of S/SSgt Bales. They couldn't imagine such aggression latent in normally functioning people – like themselves.

Earlier I cited a lecture by the Ford Motor Company's top cop. Protecting from harm the company's entire work force anywhere in the world was his responsibility. At one point he said, Look at the person sitting next to you; now look at the individual sitting at your other side. Both of them are emotional powder kegs. Given the proper circumstances either of them or both can descend into a murderous rage.

Loving and hating and everything in between, that's the human story. They surprise us when they overtake us, i.e., without our knowing where they come from. They influence us **indirectly.** All of this, be it the observations of Ford's top cop, the Free Press's touchiness in reporting on rape, the unsuspected rage within S/Sgt. Bales, a popular radio host not quite sure he's sinless, is instructive. Hidden energies all, they give us much to ponder. Yogi Berra said: You can see a lot just by looking.

The past is alive

Our past is our present. Infancy occasioned conflicts that remain consequential. We are destined to give up parent love/sex, thence to find our own partners to have love/sex with. Sometimes we can, sometimes we can't. Parents have an important task: to maintain their distance from their kids' seductive approaches. Parents need to maintain the right kind of distance. They are to give "parent" love, not "lover's" love. They are to keep developing their marriage, working at it, making certain that both work out their differences and continue to be grateful for the chance to be close to one another. Kids will pick up that their parents' love is impermeable. They feel it. They come to know that they can safely love their parents and that Mom and Dad will return it. But the love coming back will be "parent" love which is manageable. It's "safe" because they've tested Mom and Dad. They've concluded they can be trusted never to cave in to their blandishments. Mom and dad haven't any love needs remaining, only their needs to be parents.

But sometimes parents become vulnerable. Their marriages may be empty of emotional involvement. They may become a bit jealous of their children's' love for their partner. They start competing. Such parent-to-child feelings set up a huge conflict for the child. It confirms that those very early sexual strivings may very well have a chance for success. Oedipus in Sophocles' famous play was so turned off by that prospect that he geared his entire life to avoiding it. As infants the consequences of such a victory had been so frightful that they drove them deeply into their unconscious non-awareness.   Now as youngsters and teenagers, re-experiencing too much of that, they get caught with bouts of emotion that their developing psyches have little experience working through. They may turn out to be uncomfortable with love-making as grown-ups. Closeness to others can come to feel like what's forbidden, destructive, overwhelming. They might wind up as adults shaping their sex choices to fit a neurotic background. Sex with prostitutes can allow orgasms as long as it's impersonal, devoid of warmth, closeness. Some prostitutes and gigolos, who may have higher sensibilities, tell us a goodly number of their clients are depressed. Grown-up adaptations, if their parents' love-needs pushed them to become a bit too romantic, run the gamut. Some generous souls seek out monastic lives, thereby choosing to foreswear their sexual conflicts entirely.   (This is not to say that all monks are sexually conflicted.)   Aristotle may have been the one who said, **the best thing a father can do for his children is to love their mother**. If he's the one who expressed this, he had a feel for Oedipal results. He was thinking of a home life wherein Dad so loved Mom, and vice-versa, that there was no romantic need left over that can scare the kids

The Unconscious
     Freud wasn't all on his own. Josef Breuer (Paris) also saw evidence of the unconscious. Hypnosis was the path he trod to reach it. I've watched entertainers use hypnosis on stage. One man was put under and asked when he was awakened to scratch his left ear. The demonstrating hypnotist quite easily put him to sleep. With a flick of his fingers his subject awoke and scratched his left ear. The audience roared with

appreciation. The subject felt nothing unusual. He had no idea his unconscious had taken over.

Two things to notice: 1. the unconscious rules the conscious, and 2. we're not aware of its influence. We think we think freely, our minds being unencumbered. Not true. In early life, we started competing for love/sex. Not with our minds in the adult sense, but with our feelings which were all we had as babies. Awareness advances bit by bit. When we get shocked to find out that we love the same woman (or man) as father (or mother) does, the prospect of competing, and of getting crushed by these giants, proves to be too much. So we repress it, squash it. Importantly, we "forget" it. The hypnotist can open an easy door to this other section of our minds but he can't heal a neurosis. Breuer and Freud published a study in 1895, adding that they were looking for other scientists to contribute. The response was poor. Breuer quit the effort; he stayed with internal medicine. Nervous patients remained Freud's focus and I for one feel fortunate that I live this side of the Nineteenth Century and have benefited from his research. He had gotten only part way via hypnosis. The unconscious became apparent. But how to treat it? How to treat a feeling or emotion that we don't realize is "inside" somehow or somewhere? It means that treatment can only treat **indirectly.** It looks for the results, the consequences of the Oedipal experiences on our lives. (Patients get fascinated with the genuineness of what their treatment uncovers.)

Oedipal conflicts can scare infants into making unhealthy, maybe even destructive selections in later life. They may cause bodily symptoms. Mental energies early on had taken neurotic pathways. We can spot some of these ourselves. Think back to those grown-ups who took overly fixated delight for the feelings their lips brought them at the nipple, the breast. Is that why some eat or drink too much?   Is that behind the overloading with words, with subduing by over confident blabber like a Rush Limbaugh, an Ed Shulz or a Chris Matthews? Seems like a direct effect.   There's a lot of the past mixed in what we do daily. But because we've tamped down (repressed) those infant terrors along with the adaptations, compromises and adjustments we made because of them, we go through life being uncomfortable with the choices we ought to find proper and fitting. I treated a young nun who didn't think she was attractive. Or rather, as became clear, that she'd better make sure she'd look unattractive.   To her unconsciously, men seemed too much like dad. Being attractive scared her; it felt too akin to incest; i.e., sex with her father. Easier to forego marriage, love and sex altogether. A genuine call to serve the Church should arise out of conviction, not fear. It's to be freely chosen. She made a neurotic choice, to be sure, but one our society honors.   Later she found herself becoming crabby and short-tempered with the men she encountered. A cure for such fixations begins with the awakening of these early choices and writing a new ending to an old story. She could become comfortable with adulthood. (Her treatment failed. Initially she showed some interest but not sufficiently to work with the insights that emerged. Convent life suited her well and the secular world remained unappealing. She gained some value regarding the sources of her motivation and may return sometime to complete her analysis.   Her apathy illustrates that entering into psychoanalysis requires personal investment and is helped along with a free and ongoing fascination with the uncovering process.)

Failing To Heal

Hypnotism taps into unconscious areas   That's about all it does. By sheer luck, the hypnotist could come across the original Oedipal strife. But would his subject believe it?   Likely not.   It would have been artificially extracted. It would feel unreal.   It wouldn't be bound with the scary feelings one experiences as a baby. Freud's attempts as a hypnotist did yield some insights, but they didn't endure.   Besides his subjects had become dependent on him. He had sought freedom for his patients both from him as well as from their Oedipal leftovers. His job was to observe and interpret, nothing more.   He had to help induce forgotten memories. But how? Hypnotic results failed because the resultant revelations seemed unreal. They had to be felt, accepted by the patient as genuinely his/her own. He devised an appropriate technique. He'd have the patient lie on a couch, get relaxed and then start talking. Say whatever comes to mind, was his only instruction. Skimming along at the pre-conscious level was how treatment started, then deepened; it was like peeling off layers of an onion. The patient's flow of words would touch on many things, from the traffic he crept through getting to the analyst's office to plans he had for the weekend, it wouldn't matter. His Oedipal dynamics were ever present.   They influenced him indirectly and unconsciously whether he'd driven his car or hit a golf ball. His unconscious was at work continuously so it wouldn't matter what he said. The analyst decoded what was bubbling underneath.

Targeting The Immature

Mature folks welcome sexual feelings which will yield comfort and joy, mutually shared.   They contrast with adolescent feelings. Youths up until their middle twenties haven't as yet acquired a full complement of brain development. They're idealists. They're given to severe judgments about the less than perfect world they find themselves in.

The Islamic State of Iraq and Syria (i.e., ISIS) is making war on American interests in the Middle East. It's also called ISIL; i.e., the Islamic State of Iraq and the Levant. Levant refers to the territories East of the Mediterranean Sea on to Turkey. Our State Department prefers to say ISIL because it points out the radical Islamist's goal of taking control of that huge swath of land. They use the term DAISH at times, the Arabic word for ISIL. Our officials shake their heads in wonderment at ISIS's success in so far having attracted 30 to 40 thousand young people to fight and die for the cause.

They are indeed young. Watching an Imam recently eliciting recruits sounds to this analyst like his target viewership are young men who've got damaged perceptions about themselves. What they discern about being male contrasts with their idealism. He's telling them they're sinning because they want sex with women they've found attractive. He's about to offer them an alternate outlet and giving them a chance to foreswear their sexual energies. It works for the Imam only for young men who think their sex interests are evil. The Imam's offer is switching those energies instead toward aggression. They get a chance to fight and maybe die in Allah's service. They think that makes them blessed by Allah. Actually what's to happen is the transfer of their psychic energies from what they think is bad about them to what they feel is good: going to war and killing and dying for a holy cause.

The Imam is about to invite youths to enter a world-wide fight to the death to further Sharia Law. (SL is a fundamentalist background for things like male dominance, denying education to girls and women who must marry whom the family selects, who are punished if they are raped and thereby scorned by their family, who must cover their bodies, hair and even their faces under masks with tiny slits to allow their wearers to see through.   Called Burqa or Chari a woman's beautiful eyes remain visible so they're self-defeating.) I noticed the connection the Iman was making between the presumed degradation he would have them infer about sex and the praiseworthiness of the war to which he was eliciting Muslim youths everywhere.   His premise was believably built on an energy model for human psychic energy.

Limited Energy

A credible theory says our natures have a certain and limited quantity of psychic energy. It's the fuel that powers the intellect and emotions. Mental effort uses such energy so the conclusions we have from chemistry and physics apply here; terms like mystical and spiritual don't.   Psychic energy is expressed in two ways, sex and aggression.   They function together intertwined variously.   Under the sex label we list creativity, compassion, empathy, imagination, wonderment, etc. Under the aggressive title we can expect to find initiative, competition, exertion, ambitious endeavor, personal investment in all kinds of aggressive goals. We're choosing all the time. We can let ourselves get dyspeptic when we get stuck in gridlock traffic. That's an aggressive choice. Or if we've got our kids in the car that we'd prefer not to scandalize with our blue language, we hold our tongues and take a deep, controlling breath.   That's making a generous, giving choice.   It expends some of our psychic energy for love-sex.

There's plenty of overlap between the two.   Sex however can put orgasm to its service.   Fortunate are the young of both sexes who will associate their sexual rumblings with what's good in their development.   They can anticipate that their sexual feelings and orgasms will combine with love to serve a life-long commitment.   It's part of their human worth and that of their loved one. One of the saddest episodes of my priesthood was confirming neurotic guilt through my confessional grid at 8 am on school mornings.   It communicated profound disrespect.   Some of those teenage penitents would find the Iman's appeal salutary.

There's some aggression in love making (mating) but the preponderance of the human energy expended therein goes to yielding and tenderness.   Prize-fighters and baseball pitchers use aggressive energy.   That's obvious.   Discerning whether a trial lawyer is using his sexual or his aggressive powers when he's attempting to persuade a jury isn't so obvious.   If he's simply focused on winning, it's probably aggressive.   If his overriding aim is justice for his impoverished pro bono client, his psychic investment is probably a love-sex sort of energy investment.

Like Islamists?

Generally aggression is looked upon with more acceptance than sex.   Americans are not unlike Islamists.   I attended a graduation at the Naval Academy.   It was grand, a celebration with military music, snappy uniforms and hazzahs under a sunny spring sky.   Hardly recognizable was the purpose of it all, to kill.   The nation was at war and pursuing it proudly, honoring the men and women who "will put themselves in harm's way."   However we don't comfortably allow sexual matters that kind of open expression. Rather we are to express it guardedly, like my telling you that I'm going to check out in advance something raunchy to see if it's okay for you. An example of openly celebrating matters sexual (along with the aggressive) is the Academy Awards. It's noteworthy that those who tend to be more aggressive cast scorn on body-beautiful displays. The religiously scrupulous, for example. Someone asked Dick Cheney if he'd be watching the Academy Awards that evening or a football game. The hawkish Cheney harrumphed and every listener knew it was a presumptuous question.

Off To The Same Start
All this begs this question, Why do we give less dignity to sexual energies?   Sex after all is the underpinning for the best life offers: love, family, children, the exquisiteness of orgasm, of purpose to life, of generosity and dedication, etc. Yet this tentativeness toward sex is universal, in every race and culture, in every continent, East and West, North and South. The answer has to rest within what is equally universal to every living person. That in turn has to be what we all experience universally from the time we're born: we are all conceived in a womb and nursed at the breast.

There follows the total contentment and love the breast provides. It's completely providing. Baby cannot figure out that sharing is possible because its experience with living is minimal, and it cannot think. It senses that "his breast" has another lover, it hates the intruder with emotion as total as its absorption into the nipple. With a male baby, it's his father who must be eliminated. But the father is huge. Baby feels it's surely to be crushed. Just as surely it expects its huge hulk of a father to return hatred in kind. These are massive, overwhelming emotions. An infant can't handle them; it represses them into what's called the unconscious.

That doesn't mean such repressed memories don't gain influence. They influence enormously. And all the more powerfully because they are unconscious. Hidden, subliminal and unrecognized, they roam about our minds freely, at will, and wildly. That's where they'll remain for the rest of our lives unless we work them through. Generally, come adolescence, teenagers get a reality-grounded try at dealing with what their unconscious is coming up with, this time with the aid of thought and reflection within a context of a much wider world. This time around they have developing brains.

That's part of why we harbor ill feelings toward sex and love. Our first experiences with them are combined with hatred. Love and hate are co-existing. They function at odds side by side. We don't know they're rumbling around inside. But we do see the results. Most obviously that sex which brings us so much good is regarded guardedly. Ordinarily when we give thought to "harnessing our inner demons" we think about keeping our sex drives in line. But being at the mercy of anger, ours as well as that of others', is also the hallmark of maturity. Aggression can be as unyielding as our sex drives. It's dependent on how our psychic energy is apportioned at any given moment.

Women Take The Brunt Of It

There are lots of sins to list – embezzlement, torture, child neglect, etc. – but one class stands out because it hits us where we have conflictual feelings, feelings of long standing, of personal evil and failure, of attraction to what's "wrong" and "forbidden." That's sex, all matters sexual. Women take the brunt of this, especially those considered beautiful. They know their beauty commands male interest. They want it, enjoy it, use it. This offers them a variety of male choices to mate with, maybe toward making a prudent selection. But for reasons the Archbishop recognizes for his purposes- and for the prompt guiltiness experienced by the JP's of the world, and for the dynamics the Free Press is forced to handle with kid gloves in reporting about rape - their loveliness can be taken for evil and what's sinful.

Every woman is beautiful. Not everyone agrees. Appreciating this is not as simple as, say, learning to appreciate good music. Men can step up to help out. We'd like to have a generation of men who go beyond measuring the worth of women according how exciting they make them feel. Climbing up to that purview is not easily acquired. Here again our first experiences regarding love/ sex intrude. We're preconditioned to associate something evil when contemplating the place sex and therefore women occupy in our lives. The responses they occasion in us males easily get labeled "naughty" rather than as edifying, admirable and inspirational. An American man can meet with his buddies' haranguing him if they see he's seeing worth in his fiancé exceeding her potential as a bed partner. Some of our cultures demand males be dullards, merely sexual predators. Sometimes bravery, not bravado, is called for when tenderness and loving seem best to match up to his woman's preparedness to accept a full commitment. How can a man attain more sensitivity? He can become her worthy partner with appreciation for his fiancé's qualities that exceed her physical loveliness. That's to be his challenge. Does she have friends? Does she get along with her mother? Does she read? Ponder? Keep up on what's going on in the world?

Does she care and have concerns? Had she got a sense of humor? For his part he may wonder why she's hesitant to allow herself to be gorgeous. Maybe she's tried it and in return got wonderment and sometimes scorn. We should welcome the beauty she brings to our world. She is to feel accepted, admired and safe in choosing to be openly lovely. Can males help to make this happen?

Mary Karr writes in her poem, "**Carnegie Hall Rush Seats**" (**New Yorker**, May 29, 2017) about the cello, "**It speaks from the core of the tree's hacked-out heart, shaped and smoothed like a woman**." She goes on to say, "**Be glad you are not hard wood yourself and can hear it**." She's saying be glad you're not a man who's too dulled by casual, impersonal sex to hear, i.e., to be sensitive to, to be alert to a chance for deep love commitment when it comes along. Then she uses the image of sexual intercourse to communicate the enthralling beauty of the music that can pour from the cleft holes of the instrument, "**Each day the cello is taken into someone's arms, taken between spread legs and lured into shivering …all the sacred cries of saints and demons…it aches, sending up moans from the pit we balance on the edge of.**" Mary Karr had this writer sitting on edge. She seems to have worked off the infantile illusions about love and sex. She could hardly have chosen the part a woman can assume in love-making to convey what's exquisite if she didn't have a revered feeling for love-making. She's a thoroughly beautiful woman; I don't have to look at her to know this. I see her having managed to shuck off her Oedipal remnants of early childhood. She has freed herself, now she can revere sex. I wish the whole world could accomplish this.

As I write this (2016) the Muslim Sunni militants are solidifying their conquests in Northern Iraq. Some TV footage of one invader shows him spewing venom shouting from his Toyota pick-up at a young woman: Cover up your face!!! Female beauty is deemed an evil. They are establishing Sharia Law which singles out females, forbidding their education, limiting them in what they can wear and what they are allowed to work at. Generally they are to stay subdued, confined to the house caring for the male's children. Lest we think female put-downs are only Middle Eastern, look at Rome's. For centuries the Church has covered up female bodies. It has wrapped up its nuns for centuries. And should male eyes wander further on down their bodies it puts clunky shoes on their feet.

There are sharp contradictions going on. Neurotic intrusions are invading our real world. I would say they emerge from the unconscious which is still alive with experiences babies have. They had him feeling love and sex are mixed with hatred and struggle. Cover up your face! What gives a stranger driving a pick-up the hutzpah to shout out randomly to a female he's never met that she's to cover up? Answer: she's attractive. At least the stranger thinks so. She could prompt his erection. Maybe his wish to have sex with her. He must think having erections and sex is bad. Therefore the woman is bad.   Therefore women are bad. So suppress them, cover them up. What triggers his cruelty to women?   His erection – or the possibility of its occurrence. What makes it seem evil?   His Oedipal experiences.

Looking Noble

Bishops can sense where their strengths lie. They come off as willing to take on unpopular positions, willing to lose when the collection plate comes up light. They stand for "truth". We understand that "truth" to be based on underlying feelings, which feelings in turn are the result of Oedipal struggles and outcome.   "Truth" is built on unconscious feelings. There's seeming nobility here. Giving our sex strivings a lower ranking makes the bishops' stance look "good".   The Church says noble things about race and poverty. We admire it for that. Nothing however gets its juices flowing quite like its voice for the right kind of sex.   The Cardinal Archbishop of Washington, DC, Donald Wuerl, made his defense of the Church's rigidity in the **Washington Post** (1/25/13) citing the demands made constantly that it change its 2000-year-old teachings on marriage, family, sexuality, along with morality generally.   I would have you notice how closely he would identify the Church's mission with sexual matters.   In his letter "Belonging To God's Family" of January 25, 2009 he wrote: "Even if they are not active in the Church, they are still searching for fulfillment and peace."   The Cardinal wants the Church to hang tough with its sin-appeal.   It is in the guilt-treating business.   So when American nuns got chastised by Rome recently, it was for their real-life concerns for poverty and the disadvantaged.   Give due emphasis to the evils of homosexuality and abortion, the Holy Office for the Preservation of the Faith shouted. Apparently the Church thinks in sticking with sexual issues, it holds on to a winning hand.

Oedipal Stays Fresh

We value home, family, children and the love that undergirds them to which sex opens the door. Therein lays the problem - where logically no problem exists. But it's not about logic.   Incestuous desire and homicidal wishes distort our respect for our genital functioning. "Distort", the present tense, not "distorted" as in the past. These wants exist in the present. Freud found truth in Immanuel Kant's theory that "…time and space are 'necessary forms of thought'." I will offer some explanation, simply put for our purposes here. It means that the nice food you tasted last Tuesday is a feeling you had then ("time"), not now. At a restaurant ("space") nearby, not now as you sit wherever you are reading this. These are conscious thoughts. This sounds like silly talk but it contrasts well to reveal something about the unconscious mental process. The unconscious doesn't change. Not with time, meaning how many years ago things happened. Or the space, in this case the restaurant in which things happened like the taste of the food. Later on your memory about that restaurant's food will get dull, or slip away entirely. Your recall about the restaurant will suffer memory losses too. Just a few weeks later you'd be hard put to tell the colors of its walls or where the dessert cabinet was located. However all this about time and space doesn't apply here. The unconscious memories stay as sharp and clear as when they first occurred. People in psychoanalysis are surprised at the impact the uncovering of infant memories have. They bring a dream into analysis and the uncovering of its meaning feels totally genuine. They're feeling what they felt when they were 18 or 32 months old. With the feelings the same as they had then. They are actually re-experiencing what they had suppressed. They deliver the same punch as before, except this time they can decide what to do with it with adult reasoning. Until this happens, they float around freely without moorings, knocking around like a rowboat in a squall.

That's behind the policy the Free Press has to set for revealing names concerning news about sexual happenings. People over-react to sexual stuff. They have feelings about those news reports. They'll "stick" negative (read, Oedipally provoked) thoughts to the people involved, even if they are the victims of criminal assault, innocent of sexual wrong-doing.

The **Detroit Free Press**'s setting up those special policies points to another reason why Freud's free association method of uncovering the unconscious works. He instructed patients to freely associate. He meant simply say what comes to mind, No matter what comes to mind is useful. All human thinking has bubbling beneath what early love and hate experiences left behind. We are unaware of them, we don't know they exist, we don't know they take over how we think; they are unconscious. Free-floating thoughts skim at the thinking surface, often into what's pre-conscious. About what s/he knows s/he can talk about. The unconscious is ever bubbling beneath as fresh, as authentic, as influential, as when those memories first occurred.

Why does the Church remain popular? It places limitations on sex which make its mission seem holy. People embrace those limitations because their sex stirrings, they feel, require "cleansing", or redemption, or healing, etc.

Celibacy

At this point we're beginning to see that the Church sees sex as second-rate. Woman are not supposed to like it in contrast to males who are destined to be too over-eager. Those who refrain can get declared to be perching on a higher pedestal. People have a sense that it's proper policy for those closest to what's divine. Making a public promise to God not to have sex, not now, not ever, is thought to please God. That may or may not be true. One thing is certain; baby thought his/her sex/love strivings were totally wrong; God had nothing to do with baby's "conclusions." Most assuredly celibacy impresses the populace and it's the general population that the Church seeks to appeal to. People figure that Church has more of the divine about it when it can inspire young men to foreswear orgasm. Their celibate authorities have promoted numerous nuns and clerics to sainthood but we can count on one hand the married who get similar high honors. St. Thomas More was a case in point. In his youth he decided he could not maintain the "pains of celibacy…," married a woman who later on felt her husband had too much to lose by opposing King Henry's divorce, and often found himself with differences with his son-in-law. He took on the normal stresses of marriage and family. That didn't earn him Rome's praise. Rather it was his resisting the King's wish to convince Rome that he should be granted a divorce. King Henry fired him from his lofty post, then imprisoned him, eventually beheaded him. It takes that kind of drama to dislodge Rome's reflex against the sexually indulgent.

King St. Louis, also married, got top honors for leading one of the Crusades, never mind his anti-Semitism.

It never ends. Yesterday's paper (**Detroit Free Press**, 6/29/17) gave front page coverage to the Archbishop in ceremonial dress at the Cathedral with maybe 800 well-wishers. They were celebrating the marriage of three women prostrate before the altar. They were wearing bridal gowns and veils. The groom was Jesus! The women were around forty, some of whom had once considered becoming nun's, others said they had previous admirable dating experiences, had self-sustaining jobs and residences, and a wish that their celibate living have extra meaning. The Archbishop announced that they were to be thought of as Consecrated Virgins. Essential to their status was never to have had sex and promise never to have sex.

Many women – and men too – have jobs and help out with various good works like food distribution, youth guidance, touring streets for clean-up, coaching sports, helping kids with their reading, etc. They do all sorts of good and never give a thought to congratulations and applause at the High Altar. There's one difference. Celibacy! The CVs eschew sex completely; they've never had it and they don't intend to. That imparts to them an additional aura. We know that sexual impulses can be compelling! They can overtake choice and freedom. Those who can look to the past and say I didn't! and can look to the future and say I won't!, at a minimum gather popular wonderment, and probably admiration. Not incidentally that's the past, the present and the future that Catholics expect of priests who represent them before their God at the Altar. What they want to see, what they expect to see in their priests standing before them on the holy place is "…he's clean!" In intertwining sex with the Altar, in demanding sexual abstinence of its priests, Church does two things: 1) it asserts a power for holiness others don't have, for the "other" worldly, and 2) it bestows on itself a spontaneous special sort of cleanliness because sex is felt to be ignoble.

We should be asking what makes people think sex is so second-rate.

It's All Fantasy

The sexual conflict that Sophocles' Oedipus endured, insightfully written for and presented on the stage throughout the centuries, audiences recognize as striking close to home. NONE OF IT ACTUALLY

EXISTS. It's all fantasy. My dad didn't actually threaten me with castration because I loved his wife. I FELT he would. As I proceeded through life, I was consigned to find my own partner to love and have sex with. Simply reading the words about what I've just put down on paper seems like my life's mission centers around what is bad. It's one more illustration of how imminent is the Oedipal conflict I feel sure we've all gone through. It's unreal. But we feel it; it seems real so we believe it. The Church is unaware that it's serving Oedipal responses. The awareness would deny it purpose. For such it fashioned the notion of "sin". It doesn't indicate anything real; rather it's a design, an invention that describes the impressions Oedipal feelings leave us with after the battle between parent and infant has passed. As noted in his Epistles, St. Paul insightfully set up a religion to tend to people's notions about human sinfulness. He quite brilliantly constructed theses that fit, however simplistically, a manner of responding to the consequences of our Oedipal struggles. Paul would say they are the results of the "Fall", Adam and Eve's "Original Sin". Regardless of the kind of label he may fix to it, the feelings he builds on are our sense of our "sin" or "sins"..

Some Pauline Imitators

Was Paul as smart as Sophocles? Paul had the skill of a Martin Luther, a John Knox or a John Calvin. Knox and Calvin also came up with alternate teachings they claimed had Biblical support; they filled their churches in Scotland and Switzerland and other places with other ideas about pre-destination and God's loving the rich more…maybe. Present day preachers like Billy Graham and Oral Roberts recognize the appeal of the Protestant reformers and present those notions of sin and need for redemption with confidence that they will find those who will buy into it.

Many "sin" religions are out there for the asking. Some seem reasonable. Many Episcopalians and some Lutherans are such. Some are harsh. The Church of Christ, the Pentecostals, the Pillars of Fire come off as stern and intolerant.   Meeting the feelings one holds about one's sinfulness directs the choice of a religion. There's likely a good match going on someplace. People select the appropriate religious practice that fits the feeling one retains of his/her level of guilt and sin. It's based on one's relationship formerly held as infant and child with the parents. I know of no other matrix available. Some people form ideas about choices to make in life from demanding and punitive moms and dads; selecting a gentle deity wouldn't match that felt need.   Nor would a person who'd worked out a companionate relationship with Mom and Dad think of a god as being vindictive. The selecting of one's religion - or the elements one selects from some creed – contains the hope that one will happen upon some proper adjustment to one's felt sinfulness. Things normally get worked out with the parents in family life over the years with the help of an increasing capacity to think, i.e., to think through feelings. The "age of reason", as the Church labels it, arrives for most of us around the ages six or seven. Exactly when matters little. A sense for what's reasonable arrives much too late to settle scores with what resulted from one's Oedipal conflicts.   We buried them, they were too frightening. While Mom and Dad are central to these adjustments, the history of our opposing them we successfully blocked from our memory. No one automatically thinks he/she had a serious tussle with the dear old folks.

Designing God

But a god concept matches the need. First off, a god concept is non-material; parents are physical. They are plain and simple human beings like the rest of us. They are not thought to be those around whom one formed one's feelings about love and sex. But a god-idea has no spatial dimension. He can be fashioned to be anything consistent with a person's notion of what's right and proper. There are about as many of those concepts around as there are people who seek a forgiving "father."

Many are consoled that their church stands ready to bless their sexual functioning; i.e., to make it good. But a young couple however eager to use sexual expression must wait for the blessing. To have sex too early is to have guilty sex and no pious couple wishes to bring "evil" to a love commitment. Oedipal feelings won't allow that. Church leaders don't realize that their norms for sex are designed around infant Oedipal conflicts. Nor need they bother to find out. The Church's claims and rules and threats seem correct. Especially when compared to notions generated in the unconscious and infantile sexuality.

The Church doesn't like Freud's theories. His research uncovers the source of the Church's legitimacy as fantasy-based. He takes away its credibility; he removes the reason behind its too-easily-attained authority. Rome is not about to look for the wellspring for Sophocles' unbroken appeal. It likes things as they are. The Church wouldn't get very far without people's sin-sense and the guilt and fear that follows. To wit: we had neighbors with eight kids. They were Catholics. I must be careful. They may have found out that they loved the presence of children in their home. I'm remembering words to that effect spoken to my parents by some family acquaintance; she said how the presence of little feet running about made her wishing for additional pregnancies. Our neighbors "with eight" may have found similar joy and purpose through parenting.   If we were to come across other practices they subscribed to like their political preferences and the regularity of their church attendance suggesting "obedience" to authority we could make better guesses whether or not taking on the rearing children was goaded by severe consciences. Maybe they'd go through all that eight times because they were pretty sure that human sexual potential required following god-sanctioned norms. Assuming such speculation was true we might expect to find that their infant relationships with mom and dad got them to assume some rather demanding standards.

Some Oedipal Results For Women

When I was a teenager we were taking turns knocking down pins in a bowling alley. Waiting his turn was a classmate who was increasingly disturbed when he noticed a young man "hitting" on a young girl a few benches down from ours. He failed to notice she was loving it. When he'd had enough, he determinedly went over to the couple and blurted, "Leave that girl alone!!!" He was of the conviction that girls do not covet male attention. Do not because he felt they should not. That they might or do made him uncomfortable. That men seek sex he will acknowledge although he feels it's not praiseworthy. That women welcome shelter from overt male outreach fits with his conviction that women are indifferent to sexual joy. The occasional female sexual enthusiast is the exception that proves his rule. His was the simplistic notion shared by many men and it went like this: men are sexual, women are not; sex is unworthy of women.

Another dynamic is in play. If not already, women are eventual mothers. Emotionally speaking, to the neurotic, sexual desire and motherhood don't mix easily. Oedipal memories make us abhor that mix. Men are stuck with the indelible impression that any woman is too much like the first woman he loved with overwhelming intensity - his mother – and it turned out badly because the all-powerful father was part of the triangle. It leaves males with impressions that won't go away, no matter how silly or ill-fitting they turn out to be. Without reflection and insight, males will spontaneously hold notions about expecting women to be "pure", to be sheltered, to be dependent.   However much these reflexes keep showing up in society, they are nevertheless extreme. They are based on pre-rational fantasies.   Thoughtful men come to know they are wrong-headed. They also know, at least many of them do, that they hang around, keep intruding.   They become elements in the awful contradiction swirling around human love. It goes like this: as a man I want sex and I want it a lot. My love partner is to be totally willing, totally cooperative and completely joyous when we copulate. That immensely popular radio personality I've talked about said in another context, There's no greater aphrodisiac than a willing, joyous sexual partner.

Now enters the other side of the contradiction. A wife is a mother, at least potentially. Can her husband comfortably have sex with her without feeling compromised?   Neurotic feelings inform me what a proper woman should be.   A loving, willing partner necessarily surrenders that propriety. She's not to be willing and good at the same time, a purview that emanates from American pulpits on Mother's Day.

Being a mother and simultaneously eager for sex is a turn-off. My father-in-law was caught in this bind so he and his wife worked out a compromise. They had sex but they made sure theirs was God-sanctioned sex; i.e., they indulged in it in a manner God approved of voiced through his Church: the rhythm method of contraception, which means using "natural" coition without artificial devices when the woman isn't ovulating. God's way with sex permitted their feeling better about his wife's goodness, and of his own, for desiring sex. It worked to a point; they were never comfortable with closeness to each other. When my father-in-law was hospitalized a lot during his last years, his wife grieved for him. Was reconciliation taking place? Not really. Each time he returned home the tension returned. Their warmth for each other turned off and on like a spigot, on when he was away, off when he came back. I challenge those who ponder about such contradictions to come up with a more vital explanation of such going's on than that addressed by the Oedipal Conflict.

Using God

What a mess this makes of humanity's love life. People want sex when they want it. It's to have a genuine quality about it. It helps ensure an ongoing delight in each other's presence in their lives. It helps get us over the rough patches in life. Sexual genuineness illuminates the other features of the marital relationship. It can make the simple tasks and burdens of running a household pleasant. The devoutly religious are kidding themselves for thinking they can muster the heft to bring God into their sexual practice. All they're actually doing is using their religion to allow some goodness or worthy purpose to run parallel to the act they feel needs bettering.   But can it be truly thought to be honoring God by utilizing Him to becalm one's conscience? How could it?   There must be less self-focused ways to honor Him.   Should He not be taken for His majesty, His supremacy – for Himself, rather than as a palliative counter-weight for neurotic scruples?

Catholicism has surrendered itself to the service of neurosis - which is to say that it supports our unease with our sexuality by "forgiving" our guilt about it,
- which is to say it has committed itself to confronting a "fallen" sin-prone humanity - which is to say it is counting on humanity's predictable feelings left over from its Oedipal Conflicts. That's how I see it.

Religion generally depends on our universally held notions that get locked into the unconscious.

It's Unreal, The Whole Thing

Oedipal conflicts are entirely fantasy. They have us reacting to baby's imagined problems. Baby felt that dangers were present and real (but they weren't) and they were so awful that he buried them. His running away, burying them, accomplished nothing. In fact they made things worse because they became uncontrolled influences on everyday adult living. So is much of religion. Some elements of religion support the highest examples of altruism. It can however be held to the service of fantasy. Those who hold to much of religion that cannot bear up under logic or scrutiny or experimentation can be drawn to practices than defy good judgment.   Martin Luther saw the fantasy in Catholic belief that the actual flesh and blood of the historical person of Jesus Christ becomes fully available for human ingestion under the aegis of unleavened bread. Hundreds of thousands within a ten mile radius of where I'm sitting say they accept that the hundreds of thousands of little wafers they put on their tongues is each and every one the actual living flesh and blood of Jesus Christ. In effect Luther declared it to be nonsense and gave the notion of "Eucharist" reasonableness by modifying the physical presence notion of a Eucharistic Christic. He held that Christians who assemble to celebrate their union with Christ consume Eucharistic bread as a memorial of His life and teachings. He stayed within the bounds of what's credible while accomplishing the same religious effect. He allowed the Eucharist to make sense. It can be prudently assumed that those who accept the "actual flesh" theology would be more likely to believe extreme religious tenants than those who accept Lutheranism. He made sense by way of common sense.   A lot of enmity between what became two rival Christianities emerged with plenty of blood-letting to follow. Love/sex energies morphed into aggressive/hate energies. (When those conflicts first happened that mixed in those love/hate energies is part of psychoanalytic theory.) They nourished wars fed by umbrage from some that the reformer questioned their sacramental flesh and blood Jesus. But for Oedipal rage at the ready to keep up the ensuing battles, an engagement of wits may have sought for some actual theological justification for what was offered for belief.

Luther accepted however that people had an inner edginess concerning their worthiness as they approached their perfect God. The ancient notion named "sin" was the only one he could offer to explain this. He could not improve on St. Paul's accommodation to this nearly universal feeling among humanity. Throughout history religions sought to fit their creeds and practices to meet the felt human need to become more acceptable when it stood before its deities. Sophocles was not about accommodating to people's "sin" feelings.   His creative talents set to work uncovering the source that activated the sin-notion. What we'd do with it would be our business.   His ***Oedipus Rex*** shined the light on the love/sex dynamics that smother our earliest life experiences.   After the analyst pieces all these fantasies together as bound to their source- experientially and actually felt during the treatment process –his patient can choose not to be victimized any more by guilt, or some particular guilt.

Why Religion?

When I was a kid another kid asked me why I told my sins to a priest. He sanctimoniously said his religion told sinners to confess their sins to God privately as in the quiet of their room. That's fine but there's sureness I enjoyed in confessing to a priest. Admitting to my sins and hearing words of forgiveness from a God-authority seemed like forgiveness clearly rendered. The sinner is left with no doubt but that requires a structure. Some organization has to provide priests, they in turn require bishops to ordain them, who require consecrating popes, who must claim a link right back to the Apostles and Jesus Christ. Finally to His Father in Heaven Who does the forgiving. That's Catholicism's claim.

Requiring a structure is requiring religion. It's all part of bringing the deity close. People like that. They want it. We're about to see that God's biggest task we assign Him is removing guilt for wanting sex…or at least to modify it. Subduing neurotic sentiment has religions bending every which way.

Bringing God Close?

The Bible claims linkage to God. Its claimants say it's God's word. Christian Protestants seize upon it, as do Muslims to the Koran, as do Mormons to the Book of

Mormon, as do Jews to the Torah. Throughout its history mankind has sought ways to make God become real. God's having written a book is one way, a way frequently turned to. A person can grasp, can take hold of, a book containing "God's Word." God seems closer. Importantly "He speaks to me" through the words on its pages.

The manifestations in nature are another. One Church teaching says Christ ascended into Heaven, a location where live God, angels and souls of those who've merited eternal reward. Previous generations looking up at the sky may have concluded that Heaven could plausibly be up there. Especially when clouds are part of the sky a location like Heaven just beyond them seems about right, especially when God's priests and bishops assure them that it's so. I've got a friend who sees in the forces and ordered movements of nature, not to mention its beauty, a linkage to God Himself. God reveals Himself via nature, it would seem. This presents a problem all of itself. There's plenty of distortion in nature which can be violent, disordered, destructive and unpredictable. My friend doesn't address these wrongs. Perhaps they are too difficult to justify. But can he be helpful, to himself or to others such as his wife, who can't slough off a recurrent cancer, by ignoring painful facts about human existence? My friend can't associate anything bad or wrong or evil with God.

Problem: Bad Things Happen

But bad things happen. We can't dodge trying to explain balancing the God whom we assign the task of forgiving our sins with His allowing evil in His world. There are the big evils like wars and Wall Street-induced recessions. There are the ordinary ones. These occur daily, hourly, over and over. Cancers, hospitalizations, surgeries and surgeries gone wrong, auto accidents. kids bullying or being bullied, moms and dads picking at each other, car thieves, credit card hacking. And the car loaded with kids that slides off a bridge that gave way. Archibald MacLeish's Broadway play *Job* puts our problem with evil into this neat dictum: If god is God, He is not good; if God is good, and He is not god.

My mother-in-law (Josette), who was distressed with the news that her two-year-old granddaughter with retinoblastoma was to have an eye removed, organized a group of women who prayed for a miracle. They attended daily Masses and recited Rosaries for two weeks. The surgery occurred as scheduled. Josette remained Catholic. After a disappointing reversal we look for an explanation. Quite probably the leftovers from her Oedipal experiences may have prompted a sin-laden masochism. She'd become scrupulous. And cautious about over indulging. This is the same lady who practiced rhythm to control pregnancies. She wouldn't ask for a beer; i.e., her own bottle. She'd ask if someone "…would like to split a beer with me." Underneath it all she might have figured her scrupulosity fit properly her overall unworthiness. God undoubtedly had good reasons for disappointing her. A sinful person is not to expect other than punishment.

Josette's prayers went unanswered. So do all prayers go unanswered. Josette understood that her god understood her unworthiness. His ignoring her was what she deserved. The grandchild's cancer would turn out to be actually okay. Her flood of prayers guaranteed good.   St. Paul wrote something like, **For those who love God all things work for good** (Romans 8, 28). Life is rife with reverses, with strife and worrisome problems of every kind. There's no escaping them, they will occur. People say they are a necessary part of living. Paul would have us make a virtue out of submitting to adversities.

People are ever getting prodded by their Oedipal interpretations. They're quick to highlight the problems the impulsive use of sex can cause. That sex can serve lofty human purposes is to be quietly acknowledged. We're not to laud its benefits too much. Overlooked is a fact: sexual misuse for the most part contains its own built-in punishment. Messed up marriages and human relationships, reputations lost, guilt feelings and betrayal, these and more are the attendant sorrows for adulterers. Others like venereal disease come standard, packaged along with sexual missteps. Compared however to the problems white collar crime inflict on society they don't do nearly as much damage. Greed was at the bottom of the Great Recession of 2008 – 9; so far no "credit-default swap" cheat has spent time in prison. Far from it. Unethical profiteers frequently enjoy admiration from many uncomprehending observers bedazzled by their strutting in two-thousand dollar suits. Their crimes are difficult to prosecute and impossible to spell out in simple terms. Not so for our sexual aberrations which find exposure in spite of imaginative efforts to hide them. Besides there's plenty of enthusiastic interest ready to vicariously participate at a safe distance in others' orgiastic practices.

Outsized

Our population becomes enormously curious over sexual aberrations. They become big news, the stuff of exaggeration. They're like my tongue poking around the hole my dentist grinds into my tooth when he removes the decay. They're not as big as they seem. Such are sexual promptings, hardly to be compared to our world's truly big problems. Nevertheless this seeming bigness makes an Archbishop's task as the expected guardian of what's good a rather easy one. He need only piggy-back on what our personal sexual promptings call to mind. We hold them as suspect because of our earliest experiences involving them. He can basically ignore the really big evils and still look like a responsible moral leader.

But those other evils, the big ones, exist. I've listed some of them. In 2017 twenty percent of Michigan's youths under five live in poverty. (In Texas it's one in three.) **Credit Suisse** reports that ten percent of the world's population owns 87% of its wealth. Life is really tough for half the world which lacks clean drinking water. The Archbishop and most religious authorities admit such problems exist. That's about all they do. Their rationale is typically vague. They protest in long periodic sentences which hide meaning. They encapsulate moral judgment in legalese; it's hard to follow and our eyes glass over. If they manage not to be heeded in those matters, they can have it both ways. They compile a history of speaking out for what's right and moral. At the same time they're not rallying the population to stand up for a moral position. Admittedly not as easily evoked as for sexual matters, it's not that they don't know how to go about it. They could choose to get as loudly specific as when they hitch on to something sexual. Same-sex marriage is a current example. They don't have to build a constituency as with the hard work of rounding up cooperation if not enthusiasm for social solutions like bettering the lousy education inner city kids are getting. People are already soured on legalizing marriage equality. Religion has only to condemn what people already condemn. It's already there.

People support what the Archbishop says about sex because something felt inwardly prompts them to agree with his super-caution. Much of the purpose of this book is to explore why. And it asks why the truly big problems right in front of his nose the Archbishop can shunt off for others to deal with and still be considered on the side of what's moral. Massive injustices weigh heavily upon our fellow citizens; their causes have been pondered endlessly. Do we hold to real hope that religious leaders have answers? We'd like some because those they've offered so far are pretty thin.

We dig into our wallets when archbishops ask us to. We admit that they don't offer much of worth as we deal with world problems. But they do give us relief of sorts from our Oedipal guilt. For most of us that's all we want. Just wanting love and sex makes us ill at ease so we tie ourselves up with ecclesiastical restrictions. Sex requires the most personal of choices but we don't feel free to make them as free individuals. We are comfortable with sex when the Church says it permitted. Only then. We don't want to make our own decisions about our sex lives, we want "God" to give us the OK. God's church is as close as we can get to involving God when we seek sex/love that is guiltless. His Church allows us to enjoy sex honorably. If we insist on having sex, and we do, we feel a whole lot better about using it if we can get it blessed. We will do sex anyway any way we can approach it. But getting it approved by God first before we combine in physical love-making, well, that's optimal. Religions gladly oblige.

It's All The Same
I could make my point if I showed you a template for a church that does not appeal to our neuroses. This is a church that lets us handle sex on our own. It's a

little hard to imagine Catholicism taking on heavier challenges. It has been assertive in decrying contraception, abortion, divorce, masturbation, homosexuality and pre-marital sex. On such as these it shouts from the rooftops. Most people figure that's the Church's place. People insist on it, more than insistence on social justice like the right to vote, or having a voice in how we get governed, or decisions on issues of war and peace - some of the many problems humanity faces. Many feel it's the Church's purpose to set limits on when and why to experience orgasms. Al Capone, the Chicago gangster, said, We give the people what they want. He included what's illegal (heroin) or unjust (payoffs) or brutal (extortion) or degrading (child porn). The common good loses. There's a parallel to the Church's use of power. It could do much good. Instead it rewards what St. Paul figured out folks wanted when he wrote his Epistles. Catholicism assures our sin-induced inferiority feelings will meet with God's guaranteed acceptance, along with superiority feelings over the rest of mankind who haven't been forgiven. An us vs. them appeal. Infant Oedipal struggles left us feeling degraded, scared and inferior. Religions don't try to remove guilt; they build on it, then arrange for God's forgiveness.

In other places where the Church doesn't hold sway or very little, other religions pick up the slack. Islamism insists on similar rules, as do some by way of ones even stricter. American Baptists follow similar notions as do Hassidic Jews. I used to think only Catholics made laws to "protect" marriage from divorce and intra-marital sex from the evils of contraception. That was before I knew that Oedipal experiences are everyone's experiences. Many Christian creeds manage to come up with the same restrictions I got used to hearing from Catholic authorities. Then I found out that other religions come up with the same, the SAME, dependency on their deities to forgive them. I visited a Muslim mosque recently. A devout layman proudly took me through its fourteen million dollar structure. Incidentals were different. Catholics kneel, Muslims touch their foreheads to the floor; the seeking for forgiveness is the same. Generally the more fundamentalist the religion the more severe are its rules on sex.

Most religious guidance grows out of what we expect it to say. A surface reading of the religious culture would have us conclude that the minister, priests and rabbis write the rules but it's actually the congregations that control what our religions stand for. We indicate to them what we want and don't want. Consider the music we find befitting for worship. It's subdued, clear, straightforward, reverent, and deep-throated. It's what fits with our presumed sinfulness. Even if we don't sin we experience a few sexual urgings now and then. They leave us feeling vulnerable. Asking for forgiveness, however vague and indefinite, seems like the right thing to be about. Everybody is presumed to have sins and should you express doubt about that you're considered arrogant. Everybody else is bowing her/his head and shoulders, what's so good about you???

Prayer – Any Problems?

These bows and kneeling are worshipful; worship is one of the kinds of prayer. The other three, in order of importance, are thanksgiving, forgiveness seeking and petition/asking. Prayer is said to be talking to God. Is that possible? He is distant. People think of Him as living "up"; He's not to be anywhere "down". That He exists within or under the earth's surface is never considered believable so He has to be "up". Just a couple centuries ago He was easily thought to be far above the clouds simply by looking at the sky. These days His whereabouts within our immeasurable universe is difficult to imagine. There are traditions about holy people "ascending" into the heavenly reaches. Christ is almost universally thought to exist there. Elijah, Enoch, Mohammed, Abraham and Mary are also said to be there but this is disputed.

Prayer as talking to God seems to consist of thinking of Him and letting your thoughts turn into words while you "talk" as you would if He were present. It's a one-way relationship, God does not talk back. Many feel this is reasonable because He is limitless, therefore capable of listening and responding to the entire population all at once. He listens and answers. Some say the thoughts that occur to the one praying at the time of the praying are God's answers or even God answering with (mentally spoken) words. Thanking, asking sins' forgiveness, asking for fulfillment of one's needs and wants are the three other prayer purposes. Many pray and claim satisfaction with the results.

People and congregations are often praying 1) for peace and/or 2) to end abortions. These are good things or at least thought to be good things. Why do we have to pray God to do good things? If they are good why would He not do them on His own, i.e. without our asking? Maybe they are not as good as we think they are. God is to be excused for His inaction if we pray for the wrong thing, maybe even a bad thing. It seems justifiable to expect that He tell us that we're miss-informed, making prayer look like idly spinning our wheels. He does not respond in any way that I can or have been able to discern.

Recently Pope Francis got into the fray. There's a line in The Lord's Prayer that asks "our Father" not to "lead us into temptation." He says that's troubling. It presumes that God is responsible for our sins to the extent that he presents them to us. It could be seen as a test like those he permitted to be visited upon Job. The Pope observes that the Greek word for *lead* can be used actively as well as passively.   The translator for our Bible left us with the passive; i.e., we are being lead into temptation and we're asking God to stop it!   That's embarrassing; take God off the hook for setting up evil and make us responsible.   *Lead* used actively would come out to something like *We pray we don't lead others to temptation* and we'd seek God's help in doing so.

The Prayer puts on our lips another notion: *Forgive us...as we forgive those who trespass against us!* Perhaps the Pope should point those words to us out as well. It's in the same spirit as changing the words that imply that God is responsible for temptations. The Pope wants us to take responsibility for our sinning. Don't you wonder how many Catholics realize what they're asking for when they let the words of the Lord"s Paryer slip glibly off their lips?   Essentially they're saying, Lord, treat us like we treat others.   Some Catholics I know might rethink their enmity toward Muslims. It's not a new notion. Luke, 6, 37 puts it thus: What you measure out will be measured back to you.

All this begs the question: Why pray? There's no way to know if it's proper or useful. To all appearances it's a meaningless occupation. It seems correct to conclude God does not heed prayer and/or is unconcerned whether or not we do it.. It looks that way when we read about Job's experiences presented in the **Book of Job.** Job's life could be thought to have been a life totally given over to prayer which fits the definition of worship as prayer. His faith held that God owed nothing to anyone. What He permits in life whether it is good fortune or ill is His to do as He chooses. He owes us no explanation and no communication. Job accepted whatever God sent or planned or allowed. This seems reasonable. The **Book** affirms that God was completely pleased with Job who died with his faith solidly intact. He never knew how pleased God was with him. God did not owe him an expression of His pleasure. It's arguable that to have done so would have diminished the value of his faith. God's seeming to have abandoned him served to illustrate his faith's totality.

It is to be noted that the **Book** makes no mention of Job's having entered Heaven.

Sex and Mother: No Way!

Being a mother and being sexual has become a disquieting mix. The discomfort shows up in our churches' patterns for worship on Mother's Day. Mothers are lauded for their devotion to their kids and their endless housewifely tasks. Early to mid-Nineteenth century sermons asked us to be grateful for the energy and sweat they exude through plain cotton dresses. Today mothers dress up for work outside their homes so that reference is discarded. This presents a problem for heralding mom while keeping it pulpit-appropriate, i.e., sexually moderate. Men love their wives for their smooth skin, nubile leg lines, for their beguiling side-to-side sway when they walk, for their flowing hair and lovely face and eyes, but we're not reminded from the pulpit to be grateful for these. That's a little too sexy for church, including skirting mention on how gorgeous they look when they dress up in heels and jewelry. Surely not a syllable is to be uttered about their sexual desires for the men they married. Clergymen are not likely to pronounce the word **pregnant** from the pulpit but they can allow admiration for child-bearing if they can quickly add there's some punishment that comes with it, i.e., that "fallen" mankind is to bear its children "…in pain…" (Genesis 3, 16), another neurotic reminder that we are sinful creatures.   It's the sort of thing that keeps religion in business.

Kids are as adroit as the clergy.   Mother's Day sermons never titillate and they desexualize praise for child-bearing.   But kids also show skill at getting mother's praise from a safe (i.e., desexualized) distance. My sister and I were kids sitting around the supper table when one of us showed mild contempt for a crust of bread. My Dad volunteered something revealing: "We used to fight for the crust!"   He and his four siblings sat around his family table when he was a youngster. They tussled for Mom's favor and on this occasion it centered on the crust off a loaf of bread. There were many slices of bread but only one crust; perhaps the one on the other side had already been consumed. Getting the crust from Mom was getting her preference over the others. It meant she "loves me more." It meant getting Mother's love at a safe, desexualized distance.

It's the distance Mother's Day preaching must maintain or risk scandalizing those in the pews who for scrupulosity's sake are not to long for orgiastic expression. It requires however our setting aside that such expression yields what's finest in our lives. All this is rife with contradiction; it's about what we felt as babies when we came to hate those who loved us.

Here's what would pass muster as pulpit-worthy language. It's a gooey glob of sentimentality I heard when I was a kid:

Pal of my cradle days

**I've needed you always
Since I was a baby
Upon your knee,
You've sacrificed everything for me.
I stole the gold from your hair,
I put the silver ones there.
I don't know any way
I could ever repay,
Pal of my cradle days.**

The kid's mother "...sacrificed everything..." for him. She's not to have accomplished anything that's joyous by bearing a child. As for her child, he "...stole the gold from her hair..." and "...put the silver ones there..." Motherhood is for masochists. Speak only of female suffering, of the problems her children bring home which she must struggle constantly to mitigate until they grow up and can get out of the house.

That's the world the Church lives in when it celebrates Mother's Day. Can it say that women find pleasure in combining through sex with the men they love? That their beautiful bodies cause delight? That they rejoice in the pleasure they bring to their partners? That their children will come to feel the endless love mom and dad flood them with? The Church chooses the neurotic path to trod, building on the curse God is said to have applied to humanity when he expelled our "first parents" from Paradise. The Bible declares without hesitation: women are to bear children *in pain,* demonstrating that Biblical authors had Oedipal hang-ups like the rest of us.

Mea Culpa

There's irony here. Church-goers are thought to be the most moral, even scrupulous, folks in society, yet are the population most likely to decry their sinfulness because that's the way they feel about themselves. Our Oedipal experiences don't subscribe to logic.

Ever wonder what prompts thousands of kneeling Muslim men to touch their foreheads to the ground? Those are humbling acts. They tell people about their worth in their god's sight. I see the same dynamic when priests lead their congregations in cries of **Lord Have Mercy***!* Minutes later their priests have them pull out kneelers so that they can assume another humble Muslim-like position. Everyone's automatically presumed to be sinful. Those earliest impressions we experience from those months when mother's warmth was our whole world are ever present. They find their way into religious practices. Establishing those practices whether they got based on medieval custom or got Americanized as we see in Mormon rituals requires their imperfect worshippers humbling themselves before their perfect god. They didn't concern themselves why we have these feelings, as we do in this book. All creeds hue to the same presumption about everybody's unworthiness that believers everywhere accept. Not much thought supports their presumptions because they seem so fitting. Rituals vary here and there, but the intent is the same in Baptist Appalachia, Hindu India, ISIS Iraq, Catholic Boston, Muslim Egypt or observant Jews living at the foot of the Brooklyn Bridge. Readers of these pages know I think "something's going on", although it's hard to grasp because its well-spring got buried in the unconscious. A sense of having done wrong, a huge wrong, remains with everyone who's been held at his/her mother's breast. Mother's all-providing comfort and love are perfection itself. But she's already got her lover, Daddy! He's the intruder that baby doesn't sense quite yet. In the many months and the couple years that follow, he sees that he doesn't have first claim on mother's love. Murderous rage results and then terror at being blotted out by such a big competitor. Loving and hating combine within the infant. It's terribly frightening. In later life religion will offer its forgiveness to its adherents who don't feel good about themselves. Sin is the label they apply to specify the evil tendencies we inherit, at the same time offering a certainty that it can administer divine absolution. That's to meet an adult worry. For (male) baby however its huge love and hate meant treading a terrifying path, namely murdering the father, in order to get the impossible dream: mother's exclusive love.

Lording It Over Others
People who design Christmas cards and write the Christmas hymns give their believer-clients a beautified and prideful product. They boast of having the "Savior of the world." That's saying they have something better. Merely sending such messages to friends and acquaintances doesn't mean they intend what the words say, in this instance by implying superiority. It's another outgrowth of the erstwhile Oedipal struggle that keeps popping up so regularly that we forget those other times when we feel besmirched from our guilt-inflicting conflict over love and sex. Most people sending these cards simply want to share the greetings of the season. Jews and Muslims and agnostics who receive such greetings, maybe attending to what the words actually say, may or may not feel compromised. The assertions on many a Christmas card are extreme. Holliday greetings ask us to share the pleasure and relief when we can leave behind the concerns of the work-a-day world for a few days. In contrast Christmas cards say miracles happened because Christ was born; that benefited the

whole human race. A non-Christian however who is equally human can truthfully say the Babe of Bethlehem has not brought him benefits. Christmas messages can sound extreme. Their imagery reaches for the moon.

Consider these: **O little town of Bethlehem….within thy dark streets shineth the Everlasting Light…the hopes and fears of all the years…!" "Glory to the new-born King…" "God and sinners reconciled…!" "…to save us ALL from Satan's wiles when we had gone astray…" "…long lay the earth in sin…till He appeared and the soul felt its worth."**

They say we have "…**gone astray**." Even if we haven't, it presumes everybody has. **"Long lay the earth in sin**." What would have us believe this? There are real people plotting real wrong in our everyday world. But the people mailing those cards are for the most part observantly sinless. Saying they've been made sinless by the Infant of Bethlehem isn't about any real wrong they've done. It's about feeling they need "salvation"; that they've got something evil going on inside that needs forgiveness. Men get reminded of their evil when they get erections over some women they think are attractive. If desires "arise" that go further the male becomes the victim of these intrusive reactions, often at awkward times. On the other hand feelings of love and loving are the basis of what yields what's best in life and living. That can't be what the holiday cards are so happy about. They say we all should be happy about the "saving" the Babe's birth has brought us. Did his "appearance" on earth make my **"soul feel its worth**…?" Would my soul feel worthless without His bringing His redemption? That may be how the fellow with the unwanted and intrusive erections feels. Where do these feelings about needing redeeming come from?

Everybody has them hidden away. When things sexual happen in our lives feelings can arise that make us feel like we need redeeming. At Christmastide I'm guessing some folks want reminders that their sins were forgiven, or able to be.

Anne Murray sings about the newborn as "...**King of Israel**." Is a Jew to feel reassured when these messages declare Christ is his king? Or a Muslim to feel like a fellow-citizen when his Christian neighbors unthinkingly imply his faith bypasses the Real Reconciler with Heaven? Try pointing out the superiority these messages assert over others and Christians may get testy: It's just a simple, time-honored thing we do at the holidays, they say. Everyone accepts that, including Muslims and Hindus and Jews. They'll say you're too picky, take words too seriously. They'll claim their non-Christian or non-Catholic friends don't care or don't give it a thought. No arrogance is implied unless picky persons like you bring the hint of arrogance to it. Anyhow the God of truth and goodness can only approve of a True Faith, **THE** true faith, and we've got it. Some fundamentalists send cards grimly stating the entire "...**world lay in sin and error**..." but all that was supposed to have changed when He was born.

Nothing changed. The same rules and laws of nature endure now as always. There may be more nations at peace now than for a long time but that's not the result of Mary's have borne her baby. Religion purports to reverse our sin-drenched misfortune but babies still get Zita viruses and husbands still kill and get killed in Iraq and eventually we all get failing hearts and die. So why do people become religious? Hint: It's in what St. Paul appealed to.

Paul "Saves" Us

St. Paul made full use of peoples' Oedipal neuroses. He didn't realize it, of course; he was as subject to his unconscious rumblings as any of the rest of us. He saw in the human heart a sense of **something wrong** inside. He would say it's our tilt toward "sin". It had the ring of truth for everyone, everywhere. Most importantly the word "sin" refers to a god, any god anyone everywhere believes in. Those Oedipal results from those infant months and years come from baby's struggles with someone it feels is huge and overwhelming. Actually it's just daddy but to baby he feels like he's about to be squashed fighting with a giant. Something mammoth. He grows into adulthood. His dad was and is simply a person. That concept doesn't fit what it felt like when he was just a few pounds in size, but harboring love and rage engulfed its entire world. A god-concept fits the proportions quite rightly. Religion is the notion people press into service. It supplies a deity; the god of the universe is about the right size. He has the proportions that feel like what we succinctly call Oedipal; i.e., what daddy felt like back when the platform for neurotic choices got set in place. St. Paul figured out that people come equipped with feeling they were stained with badness. He started with the God-notion and fixed to it the negativity we experienced regarding mom and dad. His religion is felt to fit just about right with something everybody feels.

I'm convinced Paul and the Oedipal worked hand in glove. The hidden but ever-encroaching memories from the Oedipal strife feel like what daddy felt like back when. Something huge was what dad felt like. As adults He's the "One" with whom we want to make amends. Paul was not much about helping out one's neighbor or making the world a better place. These are nice and nice sounding but religion functions steadily onward only if "sin" gets forgiven.

God Is The Right Fit

Grappling with Oedipal consequences has to include a deity. Sophocles *Oedipus Rex* had to have a dad he killed and the rest of us did have a dad we hadn't managed to kill. His father was to Oedipus as God is felt to be by the religiously observant.

The god we fashion for ourselves is the one our neurotic needs would have us put together. Furthermore having a god makes religion a necessity. That felt need opens a can of worms. It involves contradictions like that ignored by my friend who is eloquent over the wonders of creation but is wordless about the ugly aspects in life. It twists logic. It has us wondering how a God we want to think is good can keep His distance while terrible things go on happening on this planet. St. Paul's religion (Christianity) offers some answers. His is like religions everywhere, preaching what we want to hear about the god we want to have. When we find war and disease and injustices of all kinds mixing it up with home and family and children and love, many religions will rather brazenly declare them all to be "good". We're not supposed to tell the difference. St. Paul is expert at this: e.g., he'll declare death to be "conquered" (Heb 2, 9), even as we are starring at a corpse. Elsewhere he writes: **"And we know that in all things God works for the good of those who love Him, who have been called according to His purpose"** (Romans, 8, 28). St. Paul makes a virtue of necessity. In other words, he says there's opportunity for virtue here; the evil and painful in life is actually good, even if we have trouble figuring that out. But he builds his theology on what we can't avoid, namely on what's evil and painful but essentially unavoidable in life. Thus if cancer and heart disease are as good as sunshine and flowers, all of life is good.

There's clear contradiction here. We are to belie what we see. Yet there are willing takers. It fits with the feeling of inner wrong, a pay-back for sins. To those who battle cancer or lost a child in a drive-by shooting or got caught in a costly scam Paul offers assurances that "...**the sufferings of this world are not worthy to be compared with the glory which shall be revealed in us...**" (Romans, 8, 18) Oedipal conflicts make us feel guilty, worthy of life's reverses. They were the fantasies upon which Paul sold his brand of religion.

Feeling We're "Better"
Wanting to feel superior sets us looking for shoulders to stand on. Homosexuals and African-Americans can become handy platforms. Gene Hackman played a Southern farmer's son in *Mississippi Burning*. A black farmer with some nearby acreage was doing well with the use of a mule until the mule unexpectedly died. Dad was driving past the now abandoned land. His son was the passenger when he muttered, When a man can't be better than a nigger, he ain't much. The son knew his father had poisoned the mule.

Paul conquered death and the presence of evil. Do we like his solutions? Loretta Lynn sings: Everybody wants to go to heaven but nobody wants to die. People want to believe what they choose to believe. At the funerals of family and friends promises of a future re-uniting with the deceased are offered without reservation. Many accept that - if not fully. The life we continue to care about is the one we've got. It's got a beginning and an end. It's that end part that's disturbing. St. Paul offered his solution, claiming Christ "conquered" death.

Book of Job, 1, Problem Of Evil

We're not the first to try to make sense of humanity's situation. About five or six centuries before the Babe of Bethlehem a group of thinkers? philosophers? teachers? put together a drama that dealt with the problem of evil in the world. It may be the result of centuries of tradition. They made their god out to be as good as possible while admitting that the world he created in which we find ourselves is often occasioned y sorrow. They did as good a job of putting life's loose parts into something that makes sense as any I've found so far. The **Book of Job** told the story of a man (Job) loyal to a god personage (God) who found purpose for the man's loyalty amidst hardship. It centered on winning a bet God made with the personage of evil (Satan). The interplay between these three characters details the reality mankind faces in justifying the choices its deities seem to be making while still justifying the evils they permit. In the story God keeps His distance. He watches closely but gives no indication of His interest. As for Job, he's to make of life the best he can, which presumably means cooperating with whatever may occur.

This is not the God St. Paul and the Church promote. Their template is mankind's unconscious influences.

(Important: Read the **Book of Job** at this time. You'll find it about midway among the Old Testament books.)

The **Book** is a good illustration of religion without Oedipal influences as well as religion which utilizes them. Here's a brief synopsis: God is coaxed by Satan into betting with Satan that Job is loyal and will remain so. Satan determines to inflict on Job such hardship that he will curse God. Over time with God's consent Satan deletes Job's wealth, kills his wife and family, despoils his reputation, and finally has him sitting on a dung heap with sores over his body. He dies in that condition. Job figures God gave – so He can take. His is to do whatever for His purposes which remain hidden from Job. God chooses to keep Job in the dark. They have no communication. His only connection with God is his faith which turns out to be complete - which was what God was betting on. His faith had no evidence to support it.

Book of Job, 2 , An Insight Into God
These are the attributes of the deity:
God never talks.
God never shows up.
God never answers prayer.
God chooses to stay uninvolved in man's world, in its good, in its bad, in anything.
He presumes on one's having faith; i.e., acceptance without evidence.
He chooses to remain aloof, as if He doesn't exist.
He requires mankind to accept His remoteness but live as if He exists.
He lays claim unreservedly to His magnificence as well as mastery over His creation.

These are the attributes of the real God, not the one we make up. No pretending that He is close, that He intervenes in human dealings. He exists in His relationship with mankind as if He does not exist.

The **Book** makes the case for our recognizing and living up to the real world. It's the world we have, not the world we may want or choose. It's a world

WITHOUT yielding to the consequences of the Oedipal Complex. We come to see that that's not a world we wish for. We want a world like the one St. Paul offered, one wherein we have our Oedipal needs catered to, the ones left over from infancy, the ones that have us feeling our nature is prone to evil.

Book of Job, 3, Parallels
I'll take a side trip to cite the parallels between God's dealings with my mother-in-law (Josette) and those He maintained with Job. Their only difference is the 26 centuries that divided them. Otherwise they both got the same divine treatment. During those centuries many lived and died. Maintaining His distance as always, God saw fit to deal with everyone in the same manner. He has treated all humanity the same.

By way of the measurements we glean from the **Book of Job**, God was eminently pleased with my mother-in-law. He might very well have placed a bet with Satan on the steadfastness of her faith-life quite as He did with Job.

A God Who stays distant, Who ignores prayer, Who finds purpose in human misfortune that He never tells us about, is the God all believers have. All mankind experiences Job's God as Job experienced Him. As far as I can tell, Josette accepted the fact that her God chose to be distant. She dealt with Him as He was, not as she would wish Him to be. She had to have been greatly disappointed when her granddaughter lost her eye to cancer. In exchange for a lifetime unswervingly interpreted by Catholic principles, she probably thought God would come through (just this once) with a miracle. She marshalled several friends who met every morning for two weeks to attend Mass and publicly recite the Rosary. God remained remote, unresponsive. She never complained. She may have felt that her sufferings and losses of a lifetime, not to mention her loyalty, atoned for her sins and maybe merited special favor. There had to be good coming from the wrongs that occasioned her life. Basic justice would dictate that balance.

She is dead now. There is no evidence that she is experiencing an after-life. Many are assuming her survival after death, probably for their own reasons. Her Church asserts that she does survive but it too offers no evidence. It does accept money for prayers for her quicker release from what it claims is a mid-way place (of cleansing punishment) in the after-life prior to her guaranteed admittance into Heaven. Its claim fits snugly alongside an unspoken financial motive it may have for that claim. It asserts that the deceased suffer through a vaguely defined cleansing process that hurts and that our prayers - from our side of death's wall - can shorten the time she endures those pains. It encourages collecting money for Masses to bring about such relief more quickly. Believers are pleased that they have such influence at hand; they would not have it otherwise. Masses for the dead sell well. However some kind of evidence that a status (a place?) of painful endurance exists for the recently deceased has never surfaced. It rests solely upon Catholic – which is to say Oedipal – logic: How can a sin-encumbered mortal leave this life without some stain?

Book of Job, 4, It Turns Out We Don't Like God

That is not however what many want from their gods. Not just today's believers either. There was an apparent revolt of sorts at the time *Job* was being put together as a Biblical component. The last short seventeen verses, following upon the full forty-two chapters of the main book, turn the spirit of the **Book** on its head.   They fracture the integral purity of Job's faith. They disallow God to maintain distance thereby diluting Job's faith which had pleased Him most.   The **Book of Job**'s carefully demonstrated purpose is thereby perverted.   Some Scriptural scholars conclude them to be inauthentic add-ons.

Those add-ons are titled **V. Epilogue.**   They tell a different story:
God does show up.
He restores Job's wealth. In fact He doubles what it had been.
His friends are not challenged and confused by Job's <u>sufferings</u>.   His friends and family show him every sympathy. They comfort him; they imply God's choosing Job's destitution was perverse and wrong-headed, as if it had no purpose.   Job begets seven sons and three daughters ("...**throughout the land there were no women as beautiful**..." Job V, 15).   He lives to 140, sees his children to the 4th generation, "...**then he dies...full of days.**"

Book of Job, 5, Designing A God We Like

Those Seventeen verses strike me as shameless fantasy, a feel-good melodrama like the make-believe Hollywood pumps out for patrons looking for an hour or two of escapism from life's reverses. They are willful denial of the reality in which mankind finds itself. They insist on a faith for which God repays the believer generously. It rejects as its model Job's cooperation and submission. It substitutes a quid pro quo. Quite like making a purchase: donate God some troublesome time you will agree to spend at His pleasure and expect generous rewards. Those shameless Seventeen don't require a faith which requires believing without evidence.

Job lived out a terrible life with a faith **without evidence** which God is said to have found most pleasing.   The rest of his fellows say it's quite correct that we should eventually find in God One who rewards abundantly. Such expectations however destroy the merit of faith, the kind of faith about which God boasted to Satan. God is rich, He's got plenty.   He's said to love me, I should expect a lot from a "Loving Father."

Job existed throughout his life under the umbrella of faith only and exactly because his faith allowed him to embrace what God chose for him.   For which he received no explanation.   For which he suffered immensely. With which he went to his death as destitute in personal wealth as he was of any understanding of what God (via Satan) was up to, much less any revelation from God, as to His purpose(s) for his anguished lot in life. That was much too much for the people to bear, speaking now of those who lived at the time of the *Book*'s being compiled. They are the ones who lauded the addition of the Hollywoody "17". The *Book* may be real, it may be truth, it may be the divine manner we've seen before as God's recognizable treatment of mankind. But people didn't like and still don't like living totally by faith. Quite like most believers they expect divine favors in exchange for their faith. Surely a happy after-life at the top of their list.

Maybe they put it first because other nice things they'd like God to produce He won't yield.   It may indicate that belief in a happy after-life may also turn out to be falsely placed and a disappointment.   They'd eagerly embrace a prosperous, debt-free, disease and worry-free life here on earth as the consequence of their kind of faith in their kind of god - if they can get it. Their faith becomes a bartering chip for exchange. It was not what God's boasting about to Satan was based upon. It was not Job's experience in relating to God. Nor was it my mother-in–law's. Nor was it or is it anyone else's experience. As remote as He kept Himself, she kept on attempting to relate to Him and search out what He wanted.

The **Book** contains some of the finest literature, especially the last three chapters in which God extolls His magnificence. Sharply in contrast are the last Seventeen which are crudely spliced together. Their writers were scribblers, seemingly in a hurry.

Book of Job, 6, One Real, One Wishful

The two are appropriately symbolic. The **Book** tells it like it is: a man who bears up under extremes because he believes there's a divine purpose. He's not bartering. He respects that the deity wishes to stay silent and remote and has His own reasons for what happens which He keeps close to His vest. Such faith is totally clean, abstinent of human expectations. God gives and takes away at will. It's all His to do with as He wishes. Job accepts that and goes to his death accepting that. There's no injustice involved; it's all His from start to finish. Such pristine thinking that the **Book** sets forth gets its proper due through words that are crisp and moving.

The Seventeen tell a different story while revealing the faith-hybrid fashioned by those who block acknowledging the God they've got. He asks too much. They invent the god they want, who rewards generously, doubling peoples' investment. He's the god they are willing to pretend exists. They are willing to admit to life's sorrows because they have no choice. But they hold on to their personal expectations about rewards and compensation for doing so. The Seventeen are childish fantasy, briskly and unimaginatively worded.

Book of Job, 7, It's Oedipal

"God gives, God takes, Blessed be He!" is heroic. More precisely Job thereby chose realism. He felt he had nothing coming, no merit due for his faith-acceptance. He looked inside and failed to find some worth with which he could barter with God. The ***Book of Job's*** authors, I submit, saw a persistent bent toward wrong in the human heart. It was the same dynamic that had my wife's parents foreswearing delight in sexual expression, that would have J. P. McCarthy hurrying over to his priest to admit to feeling erectile if some woman asked him to have sex with her, that puts newspaper editors on tenterhooks when reporting sex crimes, that awards reverence for the Church that forbids its clergy to have marital sex, that wraps up its nuns head to toe, and that gives an Archbishop implicit authority to condemn same-sex marriages. Oedipal forces pushed them toward neurotic decisions.

It was what the protester objected to after I had presented Cardinal Dearden's ideas on bussing at a Sunday Mass. Our suburban kids exchanging the schools they attend with inner city kids, and they with ours, was not the righting of an injustice our Catholics wanted to take on. They would not embrace a religion that deals with real life. They were Catholics for personal purposes, along Paul's designs. Sermons like mine that Sunday were a betrayal. They angered them.

Are We Better?

History hasn't changed a lot since Christianity made its way into human affairs two thousand years ago. Advances in literature, mathematics, music, and politics find their underpinnings for the Western world in Ancient Greece. Those principles evolved some five centuries before Christ. Some two millennia earlier the Egyptians built the Pyramids which continue to amaze civil engineers of our own day. Can we discern that humanity is better socially, morally or in any way since Christ's birth or as a result of the religion about which St. Paul wrote in the Epistles? The same propensities toward war, racism and the maldistribution of wealth exist today as are to be found in recorded history anywhere including the Bible.

This is not to deny Christianity's contributions to human betterment. It is to assert however that much injustice and subjugation flourished where it has held sway. It is assuredly demonstrable that human nature is no better or worse since Christ's execution on a cross. That humanity was "redeemed", i.e. "improved" in some fashion, from that point on finds no evidence in history. It is arguable that we became a whole lot better off since the Age of the Enlightenment, with Francis Bacon's **Novum Organum** (1620), ending with Immanuel Kant's **Critique of Pure Reason** (1781).   Christ's dying preceded fourteen centuries of lack-luster human attainment. Substantial achievement in the Golden Age (500 to 300 b.c.e.) showed great promise. Christ's dying didn't revive it. We are forced to observe that Christ's "redemptive cross" contributed nothing to mankind's moral, social and intellectual advancement.   Portions from the Gospels have inspired many to good, although they have us guessing what Christ meant by much of what He is to have said. Most Christians are Pauline, hoping to save their souls. They feel sin-bound and seek forgiveness. Their faith-practice like everything else in life, is Oedipally determined. By contrast Christ as far as we can tell fixed our concerns outward as His parable of the Good Samaritan would have it.

Christmas's Promise Of Peace

What's behind feeling sorry for those who don't know about the Babe of Bethlehem? Catholics like to think they're on the winning team. Christianity has evolved into many sizes and shapes. In one way or another they claim to have truth no one else is heir to. According to some fundamentalists, they risk going to eternal Hell unless they get "washed in the blood of the Lamb." The Church's books on theology I studied had chapters titled, Outside the Church There Is No Salvation (Extra Ecclesiam Nulla Salus). This kind of thinking prompts believers to do the rest of the world the favor of sending them the "revealed truth." They put a lot of their money into financing world-trotting missionaries. It's about getting heathen to switch whatever be their religious practices for what Christians think is correct practice. Supporting all that is something about which they can feel superior compared to other religious types.

Like the Islamists they want the entire world to participate in their kind of Christianity. They make it Christianity's claim. It's a competitive organization. Christians by and large don't much care but official Christendom in Rome and its other centers want all mankind to be baptized. That Islam should inhabit the Holy Land, considered holy by Christ's historical presence there, offends Christian sensibility. The plain logic of such a miss-arrangement would have nothing less than organizing huge corps of armed men at its disposal to set things right. Its armies invaded those "occupiers" with the Crusades (1095 to about 1348 c.

e.). They didn't succeed but they nonetheless felt fully justified in attempting a take-over of other peoples' lands, not by seeking conversions of the heart but coercion by the sword. Blood shed for such a noble cause is blood rightly spilt. Quoting Christ's language about loving one's neighbors as oneself and loving enemies is water cascading off ducks' backs. They could say Christ is not so easily understood and we'd have to agree. They'll pick and choose among Christ's quotes and who's to say they are mistaken? One thing is certain. People fight back when armies thrust themselves into their territories. Arabs generally remember well that Europeans tried to wrest their lands away from them and they like it not!

Making Enemies
They haven't forgotten or forgiven us for our dividing up the oil rich portions of what was to become Iraq and Kuwait. It may be instructive to show that these Christian nations were not about "Christ" and human betterment ala the Good Samaritan. Rather were they about bettering themselves over others, the very stuff of the conflict results between baby and a parent.

A case in point: In 1914 at the start of World War I British scientists found oil in southern Iraq. That was good news. Britain had been buying 80% of their oil from America. They craved a new supplier. Now they had an oil rich desert within their grasp but how to hold on to it? Impatient European nationalism was growing everywhere, grabbing land in Africa and the Middle East, so Britain figured it could similarly claim this stretch of desert belonging to Kuwait which was under British "protection". In 1915 Britain invaded Iraq and occupied Basra, the city just north of the oil fields. They stayed there until they could make it look legal. That happened with the end of the war. Britain and France granted themselves Germany's colonies, which included German rail rights through Iraq to Kuwait's port. In 1922 after Britain took control of Iraq, a British officer with a red pencil drew two red lines on a map and formally amputated the piece of Iraq that had the most oil. It was surely arguable that Sadden Hussein had some legal right on his side when he invaded Kuwait on August 2, 1990.

St. Paul has set the standard. **In a race all run but only one receives the prize. Run to win it!** (1Cor 9, 24). Christ doesn't sound like that. Paul's is not a religion of peace or coexistence. Only one wins! Quite competitive and quite Oedipal. Since Oedipal experiences are universal, no surprise that others feel better about themselves if they "win".

ISIS adherents and recruits call us infidels. To them it's sufficient cause to kill us. To most Islamists we're regarded simply as infidels, as unfortunates who lack Allah's truth. "Allah" is their word for "God".

In similar fashion Christians call them heathen or infidels. They react as we do. They too have Oedipal consequences. They don't take to it kindly when Christian missionaries arrive to preach on their turf. If a Protestant preacher seeking converts from Islam where Islam holds political power gets told by the local authorities to pack up his bags and go home, he's lucky. Imprisonment and possibly something worse awaits many such "intruders." I'll cite just one example from the **Daily Beast** of May 14, 2014. "Meriam Yehya Ibrahim, 27, eight months pregnant, wife of an American citizen from South Sudan, was a condemned prisoner on Death Row in Khartoum….the Sudanese Public Court Order affirmed that Ibrahim was to be sentenced to 100 lashes with a whip and then taken to her death by hanging…the former punishment was for adultery due to the fact that she was a Muslim married to a Christian man, a marriage considered invalid (therefore adulterous), and the latter, somewhat contradictory, for having left Islam to become Christian, which was a capital crime."

We think it reprehensible when some Muslims display extreme intolerance. That same reaction that gets written into our policies, as in the Code of Canon Law, seems quite proper. We fail to recognize how alike we are to one another. We are alike; our neuroses have the same origins.

Pride As Compensation

Those earliest periods of infant growth have love and sex as usurpers of human psychic energy. They also promptly expend it in rage, fear and competition. When it can exclude the needs religion deals with, we're glad to surrender some of our conclusions to others that seem better. About 30 years ago when the Japanese were knocking the socks off American auto makers, flooding the nation with reliable transportation, Ford Motor planners bought some Toyota Camrys and placed them at various manufacturing plants. An engineer told me when their designers ran into problems like how they might bend some metal around headlights to effect a beautiful curve they'd say, Let's go take a look at how the Japanese did it.

But if we run into competition that surrenders our sense of worth we don't give up so promptly. The two-year old male competing for his love attachment with an overwhelming force (who will turn out to be daddy) feels defeat is inevitable because he is so small. His eventual manhood must include, so he feels unconsciously, opportunities to assert his betterment over others. The lad in a scene in the movie **White Ribbon** had parents who tied his hands to his bed to disallow his masturbating. Oedipal experiences already had him on a path to self-contempt. Mom and dad were confirming his negativity. In a few years he'd be finding in Hitler's claims about his Arian superior blood-line a chance to feel better by way of state-approved persecution of Jewry.

Similar "take-charge" practices are common among Catholics. They speak of the perils of "mixed" marriages. "Mixed" means combining the spouse's "true" religious practices with those of a heretic (or heathen or infidel). Church policy in this regard may surprise you. It says a "heretic" is any Protestant, including probably many of your friends and neighbors who mean no offense by being Methodists or Congregationalists. Mothers and fathers eagerly and devotedly raise all kinds of ruckus when their kids seek marriages apart from the family religion. They'll refuse to attend their kids' marriage ceremonies, sometimes disowning them. It's to be seen within all religious types, Catholicism, Mormonism, Judaism, to name a few. Canon Law (1917) comes down hard on Catholics marrying Protestants.   If someone dares to do it anyway, he/she must seek permission from the local bishop. The prospective non-Catholic partner is to sign a document agreeing to have all offspring baptized and reared in the Roman Church or the priest handling the case must refuse to marry them. Assuming the couple signs on, even then they are to speak their vows not at the main church altar with candles and flowers and music but at a side altar with no such pomp save a few candles.

And finally when death intervenes, that partner won't be buried in "blessed" (Catholic) ground. He/she will have to be buried elsewhere. After all those years of fidelity to those promises his or her remains won't be laid to rest in the soil next to one's lover. Find some unblessed soil, they are effectively told, ever mindful that the deceased was a heretic.

Vengeance

Imagine the pain the Church would inflict if it could, if it held secular power. Its history as in the Inquisition makes that sorry point. It parallels Islam's currently applied Sharia Law. Burnings at the stake (read Mark Train on Joan of Arc), imprisonments, and torture of all sorts are cut from the same cloth.

Even the mere pronouncing of the name of a non-Catholic within church walls is to defile its sacred confines. When President Roosevelt died while in office in 1944, priests were forbidden to mention his name from the pulpit. He was a Protestant, therefore a heretic. "We ask for your prayers in this our hour of national grief..." was about all American Catholics were to hear from their priests within their church walls. Heretics were thought to be purveyors of religious falsities. The sacred confines where truth and sacred ceremony were honored were not to know defilement with references to infidels.

Another gem from the 1917 edition of Canon Law, said in effect: If our church burns down, we can use theirs. If theirs burns down, that's tough!

Aggression and competitiveness are as common among the religious (Catholics as well as Baptists, Sunni as well as Shia) as among the irreligious. There're all the same, all striving to feel superior. It's the same the world over. That similarity matches the aggression and fight for superiority everybody goes through as infants and toddlers.

Oedipally-induced self-shame finds expression everywhere with its depth measureable by its intensity. I've been seated in the living rooms of several Roman Catholics during the recent holidays. They set me back on my heels with the quick revulsion they've shown toward Muslims. Not that there's not been plenty of brutality from the ISISists in Western Iraq bordering Syria. But I don't see them making any distinctions. Everything Islamist gets painted over with the scorn we'd heap on murderers, as in murderers all. I'm quite sure if our Congress elected to initiate a campaign to wipe out every Islamist wherever he could be hunted down, those recent acquaintances would give their full support. They'd sink into their comfortable Lazy Boys, a pious regret lining their faces, with pride and thanks that once again we Americans must send our volunteer forces away to purge the civilized world of another despicable gang of thugs. We cover ourselves with goodness for financing the poorest sectors of our society to do the dirty work of war.   We forget, or maybe choose to forget, that we share with the rest of mankind much of the felt wrong we find in others. Virtues appear as well. Our similarities are greater than our differences. Include among them everyone's Oedipal experiences. We're all virtually the same.

Religious groups too often search for some handy pejorative labeling for the others' religious groups they are not supposed to like; they will not be spelled out here. Recall the burning enmity smoldering for several hundreds of years in Northern Ireland. Neither of the parties, Catholics and/or Protestants, shares much love. Injustices abound. Catholics under British rule were denied equal employment opportunities and representative government. The two religions divide themselves along political lines which neatly fit the two sides of the conflict. Religion is not rancor's source. It's the handy overlay justifying hatred and as such seized upon eagerly by all sides. Warring factions seek God's approval for blood-letting whenever they can get it. They almost always do. Among devout Islamists, Sunni and Shia face off against each other. I'm saying their spontaneous contempt for the other is neurotically-sourced upon Oedipal results.

Not long after Luther separated from Rome in 1517, human aggression found expression in wars from 1520 to 1540. His Reformation occasioned a clash among contrasting theologies but it wasn't about a how best to pray. Northern sections of Europe were attracted to Luther's independence from Rome with its characteristic Italian snobbery. An excuse to find freedom from the Church's sacramental grip became available. Offered God's word through the Bible was at the least an even exchange. Selling indulgences to simple peasants to finance a big edifice for the pope caused resentment. There was plenty of unrecognized aggression in the human heart to supply the Wars of Religion which began in 1520 until 1648, the year that saw the conclusion of the Thirty Years War. Those were a series of battles with Protestants and Catholics duking it out. The Bourbons struggled with the Hapsburgs and so on and so forth. All these wars had many non-religious motives but they found popular support by way of accepted religious differences. History's guide posts are reliably found to be wars. Robert E. Lee said: It's good that war is so terrible; otherwise we should like it too much.

There's plenty of aggression within the human heart.

Disparaging Sex Costs Us

The negativity we felt about sex has settled into the unconscious. It's a world of its own, held in place by our psychic energy because as infants we repressed our love/sex/hate for a parent.   Those experiences were way, way too much for our baby psyche to handle so we put it underground, where it hovered beneath the surface of our awareness. There's where it runs about, knocking around freely and unhinged against what we are aware of, and influencing us without our realizing it. One fine psychoanalyst put it this way: we know but we don't know that we know.   It's the area about our surviving baby sex/love wishes that the Church utilizes as its primary source of influence.

The Church is not quick to acknowledge this.   Its announced mission is to make men holy and acceptable to God.   That sells well.   We feel a bit dirty and the Church is ready and willing to make us feel cleaner. Meanwhile the Church would insist that sanctity is its goal and not, as those like me assert, a horribly neurotic appeal because it's based on primitive conclusions we fashioned about ourselves.   But we have them.   We don't feel them as they rumble around inside. But we recognize that we're only at ease when we make some conflicting choices that don't make sense in real life. It didn't make sense for the radio personality to feel he'd have to run to his priest to "confess". He'd have handled the fictional adulterous offer admirably.   Coming that close to sex, however, would have him feeling sinful. Those feelings are what he wanted his priest to make him feel right about. Earlier I've called them "sticky" and stick they do.

Many are the creeds, rituals, ceremonies and rites to be found here and all over the world that will accept being clustered under the over–reaching umbrella of religion.   The term derives from the Latin

religare, to bind, to tie. What is being bound? A number of nineteenth century religions in America required restraint. Adherents said playing cards are "…pictures of the devil…" Dancing, alcohol and even music were damned as damning, because they come too close to our welcoming whatever arousals or giddiness or excitement they ignite, supposedly rooted in humanity's fallen nature. The roots were actually Oedipal.

Those notions put about nimbly. Keeping the faithful sufficiently content even as it capitulates to their Oedipal feelings over their bent to sin means allowing some pleasures like card-playing and alcohol, items their Protestant brethren hear roundly condemned from pulpits just blocks away. Loosening such demands on expressiveness that are church-approved are welcomed. They wouldn't feel right selecting them on their own; that would risk their feeling too close to self-indulgence. Rather than think that one through, i.e. being personally responsible for what is morally right, we prefer a god signal his approval. Feeling we're sub-par deflects our trust in our moral choices. Our son was given gracious hospitality by some Christians while he was doing research in Ghana. They invited him to attend religious services with them which he did and reported back to us that he had a glorious time. It was loads of fun, but hardly to be labeled restraint. Maybe they were expressing relief. Burdened consciences rejoice in free expression as wild as imaginable only when their god gives permission. Some creeds spend their believability on the lifting of a burden. I heard a psychiatrist say he would consider his work very well done if he could accomplish the almost immediate relaxation he thought he saw in a troubled penitent after he confessed his sins to a priest. It worked like magic. I'm suggesting that it is.

I remember some lady coming to my confessional box and breathlessly whispering, I and this fellow did all the most awful things imaginable. I dutifully gave her absolution and probably a number of prayers to say as a "penance". But she remained disquieted; it was discernible in her voice. Is that all? she asked. I had handled it badly. The forgiveness I applied was too obviously magical. I gathered that she would have had me scold her, question her; perhaps interrogate her, make her squirm a bit. And require a penance more difficult to fulfill, a punishment to fit the crime. I heard a normally reliable source say on the radio the other day, It's an established American ritual. We sin Saturday night, seek repentance Sunday morning. When our son (the same one, we only have one) as a four year old picked up some candy off a grocer's shelf, we went together to return it to the manager. I suspect he felt better after that. I'm postulating that that's what religion "binds" us to, a means of feeling better about ourselves. Religions, especially the big ones like Catholicism and Islamism, require an ongoing seeking for forgiveness. The Catholic Mass rids its congregations of feelings of unworthiness early in its ceremonial with cries of **Lord, Have Mercy**! Later it will put them on their knees. These humbling bodily expressions have ancient roots but they communicate the sinner's repentant submission as unmistakably as ever. To me those have Oedipal links.

More Oedipal At Work

The unconscious takes on curious forms. As with water in a balloon, tightening it on one side simply fills out the other; the water's volume stays the same. The unconscious takes on curious forms. Jonathan Haight, in his book **The Righteous Mind**, talks about the response patterns of conservatives as distinct from liberals. Haight says liberals use three "languages", care for the weak, fairness and liberty. Conservatives use the same but add three more: loyalty, respect for authority and sanctity. Conservatives generally feel better if they observe religious ritual.

There's recent church history that makes this point. The Second Vatican Council recommended that Catholics jettison meatless Fridays in favor of choosing good deeds of their own design. People didn't like it. They wanted the security of Church authority behind the simple, and actually meaningless, abstinence from Friday meat. It offered them God-sanctioned surety that they were really doing something holy, a security their personal selection of something worthwhile, like shoveling a sick neighbor's sidewalk, didn't offer. Proof of the better of the two choices rested in the Church's slapping on its guarantee that eating Friday meat was mortally sinful punishable with Hell-fire, something that couldn't be the result of skipping the shoveling of a sick neighbor's sidewalk. God's mandates are superior to "sin-stained" (read Oedipally diminished) human acts.

Phil And Steve

Consider Phil who turned out to be conservative and Steve who became liberal. Both Phil and Steve had over-bearing fathers but they reacted differently. Phil fashioned an accommodating respect for authority from the experience and Steve who was angered at his father's use of muscle looked a second time at regulations from on high. Both did what all male infants do. They wanted their mothers all to themselves and made adjustments to the unfair fight that ensued. Such conflicts shape our ideas of what's morally right and wrong. They show up in disguised form in later life.

Professor Haight proceeds to have a lot of fun showing how we use our fixed attitudes as liberals and/or conservatives without realizing it. The latter are much more likely to respond to symbols like reverence for the flag and become reflexively suspicious of "foreign" garb like saris and turbans.

Nicholas Kristoff in his **New York Times** article "Politics, Odors and Soap" of March 21, 2012 cites some primitive leftovers from our earliest years of development. Here's a quote: "…Some research suggests that conservatives are particularly attuned to threats with a greater startle reflex when they hear loud noises. Conservatives also secrete more skin moisture when they see disgusting images, such as a person eating worms. Liberals feel disgust too, but a lot less." Anything that prods us to think of disgust or cleanliness seems to have an at least temporary effect on our politics. It pushes our sanctity buttons and makes us more conservative

A University of Toronto study found that if people were asked to wash their hands with soap and water before filling out a questionnaire, they become more moralistic about issues like drug use and pornography. Researchers found that interviewees on Stanford's campus offered harsher, more moralistic views after "fart spray" had been released in the area.   At Cornell University, students answered questions in more conservative ways when they were simply near a hand sanitizer station.

Our ideologies shape much more than our politics. We'll seek pets who reflect our moral outlook. Researchers at **Your Morals.org** found that liberals prefer dogs that are gentle but not subservient, while conservatives seek dogs who are loyal and obedient. In short, moral and political judgments are complex and contradictory, shaped by a panoply of values and personalities.

Consider with me those two men I just spoke of, both with responsible jobs but with two opposite decisions regarding the employees their decisions affect. The first is Phil. He's the vice-president of a group of Catholic hospitals around Philadelphia. He complains about having to write off hundreds of thousands of dollars each month to supplement care for the uninsured. He feels medical insurance is a privilege, not a right. The second is Steve. His story goes back a few years. He was hired in as a young engineer at General Motors and wound up with the assignment nobody liked, time-study. That meant "studying" (a euphemism) the production line and planning for its faster movement. It was the early 1930s. The Great Depression was deeply imbedded, unemployment was rampant. The assembly line kept moving unmercifully hour after hour. Laborers, sweaty and sore from grabbing parts from below, hoisting them in place and hurriedly reaching back for another, could barely keep up. Unions were forming. Steve quietly turned to their stewards for support. Typically he would say to them: I'll submit this standard to upper management. Now you back me up!

Clearly Phil and Steve differed. What made the difference? What they thought of their fathers holds a credible answer, their feelings about their dads from incidents when they were teenagers. I'm suggesting that their responses to those incidents had their bases in their pre-rational years; i.e., the feelings they took away about their dads when they found that their earliest love/ sex feelings put them in conflict with them. Even if you're not quite ready to go along with me on those infant-based struggles, what these two men must have concluded about their fathers fits my assertions. Phil would tell you that his father was a disciplinarian whom he learned to admire. In one instance, the father spanked his behind pretty thoroughly. "It was for my own good ", he will declare. Steve also was "beaten" (his word) by dad and it seemed to confirm what he'd already felt about him. He was humiliated and angry and unforgiving.   It presaged his feelings about all authority. See here, if you will, how he'd find it easier to seek out union support against his upper management that he saw as oppressive. Steve saw it as beating up on the defenseless "little guy". He was acting out his fury at his father before whom he was small, powerless.

(His father had been conscribed into Bismarck's army and became a "schussmeister", some kind of artillery overseer. His sons were years later to whisper among themselves their contempt for his muscular rule, calling him a "sheissmeister", as in shit master. Looks like all the sons came away with a penchant to dislike authority, but not necessarily. Some may have thought it best to knuckle under, thus presaging a penchant to conform to whomever is boss. Some may have come to feel "law and order" is admirable.)

Oedipal residuals leave us trying to feel better about ourselves. Ask why someone feels these needs and the truest answers will be found to be based on the battles s/he fought and lost in the Oedipal years. Steve bristled at high-handed bosses of any stripe, governmental or military or industrial. Phil saw little or nothing inhumane in his reluctance to pay for care for the uninsured. Unconscious memories determine how such inclinations are acted upon day-to-day.

Maureen Dowd of the **New York Times** loves to write about these things. In her 3/25/2012 article **How Oedipus Wreaks**, she speaks of Mike Nichols, the renowned playwright, director and comic, who "…believes the father-son wrestle is the central American relationship." All the work I've put into building the family scrap collection business, dad's will complain, and you want to be a journalist or some damn thing? She continues: "Presidential politics thrum with Oedipal loop-de-loops. Many candidates – JFK, Al Gore, Mitt Romney - seem to be running to fulfill their fathers' dream more than their own. Others like "W" (George W. Bush) and John McCain, are shadowboxing with fathers who cast a long shadow. Still others, like Jon Huntsman, are treated to a campaign by wealthy dads. Barack Obama, Bill Clinton and Newt Gingrich have lived in the shadow of their fathers' absence. Nichols says he knows so many accomplished people who can't get their fathers to even acknowledge their achievements. Joseph Campbell says "The Finding of the Father" has to do with finding your own character and destiny. He goes on: the first enemy is the father, if you are a man. As a boy, every enemy is potentially psychologically associated with the father image. Nichols said he felt he had to side with his father in a family dispute "because otherwise whom would I identify with. My father was the guy whose essence was forming who I was." Even after his father died, he kept an open channel with his dad. He had conversations with him about what he accomplished and what he failed at. "It had to be him and me, him proud of me. He was proud once when I won a horse show in school. And he was proud when I was brave when broke my arm. And man, I've hauled those out innumerable times."

Here's Dowd's coup de' grace, sounding like an analyst herself about Mike Nichols: "A psychiatrist once told him, even after he was a success, that he was holding himself back because he was frightened that he would harm his father: 'I was told Nichols had to have attained some deep regression in his psychoanalysis in order to find out that '…my problems were partly not wanting to symbolically kill my already dead father or to surpass him.' "

Viewers of Sophocles' **Oedipus Rex** through the centuries watched actors piece together Oedipus's conflict. His marriage had been normal and fulfilling. However watching his story unfold on stage elicits advance anxiety for what he was inevitably to discover. When he came to that jarring understanding, everyone accepted why he was unhinged with guilt. His guiltless sexual involvement with his mother through a marriage which he would never have entered into with prior knowledge, his killing a man he couldn't have suspected was his father, counted for naught. His revulsion sought proportion for his perceived "evil", not a real evil which didn't exist. That perception was cemented solidly into his unconscious in those first months and years of life and it felt limitless. It remained feeling limitless. There would be no way he could punish himself as he felt he deserved. For his innocent sexual intimacy, he self-inflicted an enormous punishment lasting for the rest of his life.

How It Works

Oedipus Rex is a hard to believe yet feelingly relevant drama. It's not a preposterous story. It's believable because each of us has felt love/sex strivings toward an opposite sex parent. We've pushed them underground because they are repugnant. But they cling, now amidst hidden energies that keep bubbling inside unrecognized. ***We know but we don't know we know.***

In treatment bit by bit patients start feeling some of the feelings that lead them to repress them in the first place. The conscious thoughts that cause defensiveness are likely coming close to unconscious material. (Try it yourself for a couple minutes. Say whatever comes to mind out loud. You'll feel your defenses leaping forward to shut you up.) Genuine feelings result. They supply a sure track back to what the patient had forgotten. The patient's flow of talk-talk-talk allows the analyst who is listening closely to "hear" the Oedipal past; it is ever influencing what's present. He puts it into words. The patient can feel when the words "hit the mark". Because the analyst's interpretation is accurate, he feels its authenticity.

Notice that the analyst asks his patient to say whatever comes to mind. Freud's method is the confident illustration that Oedipal hang-ups are perpetually active. Treatment isn't talking about sex. Treatment is about bringing to awareness neurotic dynamics. They are ALWAYS present and active. The analyst's job is to decode what's going on underneath at any given moment and handing it to his patient in words. Those words give his patient a firm hold on what his neurosis is doing for the moment. Those moments vary and so do the revealing words. Bit by bit the neurosis's hold is weakened. As one analyst puts it, each session is a gold nugget he can put in his pocket.

Hypnosis only seems easier. The interplay of conscious and unconscious mental forces shows up without the pained experiences that set up the fright that forced them into unawareness. Knowledge without the genuine re-experiencing attached is useless. Oedipal consequences sound preposterous in theory. No one believes them. However when they are re-experienced, they are believed because they are felt. What seemed yesterday as preposterous, today is re-experienced. It becomes eminently believable.   The patient's defensiveness allows both patient and analyst to realize the conflicted past is being uncovered. Freely talking touches on the points of defensiveness. Uncovering what had been forgotten is a gradual process, like peeling off the layers of an onion. The patient becomes constantly and intensely resistant to saying what comes to mind. The resistance illuminates what the patient had repressed. The same forces that are resisting what comes to mind are the ones the 6 month old, or 12 month old, or 18 or 24 month old found so overwhelming and therefore blocked out. Those fears, those energies, are the same ones the infant originally repressed. They remain as vigorous as they were when they were first felt.

Humility Through Humiliation?

Christ identified Himself with the population. Doing to another is doing to me, He insisted. Christians have hardly distinguished themselves with Christ-likeness, having joined in various inhumanities throughout their history. They've done plenty of blood-letting. In this respect the Church joins the practices of their co-religious opponents who speak blessings upon their military excursions as they send their men off to war. Many will say all such are flat out contrary to what Jesus required of those who would take Him seriously. Our neighbor a couple doors down I've often heard quoting the current Dalai Lama of Tibet who said, Your Christ is great. You Christians do a poor job of imitating Him.

The term Christianity does not mean Christ-like. It refers to those who attend Christian churches. Can we imagine Christ's admirers actually living as He exemplified? Turning the other cheek? Doing good to one's persecutors? Refusing to fight back when others attack? It's asking a lot - to the point that has many wondering if we're interpreting Him correctly. It's quite a world Christ would bring about if He is to be interpreted in this manner. A few of His imitators will try. Christians by and large don't. Confused, they pick and choose. Like General Lee. Like every Christian I know. Some of what He's to have said is simply too difficult to follow. He sets too high a standard. A thief breaks into my home and I'm to submit? Or he breaks into my home and threatens the lives of my wife and children? I'm to let him do that? Are we looking at an ideal the purpose of which it is to demonstrate our limitations, weaknesses, along with each one's Original Sin's tilt to wrong-doing?   Some pastors think such theses have the goal of illustrating how sin-prone we are. They purposely humiliate and so elicit our gratitude for Christ's having died for "...wretches like me...", a paraphrase of the famous hymn **Amazing Grace**.   It appeals to our presumed self-contempt which in turn is built on unrecognized but ever-influential Oedipal under-stirrings.

How It Might Look

It's on point to admit that we're not certain that Christ meant what we are saying He meant. Perhaps He spoke for His fellow Jews, meaning that He detested their merciless conquerors. His countrymen had few means to confront their Roman invaders beyond passive aggression. If His people had an army that could take on the Roman military with a reasonable chance of competing He'd probably have foresworn the advice to turn their other cheeks, to do good to those who persecute, to return hate with love. Nevertheless those Gospel passages remain in print, impossible to overlook. Not to be ignored is the success a few courageous leaders have attained by trying Christ's technique; He may have been relevantly practical. Mahatma Gandhi and Martin Luther King, Jr. are sterling examples. Nelson Mandela came awfully close to His ideal while remaining a practical politician. He set about peace-making in South Africa after a 27 year imprisonment. He began by assuring fairness in judgments over his captors, then granting forgiveness for the exposed cruelties and injustices against him and his political allies. Peace for his troubled nation became his goal, meaning he had to swallow chances for revenge. Few would have thought pay-back was an overreach.

How It Would Look

If everyone would set right the injustices in our world – or if they would try – odds are our lives would be peaceful. It's a lot to ask of human nature. If many of us - some of us? - would try implementing what we're guessing is His way, more people would share a happier life. Some of it seems achievable. We'd pour our energies into making life as good as we can make it – for everybody, friends and foe. Seeking cures for cancer, providing safe streets, replacing worn-out schools, supporting the arts. We'd put our brains toward designing better educational programs for inner-city kids. Contemplating artistry as in John Coltrane's jazz creations and Beethoven's symphonies can perk us up even as we lament reports of raw aggression and greed in the Middle East and Eastern Europe. We've got our own experience with similar kinds of disregard for human need in our own backyards.

Accomplishing what we could would be admirable and would surely garner admiration from every part of the world. Here would be a group with little money expended to build beautiful churches. After putting their resources to binding up their fellow citizens' wounds, there couldn't be much left.

Christ is inspiringly tough to live by. By-passing Paul's absorbing ourselves in personal navel-gazing over 'being saved" leaves us with what we're arriving at as Christ's alternative: love for everyone! What if Christians tried it? One result: there wouldn't be so many eager to wear the label Christian.

But those who remained:

1- would be a humble lot having experienced more failures than successes in trying to be Good Sams;

2- wouldn't be trying to convert the world; they'd exist only to help. Heroic types might be attracted to join up;

3- would focus on this planet; heaven would be a by-product. A "heaven-on-earth" might become that by-product;

4- "Others" like Muslims, Mormons, Pentecostals, all the "others", would see in them not competitors attempting to woo away their adherents. They'd see simply a willingness to solve problems and join with others who want to do the same;

5- would be welcomed for the most part. And why not? They would see in Christ's Good Sam a non-competitive and unthreatening model. GS didn't ask for anything; he just saw need and dealt with it;

6- would not be sending those Christmas cards, at least not those boasting about how much better they'd become over others;

7- wouldn't be self-promoting. Dealing with life's problems is so challenging that efforts to solve them, even with our best efforts, would leave little to brag about. Joy to the World? Well maybe, after they made a more joyous world happen.

8 – Oedipal promptings would be treated for what they are, neurotic.

St. Paul serviced sentiments for self-centered comfort, whereas Christ looked outward. By way of His Good Samaritan model we're to find for imitation someone who kept his eyes open for human need with not a hint about Pauline-like assurances to soothe personal hang-ups. The previous eight characteristics would emerge among those choosing to take on Good Sam's look on life.

Religion will survive nicely without nobility. The best among them center on modeling life around the spontaneous mercy shown by the Good Samaritan. Society would do well to follow the norms that would occur to us when we think through his response to human need. However religion survives well when it gives people what they feel a deity should be able to provide.   He is to provide for their neurotic needs. People see the wrongs in the world, but their self-interest is of primary concern. First among what they would have from God is to have their sins forgiven. They experience injustices they want set right; He is to set them right. They do not like or understand death; He is to spare them such finality.   He is to be their father who treats them as they feel a loving father should. They relate to Him with human expectations.

Psychic Energy For Sex, For Aggression

This evening's news highlighted an Imam who was famous for attracting young idealists or the disaffected or the adventurous, into a holy war. He promised what a certain kind of young man would recognize as welcome change. Youthful aimlessness rooted in an unproviding world without education and a productive future instantly has worth – and a paycheck each month. Blessed by Allah, how could a young idealist do better? The war seeks their religion's dominance by way of Sharia Law, a repressive fundamentalism. It boasts of its blessedness, over the "corrupt" culture of the West, particularly focused on the American invaders. The Imam was adorned in white garments and stood before a bank of microphones. He was reaching a wide audience. Here was his message: Take heed, you young men! Don't think because you turn your eyes from young women that you are spared. Or that the women are without blame for the evil they draw you to just because they cover their bodies in layers of cloth. If you are thinking of sex with her, you are guilty. Even if you avert your eyes and she is fully covered! You are guilty! (There's similar nonsense in the Gospels. Cf. Matt 7, 27-28.)

Oedipal conclusions are fueled by aggressive as well as erotic energies. Thomas Friedman wrote that most Imams find ready recruits among young men who've never held a girl's hand.

Teaming up

The Iman and our Archbishop are kindred spirits. Both utilize sex. Young men who think their erections prove their sinfulness see the "truth" in what he has to say - about themselves and women as well. The Archbishop is on record as applauding his Church's selecting the gender that has testicles to be the one from which its priests are to be derived. Christ chose males; how we can change THAT? he avows. His corps of clergymen who eschew sexual intercourse are his living proof that sexlessness is holy and all the rest of us copulators are second rate.

Which begs the question, why don't we openly aver sex's goodness?   And stand up for its components?   Merely saying penis and vagina and orgasm and such tightens our reflexes.   There are probably fifty slang terms for the penis ("schlong", "dick", "prick", etc.) and the vagina ("box", "cunt", etc.). They're off-putting and intended to be so. They prompt us to defensiveness. On one hand we value our bodies and their capacities for the rewards sex brings to our lives. But on the other that underlying discomfort illustrates that the Imam, much like the Archbishop, instinctively knows that playing the sex-is-suspect card gives an aura of representing something better.

Sex as the drag on our sense of worth is to be found everywhere. Some scene from a BBC show last Sunday, set in the 18th Century, focused mostly not on the newly marrieds who were dancing with friends at their wedding party. It centered on two men, one the protagonist, the other the marrying minister. The former had made some positive comment about the happiness of the occasion, to which the minister replied: Marriage is the remedy for fornication and sin.

Oedipal Leftovers Are Alive And Well.
A few months ago I sold our car to a fellow who after the sale sent me a brochure extolling his choice of a religion. He thought I should make a similar religious choice. The brochure was mostly quotes from St. Paul all of them claiming mankind's fundamental sinfulness. That prompted me to remember what Franklin Graham's daughter said a few years ago, seated among some Sunday morning pundits: We are all sinners, she avowed.

What's the appeal? The appeal rests on most people's wish to be honest and truthful. Thus if some priest or minister were to ask them to be honest about their goodness, they'd be slow to admit to some degree of virtuousness. Oedipal results deep inside make us feel she speaks some truth about our nature. Surely there is more that's ennobling about marriage unlike the scorn for sex seen in that snippet from the BBC TV show. St. Paul's advising the rest of us to admire him as a celibate (1Cor. 7, 8 -9) sounded authentic to Franklin Graham's daughter. And to the man who bought our car I recalled for him how the sale went smoothly. He had given me a cashier's check and I signed over the title. That was all there was to it. It wasn't characteristic of a deal between sinners. I'm sure I didn't change his mind. He didn't send me more brochures. Oedipal falsities don't dissolve so promptly.

The notion of sin gets pinned on us easily. That last wedding we attended was classy in an elegant setting. All was beauty except for the marrying parson who stayed remote in tone as well as content. In those few spare moments when he had center-stage he spoke a tiny phrase calling marriage an "…allaying of concupiscence…"

Sexual attraction gets mixed with feeling compromised. In reality it evokes promptings of the most generous kind. Ambitious strivers of the most accomplished sort like MBAs and MDs surprise themselves when some man or woman has them given over to a life-long commitment. Their accomplishments mean a lot and remain so. But the likelihood that some person will give over his or herself completely to love sharing becomes prized above any other good. That makes the preparation for life in those earlier years - years of self-evaluation, self-development, accomplishment and discipline – quite worth it all. The mutual giving over of all that one is and hopes to be to an equally loving partner finds no more ennobling parallel anywhere else in life. Labeling it "an allaying of concupiscence", mocks love's joyous potential.

Aggression

Seventeen million casualties, including more than five million killed outright, were the last numbers of the outrageous carnage attained from the World War I. The lethal efficiency of that war appalled world leaders. Freud took a hard look at basic human instincts in 1915, concluding that improvement would occur only at a deep psychic level. Unrealistic would be confidence placed in merely educating, lecturing, sermonizing and hand-wringing. We are to admit we are an aggressive species, much more than we realize - or wish to - even as we count the results of our willingness to kill our fellows.

There's that other side of the human psychic-energy expenditure: Aggression. Human nature has a ready reflex to inflict suffering, death and oppression upon our fellows. It's a propensity expressed through armaments and military edginess. Judging from the large amounts Americans spend on them we won't risk being without them. A journalist reported today about a lady whose son told her in 1962 that we're not likely to begin another war. She recalled that conversation and his naiveté when her son phoned recently. Mom, he said, it was a wish, a devout wish but an idealistic one. He was the erstwhile presidential candidate, George McGovern. He had said years ago that one positive outcome of our defeat in Vietnam was that we'd learned our lesson; we'd think it out completely before going into another sparsely-planned military adventure. Sadly he lived to eat his words thirty years later when we invaded Iraq.

None of this says what we'd have attained if the rest of the world joined the Christian one. It glibly declares that it will be a better one. In some parts of the world where Christianity is prominent a proportion of the population is civilized and sometimes responsive to human need. Other parts are self-serving. About the same percentages are to be found among other religious sectors. Some inspire, some dis-edify. People are simply people, whatever their religion, wherever they grow up and establish their families and cultures. Missionaries emerge and an unseemly picture follows. We find episodes like those of the minister who tried preaching in Islamist territory. He was seen as a deliberate agent of deception, a clever trickster dressing up churches to resemble mosques. Imams guarantee suffering in eternal hellfire to Islamists converted to Christianity, a strong-arm effort to keep Islam's sheep-like within its confines. This kind of flexing of religious muscle Catholics are used to. It's remarkably in the spirit of Rome's Code of Canon Law of 1917. Acting like we're better builds on a need to feel better - which need has Oedipal tie-ins. My wife as a Catholic child was distressed that her non-Catholic friend was going to Hell. She tried to make a Catholic of her – to save her soul. Canon Law labeled her friend as "heathen".

Christ And Paul: A Contrast

Christ says we're going to be surprised (Matt 25, 3 – 46) when we find out the kinds of persons who gained Heavenly rewards. They contrast with the "goats" who were figuring all along that they were the saints. He said our treatment of our fellows was our treatment of Him. His definition of a proper neighbor in His view was the Good Samaritan (Good Sam) (Luke 10, 25 – 37).

My guess is Christ wants us to focus outwardly. That sounds mature and could underpin what's inspirational. That might come off as vague until we compare it with St. Paul. He wanted us to gaze inwardly. There we were to find what needed divine mercy. Oedipal unconscious needling into important choices adults have to make was having its way as it always does. For example he would have had us feel better with assertions about his supporters' marital sex being better than a pagan's. Today it's called the Pauline Privilege, practiced throughout the Roman Catholic world. Simply put, if a "pagan", meaning someone unbaptized, becomes baptized, s/he is free to marry again if to one baptized (Christian) (1Cor. 7: 12 – 15). The unbaptized partner can be put aside in favor of sharing one's bed with a baptized one. I doubt St. Paul read Sophocles but he realized people have a feeling of sinfulness. When you're designing a church, comforting Oedipal mind-games has magnetism.   St. Paul's ego was consistent with such snobbery. ***And if anyone teaches something other than what I've taught, let him be damned.*** That last salvo is in Galatians 1:9.

Racism, Then And Now
Christ touched upon racism. The Samaritans were half-breeds, half Jewish, half something else. Mixing blood lines compromised the racial stock from which the Messiah was to be born. Hating Samaritans was an act of religious loyalty, an affirmation of a glorious Jewish destiny. Similar hatreds have occurred countless times. Again I cite Canon Law of 1917 where the mere mention of the name of a Protestant from a Catholic pulpit was forbidden. Protestants were labeled heathens and infidels so not to be spoken of within sacred, i.e., Catholic, confines. Christ hit hard on that

sort of thinking. No wonder that he found Himself hated by the powers that held sway. Admired as He was for His mandate of universal love, He thereby took away a soothing balm for bruised egos. That didn't go down well in Christ's time or in any other. Humanity feels better about itself when it can have other "lessers" to stand upon, to lord over. Surely the Jews of His time, conquered by Rome, reluctant taxpayers to a hated oppressor who returned hatred in kind, welcomed the Samaritan to tramp upon. Now comes Christ making Good Sam the model of brotherly love. If we are to universalize what He had in mind for His Jewish brothers and sisters, His would be a world of peace, everybody taking care of everybody. It would be His heaven on earth, His Kingdom come.

However it's utopian. Like losing weight is easy - simply eat less, exercise more. People have capacity for hate as well as love and can be counted on to give expression to both. When S/Sgt. Robert Bales returned to Fort Hood to stand trial for the brutal midnight slaying of 16 Afghan villagers, friends and family who knew him as a responsible soldier and family man couldn't believe it of him. Believe it we should, however, because recognizing these capacities in our nature is a good start if we're to do something about them. Hatred lies at the ready in every human heart. We see carnage in Syria, Ukraine, South Sudan, Mali, India and Iraq. Northern Ireland looks uneasy. Europe gets prickly about immigrants. Does some other citizenry come to mind?

Bringing it closer to home, road rage will envelope me unexpectedly. A mere one block previous to the spot where I now gripped my hot hands on the steering wheel I felt completely normal. That hot energy was the same sort of fuel that powers wars. It's ever ready to ignite. (This kind of close-to-the-surface heat arises for interpretation from the psychoanalyst's couch.)   Herman Goering, Hitler's right hand man, understood how to play to that energy, specifically the human penchant for superiority of others. Appealing to the aggression that "outsiders" ignite, he said: People can always be brought to the bidding of their leaders. It's easy. Just tell them they are being attacked. Then denounce the "pacifists" for lack of patriotism. It works in any country.

Loving Everybody: Why? How?

When Christ talked of love, love for everyone, love even for the despicable, for enemies, was He naive? Or did He really have it figured out? When He or anyone else takes a long hard look at the manifest examples of human aggression, of man's ever indulging in his hatred for his fellows, of history's sad record of wars stacked contiguously one following quickly after another, we can't be optimistic. Christ is reported to have preached universal love. It's not written someplace that He thought it was practical. We are challenged when we hear Him quoted that way, probably overly challenged. Christ may very well have supplied us with a solution to human aggression but having heard it we can't accept it.   It's just way too tough.

St. Paul saw the problem. He realized Christ "doesn't sell." He fashioned another approach, one he felt he could make attractive. But first he had to change things. The Cross was a problem. Christ had the courage to live out His universal-love-for-mankind theory and it got Him executed. His frontal attack on greed in high places sounded good to the populace at large. To the High Priests it was a threat gone too far. They had worked out a financially secure arrangement with the Romans. They were not to let it be exposed to a bright light.

Treating some people as better - therefore the rest are worse – is a popular intuition Paul pandered to. That's his idea of neighbor, a definition that appeals to self-interest. (I read a bumper sticker that proclaimed, Christians aren't sinless, just forgiven!) Using Christ's idea of who that is (cf. the Good Samaritan) does not come easily.   It makes sense but logic is not our first reflex. We've got an aging friend who is solidly anti-Semitic - and racist. She hates immigrants even as she'll assert, I love people! She speaks it a lot like a standard and sincerely voiced mantra.   That same phrase was spoken to us by an operator of a B & B we stayed at.   The service had been lousy and she attempted to over-charge us, confessing to a memory loss when I showed her in writing the agreed-upon price. Yet when we were packed up to leave she met us at the door to ask us to sign her ledger with words of praise. People lover, indeed! I remember as a kid riding a bus with a pair on board speaking some Slavic tongue. As they were getting off at their stop, an angry voice bellowed at them, Learn English!   A lot of these sentiments are supporting resistance in Congress to updating our immigration policies.

Paul's Tough Talk
Here's more in his Letter to the Romans, such as... ***the depravity of men whose wickedness keeps truth imprisoned...God Himself has made it plain...such people are without excuse...their empty heads were darkened. That is why God left them to their filthy practices....those who behave like this deserve to die*** (Romans 3, 9 – 20). And so on and so on.   He establishes his tough-talking self as the one with God's authority and therefore to be obeyed. Recall the occasion when he explained that we're training for a

race (1Cor 9:24). We're competitors. We are running to win! Paul divides humanity between those who believe his theology and those who don't. He shows no mercy for those who don't. Personally I'm appalled at his comfort with people "deserving" to die.

On the other hand Christ taught inclusiveness. He excluded no one.   He said He "...*came as one who serves*"(Luke 22, 27).   Elsewhere Luke's Gospel ascribes the following words to Christ. They contrast with St. Paul's harsh intolerance. **"Among pagans it is the kings who lord it over them and those who have authority over them are given the title Benefactor. This must not happen to you. No! The greatest among you must behave as if he were the youngest, the leader as if he were the one who serves. For who is the greater: the one at table or he who serves? The one at table, surely. Yet here am I among you as one who serves!"**   The distance separating the two is stunning. For decades, along with millions of Catholics and many millions more who claim the Christian label, I thought St. Paul and Christ were partners. Stories of Christ's life and Paul's writings were published in the Bible back to back. They looked to be in sync.   However a closer look has Paul's Christianity recommending a narrow respect for human potential and an insistence on basic human sinfulness.   He insists his truth is the only way; he alone can show how to profit from Christ's life and especially His death.

As he would have it Christ's death was not selected for Him by powerful civil and religious politicians who got Him tried and convicted of blasphemy and sedition, either of which carried the death sentence. Rather he interpreted His dying as His – and His Father's - deliberate choice. It was God's pitying our sinful state for which Christ willingly paid with His life. In his view Christ's dying was redemptive.   His eminent qualification as "Redeemer" centered on His possessing two natures, one divine (read, God's Son) and a human one, formed in a womb like everyone else's.   (His mother Mary is famous in some Christian quarters for her role as Jesus' mother.) His dual nature made Him the perfect fit. He was the God-man, presenting both sides of the sin offense, the humanity doing the offending and the God who took the offense.   He became our Redeemer *par excelance*; no one before or since had been better equipped to offer precise atonement to Heaven.

Are you seeing what I think is Oedipal influence at work? People start off as babies wanting a parent's total love, initially the one of the opposite sex. As babies they fought for it and lost. If that defeat feels like a loss, as grown-ups they seek total love by way of the god from which they can get or qualify for complete eternal happiness.

Mankind: Up To No Good

Implicit in Paul's theology is mankind's basic sinfulness. He claims we can't do much to change that. We've little choice but to rely on a god-man to lift us out of our pitiable condition.   Christ sees our situation differently. If anything good is going to come about, we're the ones to do it. Probably Christ saw the world through His Jewish eyes.   His people were chaffing beneath the despised Roman heel. Love of His people shaped His language about loving one's fellows. Christians apply His limited preoccupation to the entire world population.   Not a bad thesis, just not Christ's original emphasis if not His intent.

Paul makes much of the gratitude we should feel for Christ's redemptive act. Accomplished through His torturous death, His body fastened with nails on two wooden beams forming a cross, it's bound to elicit a deep-felt response. Today many women wear crosses as adornments, as on earrings and necklaces. Paul's teachings made of the cross no longer a dreaded instrument of execution used by Rome to make an example of those who fought to free themselves from its military choke-hold. He would have it be a sure sign of God's love for His creatures. The double-natured Christ makes His death a sacrifice representing both sides of the sin relationship, i.e., the one sinning and the One the sin offends. The perfect fit.

A Loving Sadist?

However Paul overlooks why God the Father should impose such a pain-ridden requirement on His Son. Strict logic would dictate that any of the God-man's acts –like merely breathing in and out - were fully redemptive. As completely redemptive as the bloody Cross. So why should Christ's Father ask for such an agonizing ransom? One could argue that God in previous biblical writings had already established Himself as vindictive, intolerant of human waywardness and Calvary was nothing new. The Flood comes readily to mind. It wiped out all mankind and all the animals along with them, except for those Noah found space for on the floating craft called the Arc. But for His own Son? That's a bit much and a challenge to Christian theologians. Mormons fashion their own thesis which I am not familiar with except that they forsake the notion of God as Three Persons. That would seem to displace Christ's divinity, a point not lost on some Baptist theologians who declare Mormonism to be an un-

Christian sect. A popularly accepted way around this problem says God's deep love for His creatures might get lost on His creatures if His Son's act of atonement looked too easy. We're advised to look upon the bloody crucified Redeemer and dispel any doubts about the enormity of God's love for us.

That's an exacting God Paul wants us to believe in. Paul says He wants perfect payback. He sets up an exacting religion to get the job done. It's come to be known as Christianity.

We're On Our Own

Christ wants us to get busy about making the world a better place. No one is going to do it for us. A tough assignment but not one that we're helpless to attempt. Not one that we'll accomplish in our lifetime, but one for which we'd require all the help we can get. It looks like Christ will elicit the entire human race in this most worthy project. As one who hesitated not a bit to heap praise on a despised Samaritan, it's safe to say He'd welcome all sorts, Buddhists, Muslims, Zorroasterites, agnostics and atheists, to put their shoulders to the wheel. It's a monumental mission. It's consistent with a goal of peace on earth, all peoples from all over, striving to cure humanity's ills, knowing they'll never see it in their lifetimes. They'd have given it what they could however, happy to turn over to the next generation such a universally beneficial target.

Lacking is the appeal for Oedipally-induced sin-threatened Christians who want to feel acceptable, i.e., forgiven.

Best of all it's to be accomplished together. That means everybody. It welcomes anyone wherever on the five continents. It's not a religion. It's a look at the human condition. It concludes that people ought to be helping people. That's what Christ did...as best He could. That's what people, any people anywhere, can do...as best they can. It's reasonable to predict that most people would admire others dedicated to bettering humanity's lot. Who would argue with that? Who would be threatened by that kind of a worldwide outreach? It would seem that our personal, individual limitations would turn out to be to everyone's benefit. It would pull us together. Everyone would be valuable. No one however unskilled would not have value.

Is Religion Superfluous?

Christ did not establish a religion. Rather did he see human needs and did His limited best to meet them. He would have us do our limited best to meet them. Some would see their worth in imitating what Christ saw as worthy of human investment. They might turn out to be Muslims, Mormons, atheists, it wouldn't matter. A certain percentage of any population would see the worth of dedicating their efforts to making life better for everyone. Call them Christians if you like, although that label has already been taken. Maybe the true imitators of Christ could be called humanitarians. As Martin Luther saw it, they could meet together for mutual support to eat bread and wine like Christ is said to have done with friends. Christ-centered do-gooders would meet regularly to burnish their standards, encourage each other, and plan how they might meet challenges. Most importantly they'd have to keep themselves focused on human need, not build themselves into wonder people, like priests are thought to be, sent by some deity with whom they are to atone for "sins" they are too easily convinced they are bent on committing. They would be people other people could welcome as humanitarians   and   certainly   not   claimants   that everybody listening better obey or risk Hell.   Not everyone would accept them as simple givers – until they'd proved themselves as givers, pure and simple. They would present themselves as looking for ways to better serve.   Ordinarily they'd be seen as a boon to society.   Most of all they would not be – or allow themselves to become – a competitive religious group. Religions focus on abstract notions like sin, "grace", after-life and other self-serving ideas like salvation. The wish to help, to serve, appeals to many.   Some may hold to a religion; it would not be seen as essential. Seeing and meeting human need, that would be essential.

Prayer would have no place.   Deities do not respond to prayer.   The **Book of Job**'s god prided himself on his subject's loyalty which Job maintained without any divine expression verifying His existence. Religions typically say we're to place problems in some god's hands, and expect its omnipotence to take care of things. It takes us off the hook. I heard a priest from his Sunday pulpit admit that poor people have needs, quickly adding that the poor boxes take care of that. They don't of course. But many take relaxed comfort in his authority that solutions to big problems belong to God's providence and they can let it go at that.   If nothing results it could mean that the deity has other plans. Why not? God is omnipotent, is He not? If He chooses not to lift a finger, if He bypasses our pleas for relief from poverty or war or sickness or whatever, that's how things should be.

We Change Our Gods, Not Ourselves

Oedipal relief is more easily achieved with a god whom we can fashion into anything we want. Dealing with our fellows is another matter.   We're often at variance with each other. Annual family gatherings often set down rules like, Don't talk politics or religion. Organizers want harmony among attendees and people can be brittle and fixed in their thinking. Scores of pastors invite folks in the neighborhood to relax on Sundays enjoying "Christian Fellowship", i.e., everybody believes the same thing. Rancor arises when favorite convictions get tested. The price however is high. There's not a lot left to talk about beside golf scores and what's for supper. Repression yields boredom.

Religion is boring. Unless it really gets into things, but that's rare. That begs the question, Why do people reliably sit in church pews even though it's boring? Notwithstanding efforts to pep things up with guitars, films, coffee and entertaining speakers. They want assurances of their worth with a god they can control. Ecclesiastical mandates to lessen human misfortune or elevate human potential find a few takers. For the most part they speak a language believers do not expect to hear and do not want to hear. They want ritual, sacraments, candles and environment, materials and gestures that are quasi-non-material suggesting intermediating power with their god who refuses to show up, the same deity they require nonetheless to help settle down those personal inner-workings we've been citing. Dealing with our fellows is tough work. Doubters need only watch TV accounts of the swirls of raucous discontent surrounding our candidates for the Presidency. Contrast that with a convenient hour spent on Sundays in the company of non-confrontational fellows and throw in a comfortable check. Include nice afterlife as an implicit possibility and it's a hard deal to beat. Oedipal intra-psychic pesterings are self-centered. They can't be otherwise.   They were nurtured in babyhood and remain fixed there. Baby doesn't know how to give in love; it's a long way from something so mature. Satisfying neurotic discomforts are self-focused. Bettering the human condition is quite the opposite. It's out-going and antithetical to navel-gazing.

To repeat: Christ is other-centered, at least he seems so. St. Paul sees us as sinners. That's what we feel ourselves to be and Paul utilizes that. We're a rather ugly lot, having "sinned" even if we haven't because we inherit a sinful nature through no doing on our part. He offers us Christ as a "personal savior". Forget about doing anything of worth personally. Paul set up a program called Christianity. Accept your worthlessness, he mandates, submit that to the redeeming Christ-god who will receive you mercifully in your pitiful situation and forgive you on an individual basis.

Personal? Distant? Which?

Personal is the key idea. The needs of one's fellows are secondary. Get yourself saved; your concern for your fellowman stops with his getting "redeemed" like you were. His theory is based on God's total perfection which Paul compares with our crummy sinful nature. He gives us no chance to do anything worthwhile. There's no way we can make up to the limitless God for our offenses no matter how hard we try. It's like trying to pay off a billion dollar indebtedness on a minimum wage job. Don't even try, Paul says. Only God can do something "perfect" (as in limitless). Submit yourself to Jesus' bloody redemptive Cross and thereby guarantee Heaven for yourself. Otherwise you'll spend eternity in Hell. So will the rest of humanity unless it saves itself by accepting Christ as its "savior". Paul includes all of humanity. So do Oedipal conflicts.

When the likes of fundamentalists, like radical Muslims, talk like this, we can see no daylight between them and Paul's adherents.   Extremism is more easily discerned when we can watch it done someplace else.

Paul's personal salvation theory requires God the Father to require His Son to suffer horribly. Paul's God (the Father) seems intent on gaining the devotion of His human creation.   His Son's pain makes that point. There's a dependence on God's part; He wants human love.   Paul makes the Creator of the universe seem pitiable, as if having created a people He hadn't planned on loving so much.   He offers us a needy God.   He shows up in Christian art.   A divine softness comes through in pictures of the Christian Redeemer.   He is fine-boned with well-balanced features and long wavy hair, Teutonic rather than Middle Eastern (an appeal to Caucasians).   Perhaps a bit wimpy.   Above all, kind, extremely kind, kind almost to the point of melting.   He bears scarce resemblance to God in the **Book of Job.** That's where we meet the God most of us meet, including the One my mother-in-law dealt with.   So do all the rest of us on a day-to- day basis. We probably don't like it. He's distant and admiring of human virtue when He can get it.   And He doesn't interfere.

A Quick Review.

It seems St. Paul had little stomach for Christ's universal love theory. He never mentions Christ's Good Samaritan as a model for loving one's fellows. He could speak eloquently about love abstractly but not in the practical manner Christ would coach us toward. Changing that around took fancy footwork.   To his converts the Cross was not just the gruesome Roman instrument of torture and death; it was an instrument of atonement for sins. Our "neighbor" was not to include everybody, just believers in Christ's redemptive act as he (Paul) defined it. The rest were hell-bound pagans.

It was as if Rome did mankind a big favor in its brutal handling of Christ's execution. It was unwittingly fulfilling God the Father's demonstration of His limitless love.

One last problem for Paul's outreach remained and it was a whopper. Every living soul before and since needed the Redemptive Cross because every living soul before and since is sinful. Humans are born that way, born dependent and needy and destined for Hell. Does Paul's theology stand up to Christ's mandate to love everybody? Even pagans? Non-believers?

Does Paul even sound Christian, meaning did Christ talk like that? People regularly tend to separate themselves from other groups. They're to be counted on to figure they might possibly be better than some others, even if in a minor way.   I'm thinking of those bumper stickers bragging how the driver's kid is an honor student.   Isn't that saying he or she has something to boast about because their kid pulls down better academic grades?   Paul is hardly requiring of his Christians the challenge Christ apparently points us toward in His parable of the Good Samaritan.   Christ on the other hand teaches that everyone can contribute positive good. And should. Others need each other and we need each other. We're to take another look at each other. It might even get us to like the other fellow more. We might be a bit more tolerant when he plays his radio too loudly or performs some other nuisance.   It's another platform for universal peace.   It doesn't always come easily.   Our beloved Constitution isn't easily heeded either. It says all men are created equal and have equal rights. Our policies are to be built along these lines. That's not what would immediately spring to one's reflex.   Should we give Mafiosi their day in court? No, says our intuition.   Yes, says our Constitution. Christ would like the Constitution.   Not so Paul. Paul wants to build a world community of his favorites.

Paul The Populist

So why is St. Paul so popular? A few answers suggest themselves: He is extremely self-assured. He hasn't a moment's doubt that he speaks for God. He thinks he's the only one ever so endowed. Ever. He sounds strong. He offers exclusive membership to what is highest and best. His church offers superior worship potential in this life inevitably leading to God's accepting us for eternity.

He offers the one true faith, in effect a religion. It permits an interpretation of our lives that elevates commonplace living into the supernatural.   Life's hardships become meaningful.

Paul's insistent authority separates believers from non-believers, appealing to the need many welcome to feel superior. The baptized fill this niche nicely. He often uses bombast.   This elicits quick emotional affirmation. He regularly plays the sex card, storming against adultery, fornication and homosexuality.   Like too many others, his hearers devalue human sexual functioning. Placing restrictions on it gives him an aura of holiness. Archbishop Vigneron plays this card.

He regularly fosters misogyny.   A celibate by choice, he recommends the solitary life for everyone. The less disciplined are to turn to marriage lest they "burn" (1Cor 7:9). Some biblical translations use that indelicate word.   He demonstrates his annoyance with sexual urges. Women are to sit apart and cover their hair so as not to look too nice during public prayer.

He's a compulsively hard worker. He wants that acknowledged as virtue. Psychologists could see it as a vice. He comes close to self-pity but never quite goes over that line. This gets him regarded as "one of them" and a "regular guy", the voice of the overlooked who feel powerless.

A Differing Approach, An Alternate Appeal

We are seeing two sides of the same issue. It happens all the time. In Congress smart and sincere legislators, alongside some elected manipulators goaded by self-interest, tussle over issues of mutual concern. They keep the country functioning while the rest of us put to use the freedoms the Constitution affords us. It stands up against the battering it sustains day in and day out. It's working. It's gratifying to have heard yesterday about the foreign investors eager to place their money into our enterprises because they trust our judicial system. They accept that the interest they get paid is next to nothing; their money is guaranteed safe. They'd gotten used to providing pay-offs to corrupt government hacks. They pocket illicit profits fully realizing that they can count on little legal protection when a competitor's cheating will do them in further down the line.

Christ and Paul represent two sides of the same issues. They're two different types. Christ did some down-to-earth things out of concern for sickness and poverty, pointing toward accomplishing a better lot for people. He seems to keep in view a goal of peace on earth.

Paul took a different approach. He founded a church seeking members, necessarily distinguishing themselves from all the others. Inevitably it became "us" versus "them". Like Christ he sought to bring humanity together but through establishing a universality of belief. Christ deliberately chose a religious outsider for His model of a humanity we all share. For His fellow Jews He described the Good Samaritan. He made no distinctions, implying everyone was equal to everyone else. Religious practices didn't matter. Importantly the religious variance between the two who walked away from a pitiful scene and the one who helped a bloodied victim were irrelevant. Paul however saw problems herein over a lofty ideal not easily practiced. Instead he cobbled together a much less taxing alternative. He appealed to humanity's insecurities. A snob appeal with Heaven as the reward.

He had it figured correctly! He established what he knew men could find manageable and would find appealing. People enjoy feeling superior to their fellow mortals. Religion can do that. Paul's Christians are convinced they have "the truth" others don't and need. Additionally he appealed to the human tendency to feel sin-prone and decrepit because of those pesky sexual impulses everybody (almost) mistakenly regards as somewhat degrading. Paul's declaring all men as sinners needing Christ's meritorious cross sounded about right. "Washing us in the Blood of the Lamb" says we're saved, therefore superior to those who are not.

. Paul stands today as THE interpreter of the Christ phenomenon throughout the Christian world. That his theology hangs together a bit too loosely doesn't seem to matter. Shouldn't people be asking, if mankind inherited Adam's sin why shouldn't it with equal simplicity inherit the merits of Christ's death? Paul has it that we got our sinner status without any action or choice on our part. Why wouldn't the redemptive cross be just as generously applied universally without our having to lift a finger?   Paul says we must sign on deliberately, otherwise burn in Hell. Quite an imbalance.

Tying Things Together

Archbishop Vigeron puts heavy emphasis on sexual matters. His and his Church's focus on this most personal of human functioning by-passes the big problems the world contends with, problems like wars and the millions of displaced refugees. Much easier (and financially rewarding) to point to people's sexual capacities. Our built-in hang-ups about sex already give the Archbishop's directives a head-start. The Church's makers of policy count on that. Recall J. P. McCarthy's declaring he'd probably get sensual promptings he'd want to confess to his priest after refusing a sexual invitation from an attractive woman. Everybody has sex urges. They're normal and we routinely handle them maturely. For many however they leave behind a reminder of "our sinfulness". The Church seizes upon these feelings as an opportunity. St. Paul showed how to use them to advantage.   It simply offers something called forgiveness.   It offers its members various assurances about how to remain in good standing with the Almighty, all the while maintaining its reputation for "doing good" by promoting sexual guardedness. The really important evils like wars and corruption and deceit and larceny it leaves to the rest of us to solve as best we can. For all its principles it's quick to proclaim, it keeps a comfortable distance from solving real problems while the rest of us struggle for answers to complicated issues. When's the last time you heard the Church offer us guidance on immigration policy and the Israeli-Palestinian deadlocked peace talks? If it got its hands dirty like the rest of us are forced to, it wouldn't look so divinely guided– as it likes to appear.

Forgiven? Forgiven!

In a residential area a few blocks from here, these words are on a Church lawn sign: "At Shrine we try to imitate Christ by praying, studying and growing together." It appears that the church is thereby imitating Christ; it's actually asking its congregation to circle its wagons. It's advising its adherents to look inward, fostering a certain groupism. Some congregations would have us view this as positive. Come, gather in "fellowship", is a typical invitation. Lost in all this is what we hear as Christ's challenge to focus on the world at large. We can recognize the Shrine's approach as Pauline. People tend to group together, seeking support in an aggressive, complex world. In this sense politicians are seen to take on St. Paul's advice to circle our wagons. The outside world is the world that is different, that practices differing religions, speaks different languages, has varying customs and rules regarding their women and the acceptable rearing of their children. Many personalities have an inbred suspicion of people who look, sound and acculturate in unfamiliar ways. These are the types Paul huddles together with practices and customs of their own. His grouping adds one more separated gathering from which it looks out onto the rest of the world.

Sin is a construct. It had us looking up, up at a God it offends. We have no evidence sin offends Him. The idea presumes God and the sinner have a relationship whereby God is ignored, dishonored, disobeyed, mocked, scorned by way of sin. That could be said of a parent whom a child offends. The parent and the child have a relationship. They see, hear, feel each other. The parent can be offended or diminished; we can see it or perceive it. But God by definition is perfect, almighty, etc. He's beyond being hurt. To say the sinner offends Him or in any way diminishes Him is to attribute to sinning an abundance of influence. Makes no sense.

Christ sees things differently. He sees **separation** as sin, i.e., the potential for problems. He would build a world of shared mutual concern. His story of the Good Samaritan makes His case. A stranger sees a man in need. He dips into his own pocket to help. Christ wants everyone, world-wide, to do that for his fellows. To present His case more pointedly, He choose someone despised as His model. He had been separated. To Christ such separations didn't count. The stranger needed help, Good Sam provided it. That was all that mattered.

Paul's base of influence counts on our sense of sin, like those that preoccupied McCarthy. Christ didn't bother about them, seeming to rely on mankind's spontaneous desire to help out when it sees human misery. He comes out on the side of man's ability to meet his fellow's problems or to at least try to. That makes him predictably less attractive. Fewer are willing to put their shoulders to the wheel when it comes to problem-solving whereas Paul appeals to self-interest. A decade or so ago a bishop talked of religion's offering "comfort" as if that were its highest purpose. Deep down few judge themselves sufficiently "good". Recall Billy Graham's daughter declaring on a Sunday talk show that we're all sinners. A lot of folks will think that's right. More accurately put, they "feel" that's right. Paul (then), as does the Archbishop (now), realized for most this feels authentic.

Compensating For A Distant God

There's another problem the Archbishop and his kind deal with all over the world. The God they promote doesn't show up. People at large don't like a remote god. They want to make Him feel close so religious authorities ask their faithful to gather in groups. They sing and pray and take support from others who also sing and pray with them elbow to elbow over the same beliefs they cling to. When deaths occur believers find their faith particularly in need of a boost. Sometimes a religion's claim lacking evidence asks too much. It may offer satisfaction for them when pre-death troubles happen but feel unsubstantial when death's heavy hand reaches into their lives. They are to believe that death imposes merely a temporary departure. Praying together publicly combines believers with doubters in a unity that disallows distinction over which is which. They all look the same and sound the same. Giving words to one's doubts about another's religious assertions would be sadistic if juxta-posed with deep-felt grief.

Many "find" their god (God?) in trees, flowers, shrubs and the order of nature. Their pictures accompany cards and notes of condolence. Therein is imminent power to be observed. Making of it a divine power may offer god-proof to some believers but an unsatisfying distance remains. The distant God is the one they've got. Faced with similar abandonment Job countered with the kind of faith his God took pride in (he remained deprived of awareness of the divine satisfaction it occasioned). The acceptance of His requirements and demands without evidence or proof that his deity truly wanted for him the lot in life in which he found himself is the trust all deities require, as far as I know. To all appearances my mother-in-law offered God a faith of Job-like quality. It still left room for self-deception; who can say for sure? Or perhaps she nursed a desperate crying-out for relief from feeling unworthy that many, happily not all, experience. They are walking illustrations of the Oedipal Complex's relentless hold.   Catholics believe their approaching their altar at Mass offers them an ultimate closeness. It's a bit of bread named Holy Communion or the Holy Eucharist. Their priests place it in their mouths or the palms of their hand, thence into their mouths. It's professed to be the "body and blood, soul and divinity" of their redeemer, the god-man, Jesus Christ. It would seem that one's god couldn't get closer.   No other reality in one's life could surpass it. Results don't bear that out. Judging from its effect upon those who eat it, it appears to be just a bit of bread. Believers are hesitant to acknowledge this. Job's faith probably left him with the same kind of uncertainty.   Catholics become indifferent to the Eucharist as well they might.   Job did not yield to indifference because God's demands on him were unbearable – except for faith. He remained a loyal believer. So it seems was my mother-in-law.

Filling In For Uncertainty
      The Gospels were formed three to nine or ten decades after Jesus' death. (The last, John's Gospel, came about somewhere between 100 – 120 c. e.) That was a sufficient span for impressions about Christ's possible divinity among the first Christians to gain impetus.   After Stephen's martyrdom (Acts Ch. 7) they became a groundswell.   As he was being stoned he professed that he was seeing the Son of Man standing at the right hand of God.   Divinity served Paul's purposes well.   A divine being who served the impoverished while excoriating the Temple High Priests for their lucrative alliances with their Roman bosses could very well mark His adherents as open critics of the

most powerful. Striving to imitate an advocate for the least influential, however divine He may be seen to be, who also managed to enrage the powerful, would be to take on a dangerous if not a life-threatening mission. Add to it all a policy of accepting no pay for one's labors and little appeal remains except for the most heroic. Paul was fashioning his Christ-mission for the largely self-motivated world of the gentile.   For that he was called to Jerusalem three times during his public ministry by Peter and James the Just, Jesus' brother. They saw no inconsistencies in following Christ's example while maintaining Jewish observances, the Law as it had been observed for centuries.   Paul's ambitions included as much of the non-Jewish world as he could envision. Jewish Law would get in his way.   To his potential gentile converts it would be considered irrelevant baggage.   Peter and Paul never got along.

Who's Best?

It would appear that Paul wouldn't have gotten along with Christ either. If we are to emulate Christ's "Good Sam", if that's the way to interpret His parable, then there are more important real-life issues.   Arguing about which set of rules from the Jewish ritual are to be followed would be not only trivial, it would be beside the point. Spending their lives "binding up the wounds" of the world, putting down our personal dollars to pay for it, and promising to pay again if more is needed, would be nudging close to the heroic. Being Christian would be a humbling experience.   It would require an exhausting challenge.

Summing up. All sorts of re-jiggering of Christ's teachings occurred throughout Christianity.   Largely these offshoots compete with each other.   Not all of them, a certain percentage have stressed His thinking about service to our fellows. The Quakers are among them. Simplicity about their personal life-style with plain frame structures thought suitable for worship and assembly, they seem humbled by the example they look to imitate. They don't see Christ as competing. Maybe they see as I do a chasm between the divine personality they see walking through the pages of the Gospels and the assertiveness, the aggressiveness they read in Paul's writings. Christ was first of all focused on human need.   Putting together his sympathy for the widow whose son had died, as well as for the blind beggar and the cripple too slowed to reach a pool in time to grab a cure, we find a personality with the milk of human kindness. A few sparse but meaningful stories of his sparing some newly-weds embarrassment over their stores of wine running dry at their party, of his capacity to relax at Martha and Mary's home, of the welcoming he found in others' homes, give us a picture of warm-heartedness.

That he would have those who would follow His example give over their faith-practice to human betterment is reasonably clear. That He cared not at all to establish a church that would out-number its competitors seems consistent with a humane approach. His people would care to find cures, eliminate poverty, support representative governments.   His people wouldn't prefer to serve some religious or ethnic group over another. Their model would be Good Sam who found a robbed and beaten stranger and dealt unquestioningly with the human need he saw.   He dipped into his own pocket to get treatment for the victim. He promised to meet the following day's costs as well. The approach Christ's contingents would assume would overlook the discrimination that beclouds many ethnic cultures living in and near our neighborhoods.

Some of these are poor minorities even as others do well financially. Muslims, Indians, Asians and Jews are among them. They're generally not well received by a large number of Christians at this point in our history. That could change but other immigrants could follow and would meet the same suspicion and quiet hostility. Our citizenry likes to measure the worthiness of newcomers by how well they resemble themselves. Language along with dress and customs is a big one. Recent arrivals get held to an impossible standard: speak like we speak or stay out of sight until you do! I've got a friend who gets livid when the recorded voice on his phone asks if he'd like to continue in Spanish. This is America! he seethes through tight lips. America to him is the nation of the early immigrants. If an applicant for citizenship is recent, by that very fact he/she is an undesirable. Christ's people would routinely try to brush such rancor aside. They'd do it even if they felt inside the same hostility. It is the challenge of imitating Christ. We're to do with it the best we can.

Paul's Christ Is Different

Being Christian generally means being Pauline. Like St. Paul it means certainty that religious truth is its exclusive possession. Others are outsiders and are sought out for conversion to The Truth. Historically that distinction has led to intense competition and often to war.

So what does Christ really stand for? We discern that he supported peace for our world. Under what circumstances could he justify war? Was he foolishly putting His life in danger in confronting the powers that held sway? Those who were attracted to Him, who followed Him, some even loving Him, also had questions: Was He the Son of God or the Son of Man?

How are we to square His Sermon On the Mount with His charging into the Temple and overturning the tables of profiteers selling animals to the devout for their prayer-offerings?

Things begin to make sense if we think of Him as a vulnerable leader around the time He was executed. Thereafter we recognize a steadily increasingly popular impression that He was divine. Paul's Epistles, which he wrote from 48 c. e. to 56 c. e., become increasingly assertive about Jesus Christ's role in the salvation of everyone born into the human race.

It seems that the follower of Christ is to be an imitator of Christ. That results in two interpretations. One concerns His devotion to His countrymen. He detested the harsh Roman occupation. Gospel quotations about loving one's fellowmen may have arisen narrowly out of His pride as a Jew. Quoted outside the Roman suppression within which He may have spoken, they sound like an appeal to the entire world. Love One Another is His message everyone, everywhere, can try to heed. It requires no particular creed; it exceeds any recommended religious practice. Eminently idealistic, no one will deny it's a heavy challenge. Christ may not have held the world view many today think He stood for. His world was His Jewish nation, His people yearning for release from cruel Roman occupiers. Love one another as I have loved you, speaks to the Jewish unity He was sure had to precede any chance Israel could have to send Rome packing. He was a Jew above all.

All that is past. The Christianity observed today is largely Pauline. It's focused on the individual believer, so much so that individuals who are not believers are considered heathen. The 1917 Code of Canon Law picks up Paul's spirit. Impermissible was even the mention inside church walls of another variety of Christian; say, an Episcopalian. A member of that "heathen" group in 1945 was the wartime President Franklin Roosevelt; he died that year. He was much-loved and elected to his presidency four times.

Christ Or Paul?

Casting aside St. Paul's "divide and conquer" preaching seems to be the authentic Christ-like thing to do. The Church's Canons reflect St. Paul's "Us versus Them" competitive edginess. They hardly mirror the One who defined "neighbor" in the context of His engaging story of the Good Samaritan. He made a point of selecting a despised outcast as the hero of the story, not to be easily overlooked by His listeners. At another time and place He said we'll be surprised who'll be among the goats and who'll be among the sheep at the conclusion of human history. Can you picture Him damning folks who'd been baptized in a different Church, not to mention those never baptised? He put it in stark terms, **When you did it to the least among you, you did it to me!** It doesn't sound like He cared about religious affiliation. It sounds like He wants us to take care of one another.

.   We try and we fail when we read through the Gospels for a clear picture of Jesus Christ. The problem is that the Gospels had many contributors in that they began as oral traditions which later on got written. Several personal impressions found their way into them. Some aggressive types may have figured His advice about making sure they had a couple swords to take along to wherever they were going sounded practical. Others (include me among them) find attractive His emphasis on caring for one another. Choosing one path excludes others which are in conflict. These oral contributions eventually found their way into summaries. Many got immutable status as if having had single authorships. A gospel entitled "Matthew" had many oral contributors.   The same for those labeled Mark, Luke and John. Mark's Gospel probably was assembled 70 to 71 c. e. The rejection Christ experienced during His trial and on Calvary was some of the Gospels' preoccupation. Jesus' handling of some spontaneous claims put upon Him suggests evasiveness or even rejection of a Messianic mission. It's confusing. Can we distinguish between what He may actually have stood for from what others read into words attributed to Him? One graduate professor of moral theology despaired of the conclusions from Scripture scholars. If they don't get you in one language, he intoned one day, they'll get you in another.

St. Paul was way ahead of the curve. He had already taught that Christ was God Incarnate around the late and early 50s c. e. His converts were to be gentiles and Hellenistic Jews. They like everyone else tended to prefer god-centered purposes behind life's complexities. For people who live with an inner sense of sin-prone feelings, it's settling on the nerves to have redemption to apply.   Martin Luther's "Protest" liberalized Rome's rigidity over sex by allowing divorce and a married clergy but he had to acknowledge the role religion can offer to those feeling sin-prone.   He offered an analogy: Mankind is a dung heap covered over with the pure, white snow of Christ's redemption. Doubts about one's worth keep popping up all over.

An increasing readiness to view Jesus as divine probably added impetus to a popular acceptance of stories like the Virgin Birth and His Resurrection and the days that followed. John's Gospel (100 c.e. – 120 c.e.) came last and was mystical, unlike those preceding it.

Stating that Christ was from all time, he claims the Holy Spirit as his guide. Theologians take on the task of trying to justify such a widening of Christian belief. Those seeking redemption wish them well.

The ninety or so years from His death, starting with Mark and continuing through Matthew and Luke and then leaping into the mystical with John, were on a continuum, with ever more and more assertions about Christ's divine essence.

What Is Goodness?

The Archbishop's Church is mostly concerned with sex. It's what people expect. It's why J. P. McCarthy would hurriedly seek out his priest. But why run to a religious personage? Because believers like JP required a deity, a god. No one else could quell his feelings that he'd come too close to what's sinful. Who else? Can a physician "forgive" him? Or a psychologist or a social worker or a pathologist or an MBA or accountant? Only a god can set him at rest – or someone whom God has delegated, i.e., has God's approval - or power. A deity's healing is measureable by how closely it feels like what "daddy" felt like when the believer was a baby. Nothing short of a god can set a sin-troubled mind at ease.

Really now, only God can satisfy the need? Things on this earth are mixed together. A lot of good is part of the make-up of a bad person. And vice-versa. So too with warring factions. Neither side is totally right- or totally wrong. So too with the communities in which we live. We like and get along quite well in places that will never get on the list of the ***Ten Best Places To Live***. But what we call home is where our families and friends share the space. Lots of good and bad co-exist.

The God idea however is different. He's perfect. He rewards good and punishes bad. Life is unfair and the world teems with injustice. God however sets it all right. We want to believe this so we make it, or *It,* into what we want.

God is handy to have around. Consider death. It happens to us all and it's terrible. It separates us from all we know and love. To be sure, life presents us with ills as well. Few of us however want to come to a place in life where things are so bad that we prefer to die. Assuming that most of us have kept life and living reasonably pleasant, death is an intrusion and we abhor it. Solution: find yourself a god. If you take St. Paul's god, you can rejoice with him along with his converts at Corinth for whom he wrote: **O death, where is your victory?** (I Cor 15, 55)

God's influence for good applies to the world about half the time. The other half, the bad half, some say is the devil's - or the Communist's or the Taliban's or atheist's or whatever. But in the hereafter, the after-life, God is said to have complete sway. His good reigns supreme. Some theorize that the injustices of this life are permanently set right in Heaven. We cannot control the misfortunes in this life but in the hereafter all will go well forever.

Aligning With "Heaven"

But it rests on the God idea. Keeping God front and center could be a challenge because He stays aloof. It's the job of religion to bring Him close, or at least closer, and keep Him there. Religions recommend prayer, acts of worship and submission. These take on many forms. Walking into a High Anglican cathedral and/or any of the magnificent Gothic churches in Europe conveys the sense of His overwhelming Presence along with our comparative littleness. The same sense of submission to The Presence is available to a religion's humblest hovels; cf. the Pentecostal gyrations and joyous outcries of worshippers in Ghana. Daily prayers, personally-worded or formulaic,   make Him feel close. So too are special writings considered by believers to be directly inspired by God. Most major religions distribute their own versions of such books guaranteed to be God's words; or at least having divine authority. Simply holding such a volume evokes the believer's reverence. Mishandling it even unintentionally or accidently, as occurred in Afghanistan when some soldiers carelessly disposed of copies of the Quran (Koran) at the Bigram Airfield in February 2012, elicited outrage over sacrilege. In the melees that followed six of our soldiers and 30 Afghans had died by March 2nd.

Paul To The Rescue

It seems clear from an observant reading of the **Book of Job** that God wishes to keep His distance. His boasts about His "servant Job" are based on His creature's acceptance that his God exists nowhere outside his faith. However Job was a rarity. He went to his death never having encountered the remote god he reluctantly but steadfastly served all his life. The religion he practiced was totally "pure", meaning it was unadulterated by creature concerns and desires.   Job may have illustrated by his life what God took pride in but most believers then and now mightily resist his faith-model. They want a god they can control, one they can keep close, one who responds to their wants. The last seventeen verses of **Job** describe a god who lavishes health and wealth on believers.   Never mind the contradictions involved.

In a like manner St. Paul pushed aside Christ's outward reach to "neighbors". Instead he recommended for our faith-belief a savior, a redeemer who could be approached on an individual, personal basis. This could tidy-up those personal feelings of sinfulness; it could permit scorn for the world's confusing, disturbing mix of good with evil. Paul knew what people wanted. His power rested with giving it to them.

Mixing In Opposites

It's not to surprise anyone that the way God is seen to be running things does not meet with everyone's approval. St. Paul is figured to have been quite successful by most students of the subject in putting together a theology that suits a large proportion of the world population. His version of Jesus Christ varies with what many insist is the personality and teachings of the Son of Man or Son of God of the Gospel pages.

Believers that God's running things look for ways to put the best face on life's mix-in of evil. The interlacing of good with evil in the world looks like God isn't running things, at least not completely. To me the genius of the writers of the **Book of Job** was their focus. They never took their eyes off the reality of trying to live life consistent with a God Who doesn't seem to care.

Wherever we stand regarding God's part in our world's co-existence of good and evil, we are compelled to acknowledge that we live amidst a generous portion of both. There's beauty all around. The warmth of the sun, the green of the grass and hillsides and cornfields, the four seasons along with our body's adapting to hot and cold, it's all quite wondrous. Much that's inspiring is man-made: architectural marvels like skyscrapers, museums, orchestra halls, suspension bridges that extend for miles, highways that wind through farmlands and mountains. Throw in golf-courses, too.

There are unhappy features too. Drought, tsunamis, earthquakes, disease, violence among animals and marine life. People can be and often are inhumane. Warring is the obvious fact of our history. So are the not-so-obvious wrongs like the secretive collusion within Wall Street traders and legislators' under-the-table dealing. In contemplating suicide, Hamlet cites the "…**whips and scorns of time, the pangs** of **unrequited love (and) the law's delay…**" (Hamlet Act 3, Sc. 1)

An episode a few years ago occurred in Sierra Leone that inspires and at the same time jolts me with its horrors whenever I think on it. A gang of marauding boys armed with machetes sadistically went village to village seizing defenseless men, women and children, dragging them to tree stumps and lopping off hands and feet indiscriminately. I can hardly muster the stomach to speak of this except for the episode about a father who had just lost his hand. Some in the gang were grabbing for his young son when he shouted something like, No, not my son. Please, take my other hand instead. They took the deal and spared his son.

If I had visited that village a few days earlier and had somehow met this father, I'm sure I would not have guessed he was possessed to that degree with parent-love. I would have observed just another undistinguished villager, uneducated and perhaps unkempt and eminently forgettable. Yet he has become for me the most unadorned hero I could ever hope to meet.

Perhaps this risks over-doing it. I present the story as a telling illustration of the combination of good with evil that is of regular occurrence in our lives.

Christ – Confused?

The Jesus Christ of the Gospels is said to have said things that dilute or even contradict His reputation for peace first, peace above all. Where does that leave pacifist Christians who quote His telling us to love our enemies, turn the other cheek and love our neighbors no matter what? They can point to Luke's Twenty-Second Chapter where He declares those who use the sword will perish by the sword.   Might they not be befuddled with their divine model when their antagonists highlight Matthew's Tenth Chapter where Christ is quoted as saying: ***Do not think that I have come to bring peace on earth; I have not come to bring peace but the sword***?   In the Twenty-Second he writes of Christ composing spontaneously a parable of a king unleashing his army to drive some inhabitants from their homes and slaughtering them like sheep and burning their cities to the ground.   Luke's Sixteenth chapter reads: ***If any man comes to me without hating his father, mother, wife, children, brothers, sisters, yes and his own life too, he cannot be my disciple***. These quotes confuse us, they contrast with others. It's not easy to figure out where and how they fit. For the moment simply notice that Christ seemed well aware of the mix of good and evil in our lives. He was a part of our world.

We Surprise Ourselves

Recall again Staff Sargent Bales who on a midnight rampage gunned down some fourteen Afghan innocents. Back home in Fort Hood his neighbors and friends were unbelieving. What they were revealing was not their dearth of insight into the Sargent's inner motives but their lack of such insight into their own.

They couldn't imagine their own fingers pulling the trigger on unarmed civilians.

They spoke from within a community they understood well. They had homes to which they and the ones they loved relied on as centers of love. They had security and warmth and friends to talk to and the easy camaraderie found among people who share a lot in common. These same folks, put into the same warzone as Bales, could be expected to feel the same pulsating jabs of rage he did. They may not have succumbed to it as he did. But murderous rage arises understandably when death happens all around, easily and efficiently accomplished with the finest technology generous quantities of tax dollars can provide. Any of normal humane counterbalances like playing with one's kids or sharing meals are remote unfelt memories.

People are constantly surprised by what they find in others. They thought they knew a friend or neighbor well or well enough. Then something, often trivial, happened that surprised: A student slammed shut her bedroom window; somebody's dyspeptic newborn wouldn't quit screaming while she was trying to study. A respectable Presbyterian driving in the slow lane found himself caught with instant rage when some high school kid with his hat on backwards cut in front of him. A friend told me he had been deeply into some research study some years ago in the college library when some drop-dead-gorgeous co-ed in shorts happened in and sat at the next table. Her loveliness grabbed onto his gaze and wouldn't let go. He tells me this years later, still a trifle embarrassed at her unintended hold on him. It startled him, catching him unawares, moments he hasn't forgotten. A patient in psychoanalysis said that at a certain point in his treatment he stopped smoking. He couldn't at the time explain how this happy consequence came about – he still had more analytic work ahead – except to say that something had been worked out and so whatever neurotic need cigarettes fulfilled for him was relieved. (I wasn't privy to how nicotine's physical compulsion got dissipated.)

Surprises happen a lot. A man we all thought was settled and level-headed may have turned out to have depended for his strength on his wife. When she died he became terse, anti-social. We were making assumptions. We were proven wrong.

Opposites Side By Side

Can we agree that everyone has feelings all of which are drawn along loving and hating? Various amounts of each show up minute by minute all day long. Little bits of warmth happen when we view sunsets, kids playing in a swimming pool, when we smell an apple pie baking. Screeching brakes signal undefined distress, all the more distressful because our imaginations go wild; what actually occurred could have settled down such imaginings. Many claim they turn off news reports because they don't want to confront the world's complex problems. They push aside what disturbs with what delights, like their children running to them joyously when they get home from work. All sorts of feelings, all with varying degrees of loving and hating, are happening every waking minute. Do they occur in sleep? Most assuredly - and revealingly, when we dream.

Dynamics like loving and hating are among our basic human energies. It matters not from what society or culture or continent or climate or hemisphere or longitude or latitude we emerged. That universality calls for a universal explanation. Blood type or skin color or era, be it pre-Hellenic or post, pre-Common Era or post, pre the Industrial Revolution, pre the Enlightenment or post, do not supply enough extension. These issues influence greatly but they don't account for the universality of our drives, those energies of ours we ALL give over to loving and hating.

The Nub Of It

The accounting for everybody's capacity for loving and hating will have to rest with what is inescapable for everybody: **everyone emerges from a womb, all have mothers.**   Those events everybody shares. They can be found to underpin the roots of an Archbishop's de facto pre-occupation with sexual matters. It can reveal the basis for J. P. McCarthy's rush to confess refusing an attractive adulterous opportunity. It could tell what's behind the Detroit Free Press choosing to report the facts about the most gruesome of murders but cautiously dispenses the details in reporting about a rape victim. It starts for everybody from the start. Our mothers held us at their breasts. I cried when I emerged from the birth canal and found immediate and complete satisfaction – at my mother's breast. There I found total love, total satisfaction, a complete providing. We hear a baby screaming its lungs out the instant mother's nipple pops out of its mouth and just a quickly succumbs to restful quietude the moment its lips get back again.   We see there total rest, then total desperation, then the quick return to contentment, all within a few seconds. Some alcoholics start jittering compulsively when they can't get their hands fast enough on a pint they've misplaced. Infantile lips will re-envelope the nipple. It takes but a moment but to the baby it feels like an eternity. That contrast between the perfection that was and its blank absence suddenly at hand alarms the helpless and needy creature. There's where it first found everything pleasurably provided. It is destined never to forget the breast's warmth and security. Every culture considers its women the most beautiful. Every feature of woman's face and body is lovely. Her breasts however are held in particular regard. Everybody loves them. Their shape and feel and texture suggest for us joyous, passionate, absorbing perfection.

These considerations sound, and indeed are, exaggerated because we brought exaggeration to them. Each and every one of baby's experiences feels monstrous. They seemed exactly right when we felt them. Whatever love experiences life is to bring our way will contain something of the first joy and contentment and warmth and fulfillment and satisfaction our mothers' breasts provided us. Our infant lips eagerly drew them in. Throughout our remaining years nothing will ever again duplicate the breast's "limitless" providing. To baby's feelings the breast is all anyone requires or could ever wish for. Furthermore for the first months of life mother's breast was the totality of existence.

Feelings Speak What's Real

Soon or soon enough baby finds her/his absorption with perfection ruthlessly torn away: the breast comes with a person! It is its mother! This more than a little complicates the relationship. What mother had provided turned out to be its entire entity. Now occurs a stunning truth: he (I use the masculine pronoun for efficiency expecting you'll include the feminine counterpart) and the nipple are not one. All the experiences of these first minutes and weeks and months baby perceives feelingly. The mind, the capacity to think, is four or five years distant. A woman's breast carries meaning beyond its physical attributes we delight in; it resonates to a series of rememberings. We bring to it our first indescribable wonderment, those days when the only things that were real were 'felt". In psychoanalysis we experience *experiential* remembering. It's that phenomenon that retains the exaggeration we first encounter when all we "had" were needy lips encircling the nipple that was "everything".

Psychologists wonder what prompts the infant to move beyond its universe, it's effortless being-provided-for comfort of the breast-world. Then baby comes to discern that one becomes two; the lips-nipple union turns out to be two persons. There are persons on both sides, one with the nipple (mother) and one with itself (baby). Its love for the person (mother) is total; it's its everything. It's not the mature love of the adult that seeks to give as well as receive. But it is love, considered simply as emotional attachment.

I may have observed it once (as her personal emotional leftover) in the woman I saw seated at a nickel slot machine. She was relaxed to the point of being encapsulated by her chair, eyes semi-closed, lips with a vapid smile, motionless except for her minimalist gesture of pumping coins from the large (imagine infinite) assembly of nickels she fingered incessantly into the very-close-by slot with one hand, with her other arm pumping the machine's armature. The flow of coins, the inter-action of the arm with fingers, was an unbroken, endless rhythm. It went on minute by minute, minute after minute. Timeless. Looked like she resented having to provide even the minimal exertion of the merest energy output to her arm. Timelessness could be said to be on display. Her face was chubby and inert, above all supremely content.

It Was Either Or

The breast-fed infant experiences calm and eternal love. It can't as yet have any other expectation. Nor does it want any other ("wanting" is an advance still months away). Notions about a heaven, an additional life after this one, will be fashioned in the adult years ahead on the nurturing, loving breast yielding restful satisfaction that will never cease. No one tells baby - nor could it figure it out - that its universe of peace and rest is only for a while. It's the calm before an impossible-to-avoid storm. That's when its universe is no longer a seamless entity. It's coming to have parts. The breast is linked to a person, a somewhat unsettling finding requiring a disquieting adjustment.

But it's nothing compared to what else is "out there".

Let's Go Over That Again!
Baby's same simplistic feelings are its touchstone to everything else. It starts feeling the difference between its existence and everything else and everybody else. It begins gradually to separate itself. Now arrives the Big One, the one who keeps on loving whom baby loves. Baby feels its smallness to father's frightening bigness. It's being outsized, it's scary and unfair. Baby's easy (simplistic) logic: he wants to eliminate me! He loves and hates and nothing is in between. Regarding the intruder, its father, the hate is murderous. Importantly baby is sure those murderous feelings are going both ways: my intruder feels them and returns them. They terrorize the little creature. Baby's experiences are fantasies of course but it believes them. They are its "reality". Dad's love for all its intensity doesn't seep through because it can't. It won't for a number of years when at last it can think and examine as well as feel.

The great paradox is happening. Baby's love mixes with hate. These opposites within our psyches begin to churn about not long after birth, maybe within a year. Hearing an infant screaming red-faced reveals what's going on inside. Baby is hugely distraught. What may seem little to us is big, really big, to it.

Our earliest months and years uncover how the Staff-Sergeant, a family man with a commendable work and military record, could find it within himself to give himself over to a murderous rampage?

We really don't know ourselves very well. There's potential for greatness within the human spirit. Great capacities for loving along with hating and everything in between. Those capacities remain throughout life but later life brings strength, a positive one: reason. The imprint of those first two, three and four years of life remains as our brains keep evolving. They develop for the next two or so decades. We can observe the power and meaning behind our feelings and make freer choices.

A friend says he didn't feel so free. He remembered times in his young adult life overtaken with compulsive, raging sexual desire. He had to learn to deal with it. Masturbation settled a lot of that compulsion, a wise choice. It prevented him from sexual urgings that intrude when he was dating. He and the date weren't ready for the commitment sexual intercourse implies. Additionally masturbation allowed him 1) to keep sexual experiences private and therefore harmless (she becomes his preoccupation and not his engorging penis); 2) to maintain appropriate sexual desire and potential, to set their excesses aside allowing space to the date's best interests and preferences; and 3) to allow his good judgment to gain ascendency. He could be relaxed on a date, sexual compulsion having been tempered for the time being. Graduate students like medical interns have years of study and training ahead. Marrying can be an imbalanced fit for the time being. It makes good sense to make a fully thought through choice in a life partner, not easily done if his date's nicely tapered body and legs beckon, running the risk of smothering his appreciation of her worth as a person with a mind and heart. Besides sex-too-soon keeps her from an increasing awareness of her beau's mind and heart. Sex is best when lovers can combine their bodies in love-making after they've deepened mutual awareness of the other's mind and heart. That takes time.

I'm disappointed with a classmate, the pastor of a suburban parish. No problems in my parish, they're good people, he declared. He's a simplistic thinker and nothing in his years of preparation will disabuse him of it. I suspect he tells them from time to time about his rather flattering impressions. Such talk doesn't help them to discover their inner roots: why they fly off the handle at their sulking teenagers' rebellions, why they find the person seated in the next cubicle at work annoying, or inexplicably attractive, why their avowed patriotism co-exists with cheating on their 1040s. The fact is there are no good people or bad people; there are just people.

Sex Prompts Nobility

We've touched upon why we fail to regard sex and sexual functioning in higher regard. And why a God-spokesman such as an Archbishop can count on people supporting his negative intruding into sexual matters. From the get-go our experiences are on track to get tied up in love/hate stresses which marked them as if they were evil. Later they get *thought* to be evil; our earliest life experiences convinced our infant psyches of that. Sadly they tend to devolve into adult feelings. Nevertheless nothing can yield more joy, more of a sense of completion, more tasks that bring out the best in us, than sex. Our love relationships prompt us to do our best, as we earn a living, as we experience the worth in giving to our children what our love for them coaxes us to give. It's all founded on sex because sex makes it all a reality. A woman thus looks at her lover-husband whose commitment allows her to run the gamut of her femininity. Her capacities develop as a home-maker as well as wage-earner. Her man, hers and hers alone, makes it all happen. For his part the man looks to his woman's specialness. Combining love they become unique, unlike any pairing before, since, or ever to happen in the future. That uniqueness is the template for their offsprings' individualities.   Her beauty, presaging her love-loyalty, on balance outweighs whatever his work world, that necessarily contains some ugliness, has in store.

If we can delete what I say is the Oedipal this may portend what's best in life. Of course her love for him elicits from his mind and heart an appreciation for the wonder that her happiness can reliably build on what he's become as lover, husband and father.   She nurtures the desire to give over in love all that she is and has. He has yielded to what he brings to the love relationship so trust results.   She finds the joy of enveloping herself in what she alone can bring to their unique dyad. Everyone would like to have the chance to give themselves over to what is truly worthy of human dedication.   Sex (in its fullest sense) supports that chance.

But Sex Takes A Drubbing

Everyone finds attraction in these assertions. Similarly most of us in our more honest moments wonder why sex that brings such good includes with it hints of "bad".   A couple years ago a promotional ad was worded: Do it in Detroit. The ad writer didn't have to define "it". He was counting on everyone's inner voice proclaiming that the "it" is sex. Sex of some sort - or any. Days later someone editorialized that we should be ashamed at promoting the city in a vulgar way. That editorialist knew what "it" evokes in us. Our first reflex about sex is badness.

Sex gets a bad rep. Notice how we generally give it a light, prissy touch. It's a polite version of "it". When our toddler came in the room with an itch on or around his scrotum, he spoke the word "penis". My wife and I had encouraged his using the correct term. My mother-in-law however who was present at the time protested mightily. My wife asked, "What would you say, Mom?" Her reply: "I'd say, Down There!" (That's become a handy bit of humor in our household. When our basement flooded in August, we smilingly questioned each other, Shall we go "Down There"?)

She was convinced sex was bad. When she found out that my widowed mother was dating she was contemptuous. I know what men want!, she avowed. Asking what that might be was implicitly forbidden; it risked outward references to sex. That would never do, especially on a Sunday, the "holiest" day, and the one we often took to pay my wife's mother a visit.

We treat our sexual factor in this tentative, guarded manner. Why? The fact is our earliest feelings got sex mixed with love – that was a happy state for a while but soon after merged with hate. Baby begins life with the totally providing breast. Nothing the years ahead will provide will come close to the bliss of those first months. But baby is in for a shock, the shock of conflict. It feels a stunning awareness. Baby, who thinks it had the whole world (the breast) to itself, discovers another had gotten there first. It's father. Sharing is impossible. Its mind (thinking) isn't to be formed for some time. For now it's an all or nothing world, a world of simple extremes like black and white, all or nothing at all. It knows what it feels which is all it can know.

Such is baby's reality. If it loves totally, so too must the intruder. The father becomes omni-present; he loves the one baby loves. He remains there and baby hates him for it. Extermination becomes the only solution to the conflict. The elimination it ardently wishes for him is extinction. Murder is what the society it's being born into would call it.

Clobbering Good Judgment

You'd think thinking would be enough. Baby becomes the preschooler and grade-schooler who constantly feels the mother-father love it can count on. You'd think that should correct any egregiously false notions. But it doesn't. Present day experiences contradict, indeed compete with unconscious memories. Today's parent love doesn't erase its having gone through the blistering intensity of those conflicts with father. It smothered those horrible memories into its unconscious. (Recall my asking for your indulging my convenient policy to review psychodynamics using only the masculine pronoun.) Psychodynamicly speaking, it couldn't bear to experience them any longer. It blotted them out of its enduring them any longer, driving them out of its awareness. Its desire is never to have to go through such terror again. Baby wants sureness that such fright will never again get so close. It succeeds. However the feelings associated with what it has buried from its awareness remain. They're at the ready when similar later-life occurrences suggest what happened in those infant years. Sex is surely one of them. It comes wrapped in many guises, some glaringly overt, some subtle, some gentle like those arriving in the swim suit edition of **Sports Illustrated**.

Blotting out, denying what's ugly, being stunned into disbelief is a common adult reaction. But they're mere carbon copies of baby's complete obliteration of the experience. It's only a little like being in your car when a huge truck comes careening at you. It's going to be a head-on collision. Your terror exceeds thought. Instinctively you lift your arm to cover your face. Your arm is at the service of blotting out what's coming. What's to happen to you is too horrendous to admit. It's not logic at work. Call it psychologic; the psychologic of the infant: if you can't see it, it doesn't exist.

Of course, I love my father, that's our protest when confronted with these unsettling assertions. But then come those puberty years. That's when a youngster starts getting hormones that lead to sexual - and we hope emotional - maturity. Memories of the original rage toward father are revived. Not memories that yield pictures; rather do **experiential** memories of those original feelings strive to break loose. Tough times are ahead for father and son until they work things out realistically. Parents are appalled. What's happened to that nice kid of ours who was so sweet and loving all through grade school?

Harold S. Keltner saw the problem. In the 1920s he and an Ojibway Indian founded **Indian Guides** for fathers and sons and their presumed shared interest in Indian lore. "Pals Forever" was its motto. It expanded from around 1935 to well into the Fifties and Sixties. Keltner was good-heartedly naïve. **Indian Guides** survived for a while, possibly because authority figures generally had more clout back then.   Those first 36 months of nurturing after birth put us through scary experiences of love mixed with hate. Declaring fathers and sons "pals forever" begins a forced march into adolescence.   Teens' unconscious anger has to be worked out honestly, recognizing the genuine feelings that surface. It will meet the contrasting love father keeps giving back.   Forcing a youth to be "pals" is pretending his hatred for his father didn't leave its stamp. He might be wondering why he's so put off - "my dad's being so nice to me."   Letting the rage unconsciously color son-to-father relationships helps it be understood.   That is to say the lad will come to realize that something's diluting his respect for dad and it doesn't match what's really going on. There should be more warmth between what he's allowing himself to feel toward his dad and the love dad holds for him.   He needs time. He's got to work through these contrasting emotions.   It's the honest path toward self-respect. He's to allow irrational rage to be felt.   It's scary and confusing but it's his path toward recognizing how ill-fitting it is within the real world he finds himself in, the world his loving father provides. Keltner unwittingly would have kids irrational rage stay bottled up.   Self-contempt could result followed by depression. Keltner's plan was well intentioned but way, way too simplistic.

Two Stories – Differing Results

Richard Dreyfus co-starred with Amy Irving in the movie ***Competition***.   The story hardly gets underway when he meets Amy quite casually in a crowded corridor.   They exchange pleasantries after which he enters a nearby washroom and begins angrily banging his fists on the walls. Confused, are you? So are the movie's viewers until they find out that Richard and Amy are both splendid pianists who have arrived unexpectedly in the same town for the same purpose, to compete with the nation's best for a prestigious top prize. Richard has been love-stricken with Amy but has postponed expressing his love for her until his full undistracted focus on his skill at the keyboard would win top prize. He'd been avoiding her and practicing hard for the contest; then suddenly there she appears for the same competition in all her unmistakable beauty. He is fit to be tied.

The true story of a 35 year old Iranian mother of seven is the no-holds-barred movie **The Stoning of Soroya M**. She was executed via stoning by her fellow villagers. At first they hesitated, tossing a few pebbles. Their daring gathered impetus as the crowd became a mob. Her husband and the all-male village bosses had already stacked some heavy rocks nearby but they didn't eagerly join in until a representative number of these unlettered, simple peasants had already drawn some blood from her head, shoulders, arms and upper body. (Her lower body had been buried waist-deep in an open clearing. An open target.) To shouts of "God is Great!" the camera spared no detail. The stones began raining over and into the bloody mess that Soraya's body was becoming. Up to and until her face had been too mashed to allow speech, she called to her townsfolk, You know me! Why do this? The film was unbearable to watch. Fellow citizens had dug the hole, calculated to the correct depth. She was to be inserted into it only to her waist, helplessly secured in place. Full targeting of the upper body's most sensitive parts - head, breasts, arms and chest bones, then increasingly the bulging inner organs - guaranteed maximum and long-lasting pain.

Her husband by way of an arranged marriage when she was in her early teens was a tyrant who had fixed his eyes on a 14 year old where he worked. He declared Soraya with being an "inconvenient wife", a charge which stuck with the city fathers. Not bothering to inform her, she came to recognize that she was to be dispensed with; rumors were forming around the village. No trial, no counsel for her defense, no list of the charges. Some women came to her tearfully, trembling for their own fates for being "sympathizers", so thereafter kept their distance. Her face showed anguish and disbelief; the film's director focused on her facial muscles, twitching, gasping for words to her children whom she was never to see again. Then we watched her limp frame dragged from them into the streets.

Not Without Cost

Both movies deal with male responses to women. Dreyfus and the tyrant represented the two kinds, broadly defined, of male responses. Dreyfus was the stricken lover rendered practically inert over Amy's loveliness. The tyrant felt he was to have total mastery over all womanhood. A man pays a price regardless which of these two wide arenas he chooses to occupy.

All of humanity bears the results of inner dynamics from early-life conflicts. Babies get totally absorbed over their love for the parent of the opposite sex. For the remaining years of life they imprint their life choices. The tyrant must have had a tough time of it. This is not to say that a fundamentalist version of Islam didn't add something; its entire culture controls women. (It's beyond the purview of this book to list the controls our nation tolerates. About that read Gloria Steinem.) But the tyrant took it to new heights – or depths. We can make some guesses about the feelings of crushing defeat as an infant he experienced from his father. They may well have been buttressed in his post-infancy relationship with him. Some experiences left him totally inept in approaching love and sex. The rest of his life found him crushing underfoot all women and love/sex experiences.

Fundamentalist religious tenants defining male superiority sanction this. They build on simplistic differences easily observed. Men don't cause sensual evil, women do. They cause stiffening penises. With those come wishes for sexual intercourse. It's all too evil. Females make sin happen to otherwise virtuous males; they must be subdued. In our culture most males hope to earn sex, even to be worthy of it. That means courting, being on one's best, and seeking deepening understanding of the attractive woman's personhood. The pursued woman therefore has power. She asks for her own chance to get to know the man who seeks to be her life partner. She looks for examples of loyalty and his capacity to stay with his commitments. She will ask for more time, time to watch and think.

That's a problem for men who along the path of their development picked up distorted consciences. For the tyrant humaneness can have no place. Women cause him sexual stirrings. He must not welcome them or he risks accepting sin's entrance into his life. Sex is felt to be sin-laden. The attractiveness women exude dare not be welcomed. Bravado can make its muscular entrance: no female is going to exert such power over me! Sharing becomes impossible.

"Proper" Sex, ISIS Style.

Certain reports of a few months ago shocked us. Young ISIS fighters rape young girls, some eight and ten years old. But they do this ceremoniously. After tying a child to a bed they kneel in prayer, then get astride the girl and penetrate her. Then they kneel for more prayer. This ritual is based on a "true faith" model. Outsiders to radical Islamism are heathen infidels and deserve to die. Killing them rids the world of evil. Abusing them with rape fits their status. The fit is precise: since sex is evil it is appropriately indulged with evil people. Females as a gender are the lowliest compared to males. Add to that their false (non-Islamic) religious practices and they become unworthy of any humane consideration. Should this sound foreign to our ears, recall that marriage counselors often have clients who cannot maintain erections with their wives, particularly after they become mothers. But they can copulate with prostitutes. The "fit" is the same as for that of the ISIS soldier; an evil function (sex) seeks an evil partner, in this instance a prostitute whom society considers lowly.

Being bowled over by those first throes of love attraction on the part of an equally enthralled woman whom one considers most beautiful is one of life's great joys. Love-making expresses this exquisitely. The tyrant in the movie wouldn't know what we're talking about. He is not to allow it because the evil that is love/sex is not to be equal to his superior maleness. Human loving is to welcome love/sex toward the service of love expression. It's to start with honesty, with oneself first of all, followed with honesty with the other. Mix in humility. At some point the surrendering of oneself to the other becomes eminently correct. It's wondrous and it's available to any one of us with the attributes we associate with self-respect and humility. Lovers humble themselves before the other. There's a sense of awe the man and the woman feel toward the love that is forming between them; and there's mystery, an unfathomableness toward which some of our greatest artists and poets have put their highest powers to express.   These are not the oedipal leftovers of an infant in a murderous striving with its parent. People become able to give themselves over to the lover's devotion because they have long since worked that through.   They find joy in giving, in surrendering. Compare these dynamics to the stilted mind-set of the ISIS soldier. He will give himself over to orgasm but that's as far as he can yield. A woman's beauty and potential for sharing in love and child-bearing is cloaked in indignity.   ISIS conduct toward women is rife with contradiction.   His relationship with them sets up a stunning compromise by way of rape mixed up with prayer. He may desire sex but only with contempt for its evil along with the evil women bring to society

Soroya dutifully copulated and bore seven children.   If the tyrant had brought warmth and appreciation to their union, Soroya in all probability would have blossomed. Mere copulation would become love-making. He could have been privy to her personal thoughts and reflections.   He could very well have loosened up, gained personal insight into his own inner motivation.   His acquaintances and the townspeople would remark among themselves about the humanity enveloping him not seen previously.   Specifically not before he encountered Soroya. Shared love can do this.

ISIS-Type Dutifulness

A number of German-speaking Bavarian Catholics became farmers in central Michigan around the mid-Nineteenth century. Their culture centered on their faith.   Many observed silence from Saturday suppertime until they received the Holy Eucharist at Mass the next morning. Over the years some eighty vocations to the priesthood and sisterhood were nurtured in this environment, a phenomenon that got some front-page coverage in the **New York Times** in recent years. This was also the milieu in which the cheerleaders at the football and basketball games wore not shorts but skirts. The boys were not to see too much skin. Actually the skirts were as flattering as the shorts. But few I imagine didn't understand the higher standards and guardedness to be inferred compared to the shorts girls elsewhere wore.

Later on dutiful mothers were to caution their daughters (they all used much the same language), Don't give him what he wants until you are married. Is it accurate to say, That's What Men Want from marriage? Whatever may have been presumed to be the daughter's motivation for marriage, it was made clear that males above all wanted their bodies for sex. These parents figured that everyone believes wanting sex is bad. Implicit is a parent-conviction that girls and women don't have similar desires, or shouldn't, that Catholic girls are not to have desires for sex, that such are unworthy and unwomanly, that there must be something wrong about a female who desires sex. Those must wait upon the Church's blessing. Associating sexual desire with anything virtuous simply doesn't wash with this group.

Sabatina James has founded the Sabatina Foundation. It acts as an underground railroad for women seeking escape from fundamentalist Islamism which enforces a marriage-or-die tradition. Sabatina's parents threatened to kill her for seeking a secular education and freedom to wear eye-liner and make-up with the wearing of pants and blouses. Her roots are Pakistani from the other side of the world. But those Oedipal feelings everyone has to deal with diminish the mileage between the Far East and central Michigan. In that sense all the world lives within a few blocks of each other. If truth be told, everybody has problems with mixing in "good" with sex. Everyone is to work that through from the neurotic distortion that it is. But certain groups like those mid-Michigan Catholics are quick to condemn the emerging sexual capacities of their youths.

A Painful Story

What's infinitely preferable is helping adolescents develop a respect for their sexual desires, to help them use them as guides toward maturity. Their bodies are wondrous, in their functioning, in their potential to become lovers and perhaps parents. Mom and dad are to take on imparting these ideals. Their kids need them. Parent embarrassment is to be brushed aside. Kids up to this point have only their earliest years of emotional conflict as their "experience" with sex. My mom and dad wouldn't do such things to each other!! Or would they? Mom and dad are to step up to the plate. Their happiness with each other does most of the convincing so they can talk with sincerity. Such genuineness speaks eloquently to kids. Embracing one's sexual nature is to become a comfortable acceptance. It's to be the base for their most important life choice, that of a life-partner. Even more important than their getting well educated, more important than landing a satisfying job.

A sister of a good friend fell in love with a high school classmate. They were seniors about to graduate and certain they were "meant for each other." Their timing however was poor. Both wanted and needed to further their education. Besides their parents would surely be a problem. One family was first generation Catholic from Ireland. They would prefer their breaking up and they dreaded dealing with youthful sexual compulsion. They could argue rightly that adolescents jumping into marriage often come to regret their choices. The couple sought out their parish priest and presented their case. His response was forthright: either break up or marry now. In no way were they to make love before they had the Church's blessing. They genuinely felt mutual love and wanted sexual expression. They told the priest to marry them; presumably that would change their forbidden sex urgings into a "good".

It would only be the start of their troubles. They had no money. They'd be depending on family and friends with help setting up a basic household in an upper flat somewhere. There was however their ever-present Church. It forbad reliable contraception methods. Babies might keep arriving amidst other obligations to their jobs…and their futures! Without further training and/or college courses for several years ahead they could foresee minimal opportunities for themselves and their children.

It's easy to function as a priest. His job is the simplest, just tout the Law. He stands for what is right and good. That's what people want to believe and so they do. Why do they believe it? Our Oedipal convictions would have it that way. Sexual expression is to be corralled above all else.

Oedipal Intrusions Hurt

What a mess they made of those young couple's lives. The priest, the parents, the school authorities (it was a Catholic school), indeed the largely Catholic community encompassing their honored Church building, were allowing their earliest experiences with love/hate to override their grown-up conclusions about what is befitting. Sexual feelings were pointing to making love. Should they? Answers are not easily come by. They had a lot to consider, their youth not the least of them.   Prudent advisors like counselors, psychologists, professionals with whom they could lay all the cards on the table play important roles. Not priests; they are committed to a stock, depersonalized dictum. Their entire Catholic community, people they've grown up with and trusted, insisted there was no case to be made for risking the possibility of sexual expression without the Church's permission. That meant consigning them to a lifelong commitment for which they may have been unprepared. The couple's love might not endure. They needed time. It was not to be allowed. Catholic influences demanded that sexual impulses even of the mildest and most appropriate sort (any of a variety of bodily motions occur normally between the sexes) were to be scorned. However should a priest bless them they become immediately "good". But not until then. It's more Church magic like turning bread into "… the body and blood, soul and divinity of Jesus Christ…", like the pouring of plain water and saying the proper words makes a baby into "…a child of God…"

This begs the question, Why do we accept scorn for the human sexual factor? Doesn't our established experience tell us sex is good? Admittedly it requires maturity over a period of time to employ it well. It's well worth the effort involved; everyday experience illustrates that fact. Two and a half millennia ago Sophocles' **Oedipus Rex** dramatized adequately the fact that our sexual natures get shaped into what's universally felt to be suspect.

Embracing Self Conflict

Back to our beleaguered Catholic high school seniors. They were confronting everybody else's sense of what was right for them. All of them, the entire community, were resonating to their Oedipal sentiments.

(While we respond to them with personal feelings what prompts them is the same for everyone.)   Their priest stood on top of it all. He was a celibate and honored as such. His bed was a lonely one, not like those of those sexually indulgent Protestant clergy. Pope Pius XII boasted of his Church's priests as superior to the clergy of other religions; he declared Rome's celibates as "…the single flower of the Roman priesthood…"   He demonstrated once again how sexlessness, sexual abstinence, in the popular mind equates with goodness and then holiness. How did we come by those feelings? A good question.

The couple might have sought out other counsel. Not that they were likely to do so. Their own Oedipal histories were actively working against themselves supporting Church authority. Their own feelings about sex and love were telling them they should have the Church's cleansing before love-making. It would have taken a good deal of independence from all they had accepted as good to have sought other solutions from secular counselors, psychologists – and, yes, certain Protestant clergy who may have been freer to personalize advice to fit their circumstances. Their priest?   Not really. A minister would be free to sympathize with their predicament. S/he may have given them choices.   They could continue their education, postponing marriage. They could put their sexual needs on hold as well. Private masturbation could override their sexual compulsive insistence when they dated, reducing the drama of their eager first love. Be-calmed dating sets up a better chance to observe the many as yet not seen sides of the other's personality.

An empathetic priest might have offered similar advice. He'd have faced a scandalized community, followed by a summons to the Archbishop's office. He'd likely be defrocked in some manner. The Archbishop would find universal support. No holy man was to allow orgasms in advance of marital vows pronounced at the Altar.   Should another clergyperson have been consulted and offered the couple some choices, s/he would face non-acceptance in the Catholic neighborhood. Suggesting that artificial contraception, masturbation, and pre-marital sex may have their places in a person's life invites scorn.

The Church Rides Piggyback
It's much to my purpose to state that the Church does not have the power to overtake people's thinking. It cannot produce the mindset shared by Catholics about sex. The Church finds itself inert to change anybody's mind on anything. What it can do – and indeed all it can do and is quite willing to do – is put its authority and colorful ritual at the disposal of what the populace says is right and proper. What people approve and require is determined by their unconscious Oedipal results. The Oedipal Conflict rules.

It's what prompts candidates for the Augustinian priesthood to accept rules about whipping their bare backs. It's why Roman Catholic clergy are required to foreswear sexual intercourse in marriage because abstinence makes them look holier than those sexually indulgent clergy who staff Protestant churches. It's what coerced those high school boys to line up at my confessional to self-accuse themselves of masturbation. It's what had genuinely-in-love couples kneel before me to declare their vows before they would dare to make love. It's why young ISIS recruits who had never so much as held a girl's hand (female companionship was forbidden because women evoke "evil" stirrings) will resort to rape if they find female partners who are sufficiently evil. Evil women they define as "infidel" which includes every other religious (or non-religious) person on earth. Christians, Hindus - or Sunnis if the rapist happens to be Shia - all these and other non-Muslims he may (or maybe should) rape. There's that good fit again: that evil (sex) should be practiced with evil women. It's quite like the quandary that engulfs some Christian husbands who cannot manage erections with their wives whom they consider "too good". Too good for sex; for that they have to hire prostitutes.

Shakespeare gave us a chance to watch Hamlet's Oedipal results impeding his love for a beautiful, cultured woman who shared his feelings of love – which he quickly denied. It will help build my case by tracing the anguished rationalizations of a couple I know well.

Another Conflicted Couple

Their relationship began when he was functioning as an Augustinian monk at a monastery on Detroit's West side. Years earlier as a student he had whipped his bare back along with his fellow classmates as part of his preparation for the Augustinian priesthood. A girl just out of high school joined a prayer club for youth at the monastery to which he was assigned. Who knows how these things happen, they happen all the time; they were attracted to one another. It was against all the rules. She was a fervent Catholic. She understood as does everyone else, she was not to fall in love with a monk. Nevertheless she did and her love was genuine. She sincerely wished to dedicate her life in love and sex to this monk. Normally falling in love is a happy event. Not however when it mixes in love and sex with a monk. The Church is intent on keeping its priests and nuns looking sexless because, since sex is generally regarded to be a second-tier practice, it makes them appear holy.

That was the dilemma the monk was faced with. Either choice would be painful. If he chose to marry the girl he'd have to jettison his conditioning for a celibate life he had felt "called to" by his God to embrace. If he'd chosen to stick with monastic living, he'd have to take on the misery of having rejected a life of sharing with the woman he loved.

After a year of soul-searching (they would call it praying) they decided that the same God who guided the monk to monastic life was now calling him to a life of love and sex and children. As for the lady her chance meeting with a monk who unexpectedly proved to be husband -material could also be deemed to be divinely determined. So he quit his priesthood and applied for permission from Church authorities to marry. Rome granted it.

It Won't Let Go

They are a happily married pair. Their friends and acquaintances consider them admirable. But one would think they would have become forever suspicious of the Church's guidance, especially regarding sexual matters. A "once burned, twice cautious" experience. Instead they remained Catholics, fervently so. This may have satisfied their consciences about entering into a love/sex partnership. But they might have given thought to sparing their kids similar sexual conflicts the Church, in cooperation with peoples' Oedipal strivings, gives support to.   If they did have second thoughts it didn't show up in how they reared their kids.

In making these observations it's easy to forget the power – and universality – of what I've found are mankind's Oedipal conflicts and the neuroses they undergird.   This religiously observant couple had to invent a rationale: that their God granted them an exception.   However others including their children would be expected to abide by the Church's standard requirements regarding sex. No (other) exceptions.

Things have worked out quite well for them for some 40 years? Five children were born to their union. One of them, a boy whose real-life identity we'll hide by calling him Alexis, entered a marriage that lasted no more than six months. It began with great celebration following a ceremonious wedding Mass. A few years later he's anticipating a second marriage this summer. His intended also had a Catholic upbringing.   Neither has chosen to be married by a priest, even given the option of having the previous marriage nullified so they could have the Church's blessing. Years earlier his mom and dad, still embracing Catholic practices, hadn't found a Catholic high school in their area to send him to. They dug into their pockets for his tuition at a nearby Anglican School. Close enough, they figured, to what Catholicism teaches.   They were responding to convictions their Oedipal neuroses got them feeling about sex, much like those of the parents who paid for their kids to attend Visitation High School. That's where I sat in the confessional at Eight AM on school day mornings to hear boys confess to their previous nights' masturbations. These fundamentalist Christian religions appeal to people who look into their hearts and think they see evil (sexual) tendencies. Their kids' sexual development scares them.   What they're actually experiencing is their unconscious Oedipal residuals, when the other side of the breast nourishing them as babies turned out to be a woman they loved and whose lover they came to hate.   These religious teachings genuinely resonate with our neuroses.   Sadly they conflict with real life.

Re-labeling What Was "Sinful"

Many parents who send their kids to Catholic schools want those kids to stay away or be kept away from sex a while longer. They may say they want them to "have a sound religious grounding"; what they really fear is dealing with their kids' maturing sexual capacities. Talking to them about sex embarrasses parents, which is another illustration of the power of the leftovers from our Oedipal conflicts. They would support their lining up at that Eight AM confessional to cleanse what their sinning fingers had wrought. Those moms' and dads' Oedipal experiences are supporting their kids' Oedipal experiences.

This is the milieu Alexis entered into. You can be quite sure his parents didn't talk up the positive aspects of his developing capacity for orgasm. Dad might have prepared him for his first seminal discharges. Don't be scared, he might have told him. It can seize hold of you but just let it happen. Recognize the joyous feelings they give you. They belong to you. They seem wrong but see if you can welcome them; let those unique pleasures instruct you on your worth. Could you ever have imagined that your body could yield these wonders? They are to be shared someday with the woman you come to love. While they are simply bodily functions, they are special in that they can support a deepening human love. Your job is to learn to respect them.

When adolescents gain respect for their bodies, they build a hedge against neurosis. Alexis didn't get that chance. Anglican authorities at school are not free from Oedipal leftovers either. In fact those vigorous neuroses resembling those of the school authorities were why his parents were sending him there. They probably forbade masturbation, the very practice that could have offered him some control and perhaps respectful acceptance of his normal sex urges. In all likelihood he'd been commanded to refrain from pre-marital sex. Living together for a while might have brought to light that they weren't ready to marry, maybe not just yet – or possibly not to each other. His older sister may have been spared a painful divorce that involved two kids if their religiously devout parents had put aside the rigors their Church would hold them to. It might have made sense to help them set up an apartment where they could share day-to-day living. It might have revealed those personality attributes and/or preferences that eventually made the relationship intolerable.

Living is easier when we regard our orgasms with happier associations. Not easily accomplished. Those earliest conflicts intrude. For adolescent males Dads could advise their sons about dealing with sexual urges which show up helter-skelter often when they are uninvited. During daytime hours at high school stiffening penises are often embarrassing. Dads could talk about their own embarrassing moments back when and what they did about them. A lot of what prompts adolescents to talk about sex with each other comes from needy curiosity. Their buddies learn from each other but often in an irreverent way. Kids don't want to admit their need for and love of tenderness so they talk tough. But dads, speaking of sex within their home which he's building upon love for the lad's mother, are **de facto** demonstrating sex's goodness. Kids want that.

Dad's Help A Lot

If you're looking for more evidence that those first love/sex battles leave scars consider that teen boys still keep ideas about their penises' badness. Squelching that often means dads should "give permission" to their sons to masturbate. Bring a towel to bed so as not to mess up the sheets, they might recommend. Here's where Dad's okay can intrude on a young man's worry that sex feelings are degrading and somehow wrong. Besides he helps dilute his son's earliest experiences with love and sex that make out dad as murderously punitive.

Are you seeing that dad is intruding on God's space in these instances? Getting an authority's okay, even one as huge as his dad's, isn't guaranteed to wipe away all guilt at first. Catholic lads can count on feeling prompted toward frequent visits to the Confessional to feel guiltless for a while. "Confessing" reinforces the notion that something sinful is involved. But the dad who advises about masturbation's usefulness thwarts guilt – so what is thought to be God's viewpoint gets challenged! Maybe diminished. Maybe eliminated.

The sin notion is to be recognized for its infant roots. Sin doesn't offend God. Why would it? Feeling that the deity is in any way involved is a construct from whatever our unconscious rumblings put together. Being a sharing and understanding Dad is enough to dissolve some of the guilt a kid may have toward guiltlessly stroking his penis to deflate its insistent demand for discharge. Dad can help his son lessen guilt over the pleasures of orgasm. An orgasm's exquisiteness can be frightening when first experienced. Dad can prepare his son for this initial occurrence.

High school boys have a difficult time dealing with dads. He is the unconscious competitor in that early and scary sex/love war. The fearsomeness of that war got sent to the unconscious. Years beyond, on into adolescence, dad's sharing with his son on these sensitive issues contrast with the immature conclusions babies form about their fathers. I'd like to tell you what I wish my dad had told me, might be a good way to start. No doubt the lad has to consent to this conversation. Dad's offer might bedazzle him. Dad may have to back off, wait for a better time. But if a boy's father can pull it off, it's easy to see how helpful it can be. Mothers are practically forced to prepare their daughters for the onset of menstruation. They want to fend off a girl's fright if she's unprepared for an unexpected blood discharge. These are splendid opportunities for mom and dad to strengthen their bonds with their offspring into the years ahead. And when a teenage boy talks to his buddies about sex, he could contribute what his dad told him. That would add a lot. The other boys would probably think they'd like to have a father like his.

We're to do what we can to help adolescents appreciate the marvel that is the human body. Among many other wondrous functions it can beget human life. When loving another is becoming a probable reality, the joys of orgasm can express shared love eloquently. Lovers' bodies can speak in their own way what lovers intend but often can't find words to express. Words say it best in that they deepen understanding and appreciation. But having orgasm to express love and commitment when they merge in sex is the additional eloquence available to them. Introducing these ideas to boys helps give their sexual urges value. Boys should be allowed to enjoy their seminal discharges whether they occur as they sleep or through their fondling their penises to bring about a seminal flow.

Neurotic Sex Abounds Everywhere

You may recognize the parallel between those mid-Michigan farmers' rearing of their youth and the culture that Soyora grew up in. Both revolved around sex. More accurately, both are centered on the hot, violent first love of our first 18 or so months after birth. Both intuitively relied upon religion to support the lasting impressions those pre-rational dynamics deliver. (Religion can be called upon when rational thinking fizzles.) Both groups were unaware they were making choices in response to their earliest fears and feelings.

We've speculated on the tyrant's likely infant experiences. Now consider Richard's. He felt for Amy deeply. He was trying to block it, postpone it for a while. He was quite sure his plan wasn't workable and this angered him. He had two purposes: first, to win the piano competition; second, to pursue Amy. Those of us watching his anguish understood his quandary - and while we felt for him, we figured things were going to work out just fine. Here was a man who had deep feelings, feelings he'd refined through his study of the high arts, feelings he could lavish on a woman he loved.

For those of us who've just reviewed the psychic dynamics of the tyrant, Richard's case appears eminently more desirable. He's in touch with himself; i.e., the full range of what it means to be a man, an artist and a lover. The tyrant conversely is confined, inhibited, fixated in a murderous aggression. Regarding the beauty and love of a woman, he is sightless. As for sex, male dominance smothers any of its growth potential. He is to be pitied.

Maybe even more than the unfortunate Soroya. Her development as a woman was crimped as was her husband's as a man. Her womanly beauty set up promptings that demonstrate she's a temptress. What further evidence need he have? He and his fellow male villagers knew well this familiar wrong that women set in motion. (So do we; we're aware of Oedipal's distortions on our own lives.) It's proper to beat her or curse her. Virtue demands this.

Fundamentalist religions cement in place these inhumane emotions. They make adult life guilt-ridden. They take our central dynamic which is sex and suffuse it with conclusions we formed as babies. Furthermore we buried them in our unconscious so we don't realize they take over our choices. But we can observe their influence. That's what we've been speaking about.

Oedipal: Doing Too Nicely

I submit that there's not a lot of distance from Iran to mid-Michigan; girls in the latter locale are told What Men Want. She's being told her beauty is not an inspiration and her lovely smile not a joyous reminder of human worth. Boys in her Catholic town learn that sexual feelings toward girls are reminders of our fallen nature. They get from boys and men what our cat Dominic gets from me when we neglect to keep his nails trimmed, a conflicting spontaneous reflex - and the opposite of what is intended from a tender, charming gesture. More Oedipal evidence.

There's something else at play here. Something beyond the distorting leftovers remaining in our unconsciousness. It's about who's boss? Who's in charge? Who's the dominant one? The male has been historically the "head of the family." He was the bread-winner, a weighty task but one that assured his status. Welcoming an extra household wage-earner meant displacing some of his authority. Women in this country were forbidden access to the voting booth until 1920. Such practices grew from an assumption of their inferiority, harkening to a general notion that they were too emotional and lacking in good judgment.

Such notions found concrete expression in the Law of Coverture which had been around for centuries. It grew out of ancient feudal Norman custom. It dictated women's legal status; it listed the rights that came along with her being feminine. But if she married those rights, such as they were, were suspended. The notion of "marital unity" had it that husband and wife were one person. That one was (no surprise here) the male. With marriage the female legally didn't exist. If she were allowed to work her earnings belonged to her husband. She owned nothing, not even her clothes. Not her children either. Should a divorce occur she might not see her children again – ever.

Other such practices were gleaned from the biblical story of the creation; it was not exempt from what I consider the Oedipal fallout. There's a strong implication, a very strong one, which has the serpent (the devil) slithering up to Eve, the first woman, and inducing her to eat a forbidden fruit. The story goes on to say she did so. But the Bible's story has it that the world's equilibrium nevertheless stayed intact. It was not until she took it to Adam, the first man! that "sin" entered the world. Henceforth man had to earn bread by the sweat of his brow and women were to bear children in pain. A grim picture that would not have occurred if Eve had been the only apple-eater. Women didn't count…except as sources of evil.

She was the impetus behind the man's "sin". (According to the Imam soliciting recruits for ISIS she still is.) She didn't have the status God gave to the male so her eating the forbidden fruit didn't carry a lot of weight. But sin, that she could do – and induce! Getting the man to "eat" what God said not to, getting her man to sin, only for that did she have capability! She didn't count as much with God as her male's partner. She was able however to induce him to do wrong. There was a similar imbalance in my wife's forsaking her name at our marriage ceremony and assuming mine. That inequity gets uncovered by way of the notion that I might well have assumed hers. Had my wife and I had agreed to this last choice, it would have highlighted the neurotic imbalance with its tilt toward male superiority. Genesis's long reach into our culture carries the additional clout of religion (God), no small authority. Oedipal consequences on mankind's psyche explain the consistent downgrading of sex wherever humanity made earth its home. I've found it interwoven in every patient I've treated. It's ever and always the same. For me some but not the only fascination was observing each individual's personal style in grappling with it.

Oedipal influences were as alive then as now. It's instructive to recognize its familiar strength when the Genesis's stories about our human origins were written around 1440 b.c.e.

Woman's Beauty…Dealing With It

It would have revealed another early infant influence. Women occasion sexual attraction – and erections and male sexual desire. The attendant pleasures should be welcomed except that those infantile love/sex conflicts got us all off to conclude love/sex was evil. As a man I'm left with either of two choices. Soyora's husband exemplifies the one; woman's beauty leads to sin. The other speaks to the joy of the sexually embellished love Richard found with Amy. Did the Genesis' writers think beyond the culture of their time? Men then as now respond to womanly beauty, some with gratitude, some with guilt. They concocted a story of and for their time. They had a certain theology to impart. That women came off as temptresses was an unhappy by-product of the early attempt to account for humanity's "fall". Readers who've gotten this far recognize the composition of that "fall" they were dealing with. It was the familiar Oedipal, a sense of "sin" accepted everywhere, and not given much thought beyond what felt authentic. It sounded about right. Everybody had his own after-infancy neuroses hidden inside to allow it to seem that way.

The creation story is obvious allegory to many scholars. To others, it's taken as historical fact. For some fundamentalists currently, it remains a God-sanctioned proof of woman's lesser status and moral and intellectual weakness. Hence the saying, Through woman evil came into the world. Women have had to try to live that down ever since. The colorful Fr. Fitzpatrick, a professor on the Sacred Heart Seminary faculty in the '20s, was unchallenged when he regaled his students with authoritative observations such as, Since women's suffrage, Heaven without hats would be impossible. He sounded like he'd have denied American women the vote. Humanity's mothers have endured subjugation since our species evolved.

J. P. McCarthy was the much loved Detroit radio personality for 30 years. He often concerned himself with the Catholic life of the area. Two of his interviews concerned priests, coincidently both nick-named Bill. William X. Kienzle was one of them, a crime novelist, a former priest and at the time married. Each year he published another novel in his **Father Koelzer** series. Each year McCarthy would invite him on his show to talk up the book and other topics. Bill saw a lot of unrealized potential in the Church. He commented to JP, Look at its organization. Personnel well-arranged from top to bottom, from the Pope through the bishops and priests to the people all over the world. It's all in place. All we require is direction, leadership.

Significantly, Bill left the service of the Archdiocese because he felt conscience-driven to re-marry divorced Catholics. He's said to have asked the Cardinal (at the time) about resuming work as an active priest. Or maybe someone in the Chancery took the initiative to ask him to come back. Setting aside who was pulling whom, he declared his willingness to accept his former ministry but only if he could re-marry those he felt should be. No, was the reply. That would be pushing too far. Once more the Church is found forsaking the general good, retaining its posture toward rigid sexual standards. It remains its pre-eminent focus. It offers no similar searching for answers to the big problems we face.

Reaching Outward...

Another of JP's interviews with a priest whom he invited to his microphone featured Father William Cunningham. Cunningham had been assigned as professor of English literature at the Sacred Heart Seminary. But Father had imagination and leadership and a talent for motivational speech. He saw great need in the inner city. The classroom was too confining. Just give me any broken-down church in town, became his successful pitch to the Cardinal, and let me get to work. (The Cardinal at the time was John Francis Dearden. He'd been greatly inspired by the Second Vatican Council and Pope John XXIII's progressivism.) Cunningham accomplished a great deal. **_Focus Hope_** was his most imaginative project and it's still functioning. It converted some old warehouses into a series of machines and shop benches which are still giving youths real-world work experiences. In that interview he and JP were lamenting the shortage of vocations to the priesthood. Implicit in Bill's feelings about how things were going with the Church was his boredom with parish life spent with novena devotions and Bible studies. He felt sure we'd find no shortage of zealous clergymen if the Church got busy about important things like patching up crumbling city schools, influencing legislators to raise the minimum wage, organizing suburban adults to tutor grade and high schoolers in the inner city, improving community relations with the police, bringing into town timid suburbanites to meet Blacks in their homes, forming neighborhood fix-it teams, promulgating better nutrition via several recommendable approaches. Scores of needs can be met when our churchmen put their brains and zeal in imitation of that Christ who sought the challenge of reaching out to our fellows, was Cunningham's assertion. He was about real solutions to real problems. His Church however was and is mired deeply into attracting neurotics seeking relief from Oedipal discomfort.

(Some said the Cardinal or his successor offered Cunningham the monsignorate. Bishops award the honorary title of "Monsignor" to priests they wish to point to as standouts among their peers. Many clergy seek it and the laity is impressed. The title comes with red-robed garb, quite elegant. Cunningham is said to have refused the honor. We can speculate why. I'm sure he had well thought - through reasons.)

And Inwardly...
The local church that touts on its signage that it prays, studies and grows together makes a virtue of being on an island of its own making. It sounds like an encouraging of Catholic exclusiveness. Parishioners are A – OK even as

they seem unconcerned, even oblivious, about strangers, about other differing peoples and cultures. They can feel better than the others, Oedipally induced, of course. Its light years apart from the Christ who talked up the despised Samaritan who patched up the wounds of a total stranger and took him to a place to heal, all at his own expense. The Church says seemingly good things but there's a big world out there with big problems from which it separates itself, in effect declining to help fashion solutions. . It doesn't have to. It's got ongoing patronage as long as it forgives our sinfulness and fashions practices that resonate to peoples' neuroses.

In Cunningham's Mode

On March 1, 2003 Pope John Paul II sent his personal emissary, Cardinal Pio Laghi, to intervene with President Geo. W. Bush to urge him not to invade Iraq. The President countered that he was "...convinced it was God's Will." The Cardinal argued that three consequences would result from such pre-emptive military action: 1) many lives would be lost; 2) a civil war would result; and 3) It would have dire results for the world at large. (We are bearing and will continue to bear for many years the wrongs the president's aggression has wrought.) In walking the Cardinal to his car, Bush asked the Cardinal not to be afraid. It will be over soon, was his assurance. The press corps was on hand and the Cardinal was available. But the Administration forbade the Cardinal to be questioned in this public forum. It was clear that the Bush Administration didn't want the Pope's strong objection to the President's war plans to get that kind of publicity.

Previously on September 17, 2002, the United States Catholic Bishops stated officially that a "pre-emptive, unilateral" forceful invasion of Iraq could not be justified.

A month later my wife and I took my mother-in-law to a Saturday evening Mass. War-talk was in the air – but not inside Catholic churches. There the talk was "…make straight the way of the Lord!" It was the same claptrap, vague language, deliberately nonspecific, Don't-Rock-Anybody's-Boat language. Not a word about their bishops' plea. Most Catholics knew nothing of the Vatican's ongoing opposition to the President's plans to invade in the Middle East. What a disservice to our nation! Great harm to America and to the world could have been deterred if the bishops united with the Pope had been heeded.

Pulpits Sounding Good - But Not Very.

So what might have been done? Perhaps a letter from our bishops to be read from every Catholic pulpit. It could contain the Pope's reasoning and warnings. That might have been enough to stop the President's war planners but judging from Bush's response to Cardinal Laghi, probably not. The bishops could have waited for the White House reaction. Were it weak and negligible, another letter a couple weeks later could follow, this one with teeth in it. The bishops would ask every American Catholic to pledge to withhold paying Federal taxes unless the military withheld the invasion. It would have put up quite a stir. Some citizens may have pronounced the Church unpatriotic. Fox News and Rush Limbaugh would cry foul. Maybe some Catholics, those who followed their bishops' request, would face jail-time. Should the invasion have been cancelled, the horrors that followed after and the blood and treasure we'd have spilled into it could scarcely have been imagined. Our citizenry would never have known the wearying disillusionment that depresses us today. But the debate would have begun. Some appreciation of the likely tragedy about to occur was emerging. Catholic bishops might have called on some others to join in. The Methodist bishops had urged both the President and the Vice-President to call off the invasion. George Bush and Dick Cheney would have found such solidarity difficult to fend off, especially because I'm told both were Methodists.   Admittedly most Americans could hardly have been expected to appreciate fully the tragic outcome that our venturing into Iraq was to heap upon us.

Afghanistan got bungled as well. Those two wars cost us trillions of dollars, an expenditure that would become a bloodless measure of the hordes of lives lost in the conflicts. Protest would have been worth trying. The White House said the war would be cheap, costing about 40 to 50 billion. Our troops would be home in August, proclaimed the White House propagandists. The Iraqis will welcome us, toss flowers on our tanks, promised Bush-Cheney advisor Paul Wolfowitz. (He actually used those words.) Other officials like National Security Advisor, Condoleezza Rice, talked about mushroom clouds over America if we failed to invade promptly.   Those horrific manipulations could have been contrasted side by side with the Pope's researched thinking.   Open dialogue might have followed. The betting is that most Americans would have questioned openly the "wisdom" behind that ill-fated day, March 19, 2003, when our military plunged over Iraq's borders on its way to Bagdad.

American bishops sit upon a higher perch than mine. There may be excellent reasons why the protest I've imagined would be ill-advised. But doing nothing when our armed forces were about to pre-emptively strike a sovereign nation that had done us no harm looks like immoral negligence. How is this not cowardly? Set up to do so much it does so little. The Church regularly takes the easy way out hueing to sex issues which our unconscious dynamics tell us needs perpetual vigilance. It's the province we assign to religion. Bishops don't face jail time for feeding into our neuroses. Going about the usual cautions for sex and sexual practice and expression don't incur the government's displeasure for telling hot-blooded teenagers to "just say no!" Everybody has to tussle with results that combine love and sex with hate as its murderous counter-weight. They leave behind heavy emotions, indeed. Church practices follow their lead. They're neurotic and neurotic policies are built upon them. I had been the Church's unwitting accomplice, having been assigned to that parish with a small high school on the West side. It was awful. Such a personal thing as a kid's orgiastic practices got to be on public display. They all had the same sad story, in essence an "I beat my meat" guilty admission. My job was to run this sacramental turnstile as rapidly as possible. Why I cooperated in this sham, this public exposure, says that I had largely bought into the Sacramental System. What occurs to me now did not at the time.

I Was Blind-Sided

The public exposure mixed into the sacramental process at the high school never occurred to me; I hadn't given it the merest advertence. I assumed all was well. I had been born and raised in the Church, felt privileged to be one of its priests and convinced that I was distributing good. Besides I too had masturbated. Seminary authorities told me I was to put at least five years of abstinence between my last self-evoked orgasm and my acceptance of ordination to the celibate priesthood. I had felt the same guilt those lads experienced when they lined up seeking forgiveness at my confessional. I too was Oedipally vulnerable. I believed orgasm was an evil to be kept at bay until marriage. Even then sex will be justified only within the Church's restrictions. Seminal buildup is part of the raw material that is one phase of adolescent growth. Brain development along with that of bone and muscle are some others. It's another demonstration of the power of our Oedipal conflicts. The orgiastic as evil becomes insistent, subverting the adolescent's pride and wonderment about his bodily advances. Declaring its urgings to be sin-prone is an easy sell thanks to a boy's infant experiences. Telling him that his growing toward adulthood necessarily is a sin-prone phase is a cruel link to attach to adolescence, already challenging enough. Oedipal influences have previously polluted the term "adult" in the ads he read for movies. Is it too much to expect that the girls he's drawn to are to delight and inspire him?   Their girlish style, their lovely hair and faces, their engaging moves of body, arms and legs arc to summon a man's eagerness to shoulder the ups and downs of a shared, purposeful life, not to be taken for granted. Most assuredly sex attraction is not to be affixed to what may be ill-advised, much less sinful. A girl's attractiveness is not to resonate with those inferences he gleans through what his Church and his parents feel are virtuous.

Unmerited Influence

Actually the Church hasn't got that kind of power. It could, if it chose to, marshal some citizens to try to copy the great-heartedness Christ illustrated in his parable of the Good Samaritan. That would be a tough sell, the one St. Paul carefully avoided. The bishops would be among the first to foresee that there's not a lot of money in it. Most among our species are not given to heroism; its membership would sharply decline. The profound influence on our lives falls to the Oedipal Conflict, to universally experienced conflicts following birth. Distortions result. We're left with what remains from our conflicts over love and hate that occur mostly before we reach our 48th month of life. Those remnants will make war on mature, reality-based choices. St. Paul cozied up to this masterfully. He required Christians to admit to basic sinfulness, then throw themselves on the mercy of God the Father by way of the redemption provided by His crucified Son.

Dads can step in. It may not be his intention to exclude the Church. That might be the unintended consequence. But in confronting his son's distortions formed in babyhood which the Church builds its appeal around takes away the sex-disparaging mandates it imposes on us. As a parent he's one human being talking to another about a factor in his son's development that's too easily associated with a feeling that something's gone wrong. The Church will call it sinful. However, not that he intends it, dad necessarily will counter his son's Oedipally-engrained feelings the Church capitulates to, on which it bases its sin-concepts. He represents pride in manhood and that doesn't mix with the sin-notion. He's to tell his son that there are many aspects of growing up that he can take pride in. His intelligence is growing, his memory is a sponge that dad says he envies, his eyes are keen on girls' fascinating movements and sometimes puzzling delights and joyous screaming, his expanding curiosity is feeding on learning from teachers eager to educate and maybe to inspire. He will come to know what he'll prefer among the arts and sciences. He'll find methods to settle down his sometimes unruly penis that embarrasses him. His dad can tell him to masturbate, calm down these new compulsions. His goal is to appreciate what these high school years offer beyond mere, albeit delightful, orgasms which belong to him and are his to accept, even enjoy – then learn to set aside and/or be undistracted by them. They are definitely not to be numbered among suspect pleasures for which he is to seek absolution. In other words he's not to allow the Church and a lot that's in his general societal environment to tell him sexual impulses are bad. He's to count them among many proper bodily responses.

(If dad and son interrelate satisfactorily, he can help the boy with other bodily matters like constipation which kids don't know how to deal with. Dad can say bowel movements should also be pleasurable and if they're not going well he can suggest diet and exercise solutions to the problem.)

What Did I Do!
Then came that unforgettable Saturday evening about six months after my ordination when the lady who had borne eight children and had been told by her gynecologist that another pregnancy would rupture her uterus came into my dark confessional and took the humbling kneeling position so she could whisper into the screen. If she selected a young priest for his presumed liberalism, she might as well have talked to a stone. What she got back at her through my side of the screen was the kind of language she'd have found from her reading of Canon Law.
Her unconscious feelings were ruling her life choices quite as they rule the rest of us. This wondrous

thing we call sex gets us off to a rough start. On both sides of that confessional screen sat two people both convinced that only the Church's blessing can make sex permissible. I surely was convinced of its needing cleaning up. But so was she. Using condoms or some such preventative method meant sexual enjoyment deliberately chosen to delete making babies for God. That meant removing what makes sex honorable. That makes it sinful. Sinful once again! They had reason to conclude they'd solved that one on their marriage day. They got on their knees– as though their love desires were awful - before God's agent who blessed their union. Sexual expression became permissible but another problem came with it, controlling pregnancies. Catholic thinking goes like this: God uses couples to make babies. That gives sex lofty purpose. The sexual act we feel degraded by now becomes God's functioning. For the first time the lovers feel free, i.e. sinless, to use their bodies to express love. That's a relief. But now came multiple pregnancies. The woman who approached my confessional had seen eight pregnancies through to successful deliveries. She would have dealt with more but for an emerging dilemma. She could very well face death. No need to count the results that would impose. All those children motherless is one, a fractured home and a hopelessly burdened widowed father is another.

How about the other party to this tragedy, the priest on the other side, comfortably seated vis–a-vis his kneeling penitent? Her unconscious, in conflict with her common sense, put her into this terrible fix. She needed God to take her out of it. As His agent, I could have done that. But that would have put me in the same fix. I was not about to put my God aside for this woman's love needs. That would be unthinkable. It's easy to be the

Roman Church's priest. Be its automaton. Conduct Masses, distribute Communion, "hear" confessions and recite the formula of absolution. Don't think, just do!

Wisdom From A Kid

That lad among those lined up at my confessional on school-day mornings made sense: if I don't relieve myself I can't sleep. I toss and turn and then I touch myself because I have to. Having mortal sinning so handy made it horrendous to have a maturing penis. Growing into manhood, wasn't that good? Or was his maturing body prodding him toward Hell?

How's he to be alert in class the next morning if he'd restlessly spent half the night fending off orgiastic urgings? The Church is way off in its handling of sexual issues. But it takes this easy path; people's minds and hearts are already tilted toward making something bad out of sex. As the Church would have it, the grinding human anguish that follows for the lad is merely another indication of the human tilt toward sin. As I see it, it's a demonstration of the lad's infantile fix over love/sex that's pushing aside appropriate real-life thinking.

The question keeps emerging. What gives Archbishops who speak out against marriage equality - or priests condemning masturbation and pre-marital sex and contraception - such great influence? On just about any other topic, be its protests against pre-emptive war in Iraq or supporting workers' rights to form labor unions, demanding good stewardship of the climate or the re-distribution of wealth, the Church is mostly ignored.

It doesn't seem to mind being ignored, maybe because it would embarrass itself. It hasn't any special insight that would give it influence on other matters. But on sex it shouts from the rooftops and keeps on shouting. There it appears to have lots of power.

Hitching a ride on people's hesitancy about sex buttresses its heft. It's banking on our neuroses, our hang-ups. It's not that the Church's sexual mandates are easy, they're not. Just ask the boy who tries to fend off masturbating. Or the lady with the potential for a ruptured uterus. Or the kids lining up several times a month to confess to masturbating. Or the gyrations the personages Nicholas Kristoff and Maureen Dowd cite as curious psychic goings-on that make fascinating reading. Something else is supporting the Church's laws for which it gets reflexive obedience. There's the feeling that God doesn't like my sexual tendencies and the Church is to require what will set them right.

The worse people feel them to be, the more punishment they expect their Church to mete out. Recall the disappointment a penitent expressed ("Is that all…?") through my confessional screen. (She had said something like, My boyfriend and I did the most awful things with each other, etc.) I pronounced the words of absolution and probably required of her some prayers as a penance, maybe reciting a Rosary. Although the theology behind absolution meant the sins were taken away, this time she felt it wasn't up to the task. The punishment didn't fit the crime. I presume she accepted the instantaneous effect to be had through the other sacraments she'd encountered when she witnessed a baby being baptized or when she'd accepted the Holy Eucharist wafer on her tongue. But this time getting forgiven through a sacrament's absolution didn't look like it measured up to the task. Probably she'd confessed her sins since she was in the early grades at school and never gave a thought to having not deserved forgiveness. This time she felt unsure.

Almost always loyal Catholics practice "confessing" because it's another way to stay close to

God by way of holy rituals, others being abstaining from Friday meat, making sure to attend a Mass each weekend and saying prayers at meals and bedtime. These are routine, have minimal consequences if they are missed, and getting absolution from the priest seems proportionate. But sexual acts feel larger. Our first experiences with them incorporate feelings of love and hate so vicious that they overwhelm our tiny psyches. Our minds and hearts can't take it. As adults we're unsettled when we have to deal with it. The result of such neglect is a lack of respect for sex. We try to reduce its worth in our lives. But that would be to diminish what can ennoble us if we think about it, discuss it with friends, read of it from trustworthy authors. But who gets that chance? Catholic authorities are probably the worst to consult. Inevitably sexual feelings and opportunities come along and we're overwhelmed. They grab us at our core. Sheer inexperience renders us helpless. We've never given ourselves a chance to establish an alternative to those negative infantile impressions that stick like glue. These concerns are pre-occupying and annoying. They are not likely to point me to join the activist Church Keinzle and Cunningham wanted it to be.

Dad As Hero

Being a helpful dad to sons riding through rough adolescent waters can be rewarding and embarrassing. For both parties. A kid is resistant and equally embarrassed even as he admires dad for his fumbling ways with fears and conflicts that come to the surface. This is real. It's not neurotic fantasy, not an imagined God-displeasing offense that the priest absolves. It's father and son working together, being real with each other while running directly against fantasied fears. Dad can easily be real when he advises his kid how to install a fan belt on his car. Or helping him soothe a pulled hamstring.   But dealing with penises, with seminal discharges, is hugely personal but, as we have discussed already, much more than that.   Feelings regarding sex churn through surprisingly conflictual feelings.

Maybe father and son should quit for the time being. But maybe they should keep at it. Some kind of a reasonable grasp of the turbulence they face hopefully should reward dad and son's early attempts. Otherwise they may not return to their noble effort.   They are amateurs and they're on to a hot one.   Could the two of them take a step back from what they have occasioned and find reason to laugh a bit? The very primitive nature of what they are experiencing together can surprise them both.   There's insight to be had here.   They are solving common problems.   So is the training in the gymnasium of one's reflexes for playing Second-base. But getting smart about one's penis stiffening during class takes the lid off, releasing a flood of feelings that make just plain talking so inhibiting. Taking a step back when these happen - pausing to see what's going on - occasions insight and possibly comfort.   Pausing to observe the contrast helps: on one hand their shared wish to get practical, on the other the rush of feelings that are roadblocks.   They are shared roadblocks, however, and that can build a sound relationship.

Can you recognize here a dramatic demonstration of the power of Oedipal dynamics?

This Oedipal Stuff Is Tough.

A friend displays a small glass figure.   It's a charming image of a six or so year old child kneeling in line for a priest to hear her confession. The charm is in the girl's tender youth and the little nothings she is about to seek forgiveness for. The popular inference is that she's not old enough as yet to sin. Sin doesn't happen until after puberty; so goes popular thinking. Actually newborns and infants go through a lot that terrifies them and it's sexual. The loud screams the little ones emit come from something they are feeling at the moment. But mom and dad are relaxed, feelings that communicate to baby that it's safe. Those who created it are providing a secure world. Baby however feels massive loss when mother's nipple slips from its mouth even for an instant. Once replaced it's back into total peace…until the next reversal occurs. A year or so later comes the really big conflict with its opposite-sex parent. It's an unfair fight. Infant terror pushes it to block completely any memory traces from getting into its awareness (consciousness) ever! There it remains for the rest of its life. But remaining unconscious gives that unawareness free reign. It's a sad fact that baby's fears of which we are unaware survive to compete with adult life-choices. We face a dilemma. On one side we seek a comfortable and settled conscience about urgings we want to utilize properly. We want to become realistic and that takes time. But on the other our prudent judgment is mere brain-power and common sense. That's mighty puny muscle facing an alcoholic compulsion or an insistent adulterer's seduction. These are David versus Goliath battles. They can ruin our lives.

Knowing this, recognizing that these dynamics add up to the potential for wisdom we want answers that fit our adulthood. An Archbishop's decrying about sex resonates with what we felt as maturing babies and infants. Acting as if those early frightening memories befit us as adults is the very definition of neurotic thinking.   They *seem* correct.   The Archbishop unwittingly uses our suspicions of inner evil as if they are to guide grown-up choices. Not that he intends to do us harm. He doesn't realize he's got his own unconscious promptings he's following; they are as neurotic as everyone else's in the world. His lofty position mirrors the image we felt toward the first Big Guy (daddy) with whom we tussled. It gives him (unearned) authority. We assume our feelings are based on what's real. They are built upon feelings we've repressed since we were little babies when we got into serious face-offs with our parents. Those repressions act out everywhere and always. They govern what and how we make choices. Whom we marry, the jobs we seek, and the friends we have, the cars we drive. They jump on, hem in, pounce around and stomp into every facet of our living. We're clueless why we feel at times depressed, confused, conflicted. We only know that they don't fit very well. Don't fit the real world we live in. Don't fit what we commonly call commonsense. Don't fit what is in our best interests and that of those we love.

Decisions Explained

There are many skeptics. They doubt that feelings we're unaware of could have such impact. It looks like over-reaching. But then we remember George W. Bush. And Barack Obama for that matter. And John McCain, whose family held high rankings in the Navy. These men seemed constantly working out their feelings about their fathers. Some psychologists figure the second President Bush's enthusiasm for invading Iraq was repeating his battling with daddy when he was a two-year old.   He resisted the eminent Brent Scrowcroft's countering advice about the Iraq invasion and took the opposite action. It turned out to be ill-advised. Twelve years earlier in 1991 Scowcroft and his father, the first President Bush, concluded that invading further North to Baghdad would be unwise. They settled for simply pushing Saddam Hussein out of Kuwait. When in 2001 Scrowcroft tried to discuss the merits of their decision with him, George W. must have felt eerily uncomfortable. He just didn't know why. At the family's summer home in Kennebunkport, Maine, reports have it that "W" rushed out of the room slamming the door on his father's eminent advisor as he left. Some see here the son's wish to show up daddy; that's how neuroses work. This may be mere speculation. We can't be sure apart from "W" consenting to entering into his own psychoanalytic treatment. Not likely to happen.

There's a probable link between what Dubya felt about himself in reference to his father and the consequences for the rest of us as a consequence of invading the Iraqi people's nation. I'm saying flat-out that prudent governing, admittedly less glamorous and muscular, got steam-rolled because our president's Oedipal residuals took over his decisions. Conclusion: Oedipal consequences rule the world.

Thinking About Mother

Carmen, the ***fem fatale*** of Bizet's famous opera, drew the restless, agitated and impetuous Corporal Don Jose into her always-temporary love interests. We've seen this dynamic many times over among our friends and acquaintances. When we see it played out once again in expressive music and choreography, we find ourselves as helpless observers pleading with him, Don't' do it, Don Jose! He could and should have made of his love life an enduring and loyal partnership. Michaela offered this. She was present and available, simple and beautiful; a country girl, not the raging, fiery, independent, voluptuous Carmen. The opera doesn't go into the intra-psychic. All opera-lovers need realize is that Don Jose couldn't help himself. He's about to make a neurotic, destructive choice and will die in prison. He's entranced by a woman whose beauty he finds overwhelming. It will destroy him. He realizes this but is helpless to resist. Analysis could have focused a spotlight on his primitive attraction to the "breast", pursuant to his destruction by an authority (dad) disallowing the sharing of the woman. We're curious to know why his destructive behavior happened; each person is possessed of his/her own individual series of dynamics. .We also know that if he'd married Michaela he'd have lived a happy, uneventful life and probably died in bed. Bizet doesn't supply sufficient meat on the bones of his development of Don Jose's personality to allow us to figure out why he chose what he chose. Bizet seized upon a story about which to write gorgeous, captivating music. That's why we attend opera and not to be lectured at about someone's psychodynamics – as does this book.

Shakespeare however does give us plenty to work with. Hamlet, the lead personality for his play of the same name, is as self-destructive as Don Jose. His relationship with Ophelia is revealing. It shows the author's genius: it also shows how a neurosis can rule a man's life-choices, much to our purposes here.

A Neurotic Conflict

Hamlet was a prince, the son of the king (Denmark). The first glimpses we get of him suggest a troubled, agitated young man. He had no doubt that his uncle, his father's brother, murdered his father, then ascended to the throne. Troubling indeed. Here's how we would see it. Hamlet was the prince. From his political pinnacle, he could have marshalled legal experts, put together a solid case, gathered the evidence and set up a murder trial. He could have done it all and had it all. He might have become king. He was in the line of succession as the king seemed pleased to point out (Act I, Scene 2). Importantly he'd have provided punishment for a murderer through a transparent legal process and displaced him from the throne. The path of justice was open, his revenge on the hated uncle easily achieved while covertly intended. It need hardly be mentioned as the executioner's ax was severing his neck from his body.

Hamlet however saw (read *felt*) things differently. This is to say, he brought neurotic distortion to his plans. He saw his uncle as his father's murderer. But he also loathed his having entered his mother's bed. The murder he saw as clearly perverse but the marriage enraged him. It was entirely too close to his own infantile wishes toward his mother. True, such wishes he had long since repressed, as indeed do we all. As such they (1) remained hidden and (2) ruled his unfortunate choices. Shakespeare lived four centuries before Freud brilliantly put all this together. But he was a profound observer of the human heart.

So also was Sophocles two millennia earlier when he composed **Oedipus Rex**. Sophocles insightfully wrote of a man who unknowingly and innocently married his mother through a complex mixture of circumstances. When that fact eventually confronted him, he became unhinged. The very idea of sex with one's mother is upsetting to every man. Unfastening her golden broaches from his wife's (mother's) deceased body, Oedipus plunged them into the sockets of his eyes, rendering himself blind for life - brutal punishment indeed matching his self-scorn and displaying to his citizenry his bottomless regret. They would understand; incest is spontaneously scorned and universally abhorrent. As Hamlet saw it his uncle by way of murder took his father's place bedside with his mother. Every detail mirrored too exactly his early primitive desires toward his mother and father.

The Oedipal Took Hold

These are the feelings that put force behind the words Hamlet spoke to Ophelia. The hurried pace that left little space between the murdered father's funeral and his mother's re-marriage drove him to frenzy. Mother probably had sent love-needy signals to his uncle. And perhaps he to her unless his ambition for the throne was exclusive. Uncle hadn't married, so it seems. Hamlet says his father was gentle. Maybe mother concluded their marital bed didn't reverberate sufficiently. She could have sensed more vigor within a man with murderous aggression. However they may have felt it, Hamlet saw what was loathsome. His previous urges to kill he'd repressed into the oblivion of his unconscious. He was certain that he didn't want mere justice. That was too fair-minded. When a chance to kill the uncle showed up (Act III, scene 3) he put his dagger back into its sheath. No, he would wait until he was mortally sinful, as when orgiasticly occupied among his "...incestuous sheets..." (Act 1, scene 2). That's how he would dispatch him to Hell. It was the chance worth waiting for.

As for his mother she had scorned him as an infant in favor of his father. This is the fate of all male babies; we males are consigned to find our own women to make love to. But there's this overriding angle to the story - his uncle had performed what he (Hamlet) had wanted. It had been his first murderous desire. His uncle had murdered the man baby Hamlet had wanted with all his being to replace permanently. In the years to follow he would realize his father was not his competitor for his mother's love. That realization however would not delete unconscious memories mixing extremes of love and hate. They impinge on his emotions, all the more influential because they remain hidden and unrecognized. They are what make our depression or anger or dissatisfactions or incapacities or inferior feelings difficult to account for. They keep impinging on our happiness. You can measure the scope of his rage by the depth and range of what he was waiting for, the chance to destroy the detested uncle. He was not just to cut his life short. He was to have him exist endlessly in fire. That's revenge in spades.

Sex: Self-loathing

Would this bring him peace? Hardly. He's making plans as if he had not been a baby whom mother and father loved as their own. His choices are based on fantasies he formed as an unreasoning infant. As an adult a real world presented itself centered on his fratricidal uncle. He could bring him to justice. Should he succeed he'd win the support of citizens who seek virtue in those who govern. But his unconscious is directing his choices. He is coping with his neurotic, infantile conclusions. They are taking over. Murder, not justice through the civil courts, is what his feelings tell him is the method he fervently intends. Uncle has succeeded his father with his mother in the ***manner*** Hamlet had once wished to succeed his father, i.e., by way of murder. That presents a big problem, typical of neurotic conclusions. In designing plots to murder the uncle he must necessarily feel he merits the same fate:

he too had sought to take his father's place with his mother by resorting to murder. For that he too deserves to be murdered. Self-loathing emerges.

As this story unfolds keep in mind the ruthless hold his unconscious maintains on his choices. Think of your friends and relatives who've done similarly zany things (probably not so extreme).   Neighbors and acquaintances find unceasing wonderment in the choices that puzzle them when people marry.   What does he see in her? (Or vice versa: He's a looser, why did she do it?) Our daughter married an alcoholic and a high-school dropout because she felt she could provide for him "…a happy home." A friend's son quit a good job in Chicago because he couldn't "click" with his boss. Shouldn't we wonder what that was about? Some ex-priest friend, whose Augustinian development included some whipping of their bare backs so as to keep their sexual urgings in check, "knew" God wanted of him the "Gift of Celibacy." Years later he fell in love, this time "knowing" God sent the woman into his life. Was God inconsistent? He might counter that he was totally at his deity's disposal. "Whatever You want God, I do". It reminds me of a friend's quip, I practice celibacy fifteen minutes a day.

Her Beauty vs. His Self-Scorn

Hamlet's self-hatred becomes apparent when next he meets Ophelia. In some direct quotes we notice a couple things. She's intelligent and beautiful, tender in her efforts to empathize with his persistent depression. She sees beyond his clumsy rejection while she watches his painful inner destructive forces taking command. He had just put aside suicidal intentions for a while when he notices Ophelia is close by. He is taken with her beauty, the words **nymph** and **fair** occur to him spontaneously. He asks for her prayers.

Hamlet: Nymph. In thy orisons (prayers) be all my sins remembered.

(Everyone's Oedipal leftovers make him/her feel "sinful." With the fact of his uncle's murdering his father and marrying his mother impossible to suppress, his personal leftover infant desire to have done the same stares him in the face. His unconscious has him feeling sin-laden.)

Ophelia: Good my Lord, How does your Honor for this many a day?

Hamlet: I humbly thank you, well.

Ophelia: My lord, I have remembrances of yours that I have longed long to redeliver. I pray you now receive them.

Hamlet: No, not I. I never gave you aught.

(He had sought her love when he had felt better about himself.)

Ophelia: My honored lord, you know right well you did. And with them words of so sweet breath composed as made (the) things more rich. Their perfume lost, take these again, for to the noble mind rich gifts wax poor when givers prove unkind. There, my lord.

(She senses his nobility – which he cannot.)

Hamlet: Ha, ha, are you honest?
Ophelia: My lord?

Hamlet: Are you fair?

Ophelia: What means your lordship?

Hamlet: That if you be honest and fair, (your honesty) should admit no discourse to your beauty.

(He unknowingly – i.e., unconsciously - is illustrating that the neurotic results of his infant love/hate/sex conflicts make the trappings of sex, normally welcome between lovers (erections, orgasms, penetrations, secretions), unfit for his lover's goodness and beauty. In some religious cultures the truly good woman is the distant, untouchable, heavenly "virgin", unbefitting sexual intimacy.)

Ophelia: Could beauty, my lord, have better commerce than with honesty?

{Notice how gently she goes right to the heart of the conflict. In Ophelia's mind her beauty (i.e., sexually desirable) combines with honesty (i.e., virtue). Quite in conflict with Hamlet's feelings about his – or anybody's - sexuality. She's a more mature person; she shows how incompatible are his neurotic energies with right thinking.}

Hamlet: Ay, truly, for the power of beauty will sooner transform honesty from what it is to a bawd than the force of honesty can translate beauty into his likeness.
This was sometime a paradox…I did love you once.

{Notice the fruits of unresolved Oedipal dynamics. He's saying that in his judgment, women's' beautiful bodies overwhelm virtue (e.g. honesty) leaving just sin in their wake.
Tragically Claudius's (the uncle) using murder, then marrying his mother revives his infantile love/sex/murder energies; no room remains for love.}

Ophelia: Indeed, my lord, you made me believe so.

Hamlet: You should not have believed me   I loved you not.

Ophelia: I was the more deceived.

Hamlet: Get thee (to) a nunnery. Why wouldst thou be a breeder of sinners? I am myself indifferent honest, but yet I could accuse me of such things that it were better my mother had not borne me: I am very proud, revengeful, ambitious, with more offenses at my beck than I have thoughts to put them in, imagination to give them shape, or time to act them in. What should such fellows as I do crawling between heaven and earth? We are errant knaves (all); believe none of us. Go thy ways to a nunnery.

(He can't make love with Ophelia. He's already experienced love/hate as we all have as infants. That makes love/sex an evil making her too good for sex so he distances himself lashing out at her angrily. He'd never worked out his infant fixation with his mother who like all good mothers denied him sexual love. The uncle designedly

murdered his father. Hamlet had had murderous rage toward the same man the uncle murdered, the difference being the uncle succeeded where he as an infant failed. It included replacing the father as mother's sexual partner. It was all much, much too ugly. He feels despicable for seeking love and sex with a noble and beautiful woman who would physically cooperate in returning love. Sex started off yielding unhappy results. Most of us allow life experiences to mature us, to allow us to cherish love making. It remained for him a degrading evil.)

It's Everywhere

It remains evil for scores of people. It's what gives an Iranian stranger the hutzpah to shout scorn from his pick-up at a young woman because she's too attractive even in her almost totally enveloping garments. It's what's behind the **Detroit Free Press**'s policy to wait several days in reporting rape before including the name of a rape victim; she could be judged by some readers as the evil doer. It's what made J. P. McCarthy say he'd feel sinful even though he'd decline an adulterous opportunity. It's what gave the "grab" several years ago to the city's promotional slogan, Do it in Detroit! The professional advertisers who composed it and displayed those words on freeway signs were counting on readers having unconscious baby conflicts. People can feel what else the "it" refers to. It reaches for the negatives we harbor for our sexual potential and they are not flattering. Sex gets off to a bad start and it's important that we know that. Buried as they are in the unconscious where we can't deal with them directly, they're free to distort human love. That means we'll never not respond to it. *We know but we don't know we know*! Everyday life and living tells us that sex used responsibly yields good, often great good, but we're slightly ashamed of it. That's neurotic. We can measure the depth of the neurosis by the amount of the shame it occasions.

St. Augustine

Stephen Greenblatt, writing for the **New Yorker** (June 19, 2017), says Augustine "...went on to shape Christian theology for both Roman Catholics and Protestants, to explore the hidden recesses of the inner life, and to bequeath to all of us the conviction that there is something fundamentally damaged about the entire human species."

He and his father had attended a public bath one day in the city of Thagaste which today would be in Algeria. It was in the year 370 c.e.; he was sixteen and it was in that bath that he had had an erection. What impressed him most, if not quite at the moment, was not only the embarrassment it occasioned. It was that it was involuntary. He couldn't control it, it just happened. And it kept happening thereafter. Teenagers who get these stiffenings in their pants know what Augustine was talking about. One teacher accepts answers from boys in class after asking them to respond while seated, decidedly to spare their embarrassment because erections occur unpredictably. Again and again Augustine deplored his unruly penis overtaking his choices; it was taking away his freedom! In later years he compared its unwelcome intrusions to the freely chosen control he had over his other body parts, his arms and legs, his head and shoulders, as well as the other movements taking him where he wanted to go. The worst of it was the evil he felt sure his penis was drawing him to. He could never thereafter associate his penis's urgent demands for seminal discharge with what was good and proper.

He put his superb intellectual powers into what amounted to a search into the Adam and Eve narratives in the **Book of Genesis.**   He was looking for a confirmation to what his sexual urgencies were propelling him to accept about humanity's basic sinfulness. To Augustine the happy state in which God placed Adam and Ever meant they did not need to experience lust in order to beget offspring. Greenblatt quotes Augustine from his famous **Confessions:** "…why should we not imagine that Adam, in his uncorrupted state, could have quietly willed his penis to stiffen, just enough to enter Eve? It would have been so calm that the seed could have been dispatched into the womb, with no loss of the wife's integrity, just as the menstrual flow can now be produced from the womb of the virgin without loss of maidenhead?' "   They failed however to obey God, therefore Adam never got the chance to impregnate Eve lustlessly. Regrettably he had to have lust-filled sex if he and Eve were to beget children.   Furthermore she was to bear children in pain; his labor to provide for his beloved wife and eventual children was to evoke perspiration which in turn was to be seen as a consequence of his sinful disobedience. Augustine linked work with punishment for sin as he had done for orgasm. If he could have discussed this with Sigmund Freud he could have come to see things differently.   He might therefore have lessened guilt for Christians yet unborn. He couldn't have eliminated quilt altogether, the entire notion that lust-filled sex/love is the hallmark of Original Sin was his conclusion over his penis's uncontrollable meanderings.   Freud and Sophocles' writings might have instructed him. He might have observed that our infant struggles about love/sex left us with infantile impressions that don't fit adult reality. Ridding our orgasms of guilt means freedom to delight in sexual expression. All kinds of rewards follow including opening our minds and hearts to increased love-sharing.   But that's a subject for another day. For the moment recognize that sex is to be at the service of lovers.   So is human labor.   Freud saw labor as a benefit. Someone is supposed to have asked him for a proper platform upon which to build a full life. I'm unaware when that question was put to him or where but his supposed response is famous: lieben und arbiten, to love and to work. There is pleasure in orgasm; not to be overlooked are the pleasures of the mind.   No place for Original Sin in either sphere. A farmer's pride seeing in acres of emerging strawberry patches the results of his prior-planning, the accountant's satisfaction when his records on months of commerce balance to the penny, the useful insights on film that the movie director's patient sensitivity arranges for popular appreciation, all such as these, not to mention the labors of teachers, pediatricians and landscapers, prompt justified satisfaction.   And frequently joy, because they bring home to their spouses and children security and the means of following up on their opportunities.

Augustine was convinced that lust was an evil experience and the sure sign of mankind's inherited corruption which he labeled Original Sin. The lads who lined up at my confessional at school day mornings so they could admit to their failures at fending off urges to masturbate would recognize what Augustine was talking about. He would say, Do you want proof of mankind's having inherited the effects of our first parent's Sin? Consider the free-wheeling penis with its insistent calls for discharge, a virtually irresistible and exquisite bodily pleasure.   Freedom of choice is surrendered.   Unlike

Adam before his disobedience, the penis stiffens with wild abandon, dragging the unwilling male into lechery with its miserable consequences. In harboring despised sexual urges as ignoble Augustine could count on his fellows everywhere who also enter life with negative impressions about love/sex. Christians thereafter would find little to dispute or deny. It was Augustinian thinking that buttressed the words of the minister at the classy wedding we attended. He said marriage's purpose was the allaying of concupiscence.

(About a month before he was to ordain us Cardinal Mooney made an additional demand beyond our spiritual and academic preparation. He required that we pledge abstinence from distilled alcohol for five years. He might have wanted to ask for our refraining from all alcohol but that would mean we couldn't offer Mass, a daily practice in the parish churches to which he was to assign us. Wine was consumed at Mass. The back story was the large number of his priests who were over-drinking. The laity were reporting to him their scandal in watching many pastors staggering at the altar during public Mass offerings. Additionally some priests were expiring long before their time of alcoholism. Fr. Thomas Garvie died of it in his early 40s. I knew him personally.

I submit that the issue was not alcohol consumption. It was celibacy. Men keep producing and discharging their sperm regularly, usually during sleep at night unless of course they have sex which most arrange to do. The discharge elicits at least some venereal pleasure, which will make some priests feel sinful as in, Did I cause it, Did I touch myself a little bit? Did I allow myself to enjoy it…even a little? St. Augustine would know what they're talking about.

There's a general tendency to tie penis-pleasures to wrongness. One way toward repression is dampening stiffening erections with alcohol. Married men who became hesitant about penetrating their wives after they became mothers know about this remedy. Another group that used alcohol to quell guilt along with squelching their penises was some priests who married and, for any of a variety of reasons, got skittish with holding in intimacy a naked woman. The Cardinal's demanding the pledge of the newly ordained poked at the surface of the problem. Most priest-alcoholics face a choice; either is destructive. Keep battling sexual urges which they can't forestall or remain chaste and therefore priestly with alcohol.)

Would that Augustine had had an awareness of the unconscious. There lays buried the dynamics that surround our earliest experiences with love, sex and hate. They became our first impressions of love, to which we had given ourselves entirely. Hatred got put into the mix when an "intruder" seemed to compete for the one we loved. We buried our terror over the uneven, unfair and terrifying conflict that threatened. We managed to retain no memory of them; had we not obliterated them into unconscious unawareness? Actually all we accomplished was memory loss; they became merely hidden. They remain freed to mix a man and woman's shared love and sex with the evilest of primitive associations. Had Augustine understood the direction our psychic energies take in early life, he might well have welcomed those insights. He writes in his **Confessions** that his mother persuaded him to forsake his lover of fourteen years, a love union that he wrote got "... ripped from my side." He could hardly have realized that his mother and he were victims of their individual Oedipal conflicts. She appealed to his unconscious promptings while supporting her own. She wielded power over her son sufficient to break apart a love partnership that lasted fourteen years. Neither he nor his forsaken lover maintained any other intimate relationship for the rest of their lives. Augustine from that point on gave himself over to celibacy. It looks like they had built an enduring love.

How sad! For all his deep speculation about his and indeed mankind's sexual magnetics, what he accomplished was to give justification to the neurotic hold over our early and mistaken neurotic feelings which we later apply to human loving. Christianity gave its "divine" authority to such feelings. We can speculate how Christian history might have been upgraded should Augustine have had psychoanalytic treatment available and the personal insight it provides. He could have come to respect the erotic sex he had shared. Instead he managed to cement further into our adult reflexes everybody's already established disparagement of sexual functioning that arise from the terrified experiences of a toddler.

Monica

His mother's name was Monica. She is lauded in Catholic lore as the one whose continuing prayers for thirty years saved her son from the grasp of lust and gave Catholicism one of its greatest theologians. Actually what she accomplished was wresting him from another woman's hold. Her relationship with her husband was reportedly contentious probably over his wish for a grandchild which had to have involved a woman other than herself. At her most basic level every woman would wish to keep for herself the sons she produces. Their seeking love with another leaves her with a sense of loss.   Most mothers hope for their sons' happiness but that means their building a family apart from the home they lovingly rear them in.   My mother became the victim of her own lack of insight into why she disliked my wife. In this respect she is like mothers everywhere. But her conflict went further than most and it resembled Monica's. Monica failed to recognize how irregular was her closeness to her son. It suggests that she wanted to be his sexual partner. She may have observed in her son's revulsion to sexual stimulation the platform upon which she could build her own style of intimacy with him. Greenblatt recalls a moment mother and son shared as "…the most ecstatic experience in his life."   He cites the novelist, essayist, feminist and journalist Rebecca West (1892 – 1883) who wrote of this without a hint of exaggeration, that it was perhaps "…the most intense experience ever commemorated." Monica wanted to possess her son. To a considerable extent she succeeded. She pressured her son to forsake an enduring relationship with a woman he loved. That might have evoked her regret for the painful separation her demand was occasioning for her son and his lover. She need not however have looked that deeply into her heart. She needed simply to look around her at the Church - which had the support of the influential bishop of Milan, Ambrose (who came to bear the title of Saint) – which finds its support in people's Oedipal leftovers. When religion (God) supports the feelings, looking inward for personal motives can be seen as small-minded.

Roman Catholicism sees things in its own way. It declared that the unrelenting hold sex had on Augustine got broken. That freed his superior spiritual and intellectual powers to eventually confer on Christianity an impregnable theological foundation. A tradition has it that his mother accomplished this through her prayers (of some 30 years duration.) We are to conclude that Monica harbored no other motive than saving her son from sin. She is the arch model for Catholics to persevere in prayer. It was simple cause and effect. She prayed and her son became a celibate. Overlooked in the scenario is the accommodation Augustine made for his sexual compulsions. His sexual exploits were varied until he wound up with a woman he loved so deeply that giving her up as directed by his mother, quoting Greenblatt again, "…felt like something ripped from his side."

I'm sure my mother thought encouraging my budding priesthood was doing God's work. Her actual motivation spun around her low opinion of femininity ("Why did God so curse women?" she said more than once), a distaste for sex, her possessive love for me and a search for compensation though money and social position. The priesthood, specifically the celibate priesthood, fit her goals. The skill and precision of our unconscious forces continues to amaze psychoanalysts. Those forces apportion exact measurements which mom could scarcely have understood were fashioning what was really going on in her. One hint might have been her continued gloom even after my priesthood occurred. But looking inward can hurt. If her analysis had come about, many sessions of cooperative effort with her analyst may have brought her to recognize the underpinnings of her possessiveness. She could become self-aware with the method that uncovers her infant-centered goals, allows her to welcome her son's individuality and grants her the personal freedom to become a happy grandmother.

A lady friend found out about my mother's displeasure with my marrying. She took an opportunity to speak with her when my mother was visiting us, having traveled from her home near Phoenix, Arizona. Look at the love your son and his wife has brought to their home, the friend avowed, and the security that love permits their two children to experience. The lady was well-intentioned. She thought the warm and supportive affection that my mom would find palpable in her son's home would gladden her heart about my marriage. Quite the opposite resulted; she couldn't have suspected mom's powerful unconscious motives no more than mom could fathom her hidden dynamics. Actually the lady's assurances of my marriage's presumed success infuriated my mother. My mother had nurtured for years her desire to be my partner in life. (She thought, after my father's death, that she would spend the rest of her days as my housekeeper of some church residence.) Not that she wanted sex with me; that would be grossly forbidden. But she devoutly sought to preserve her fixation that no other woman in the world would be as happy married to me as she would be. No woman could wallow as joyously in the possessing of her son as she could. That such a woman not only existed but was to her eye also really and truly married to her son evoked her wrath.

Dissolving Guilt

David Brooks observes that while religion is currently less influential, guilt persists. In his article "The Strange Persistence of Guilt" (**NYTimes**, 3/31/17) he notes how people seek methods of guilt-relief, one of them by becoming victims. Victims don't have to be responsible; someone or something else "did it to me." Original Sin is a famous one.   We take it on automatically simply by being born human. Catholic theology would have it that Baptism removes it instantly.

To die without it would be to be denied Heavenly happiness for an eternity. However it's to be noticed that the baptized are as subject to guilt feelings as anyone else. Baptism's "instant forgiveness" may remove what we inherited from Adam but our doubt about our worth adheres. Removing guilt starts with acknowledging its source in the infant's fantasies over love and hate. Baby is as yet too psychically undeveloped to recognize them as untrue and as unreal (its parent doesn't actually compete with it for mother's love). The best way to dissolve those infantile feelings over loving and hating is psychoanalytic treatment. That's how those initial conclusions we made about life and love get feelingly re-experienced. We re-experience again, now with our adult perception to shine the light on what really was going on, that what we felt − and continued to feel - guilty about has no reality to support it. It doesn't fit into living as an adult. Oedipus felt self-damning for having innocently married his mother. Similarly it was a justifiable conflict in which he slew a man who just happened to be, whom he realized later turned out to be, his father. His innocence is the point: it didn't prevent feelings of the most intense kind. You'd think it would squelch or at least modify their intensity but it didn't. Lining up against him were the facts: he actually killed his father and married his mother. The rest of we males have the advantage of our personal history chipping away at the foundation of our neurotic downgrading of sex; we didn't actually kill dad and marry mom, we just wanted to. We can compare what we felt as babies with what makes sense for us now in our adult world. We're to make choices based on that comparison. The Oedipal feelings however still hang around. Re-aligning them completely requires many hours on the psychoanalyst's couch. Oedipus was

Sophocles' invention to make a point about human psychic development. But had he been a real person, would he have been helped through psychoanalysis? Probably. Everyone's feelings differ; he felt overwhelmed. A person with duller sensibilities may have sloughed off residual guilt or just learned to live with it but Sophocles character didn't, presumably because the fact of the incest and homicide actually having occurred was too imposing. Psychoanalysis offers enlightenment through feeling again what we felt back when. He'd get a feeling-hold about matters in his life that were disrupting which he couldn't let go of.

A friend who's a medical doctor and made a lot of money at it tells me he got bored. His brother, an orthopedic surgeon, arrived at the same complaint. It came as a surprise although I'd heard it before. I'm recalling a heart specialist who started making movies and loved it. He got tired of exchanging patients' blood over and over, like "...changing crankcase oil..." (his words).   I compare that with the ever-questioning zeal of psychoanalysts I've known. Even with many years of experience behind them they meet to discuss cases every week. One of them told me, No one knows everything about this field.

Other Treatments

Many modes of psychotherapy treat mental issues like depression, panic and anxiety, phobias, eating disorders, etc. They employ parts of Freud's techniques and theories. There are the talking therapies that access the unconscious, the Cognitive which establishes short-term goals, the group and family therapies for learning about others and learning from them. Behaviorists set up constructive response patterns in lieu of destructive ones. Psychotics and schizophrenics generally face a cocktail of medications which coat synapses in the brain. Patients don't like them because it depersonalizes. Their resulting choices take them over and feel inauthentic.

The psychoanalyst has nothing to offer beyond what the analysand communicates. He listens and observes. He doesn't speak until he can put in words some uncovering the patient discloses without realizing it. It's totally personal. Each patient writes his book. It takes a long time.

The longest way is really the shortest.

The Past is Alive

We began with an Archbishop who thinks he's accomplishing what's pious. We beg to differ. We contend that neuroses support his authority in these matters. He harkens to the infantile thinking that survives unconsciously in our psyches, making us feel like Oedipus, guilty about our sexual tendencies and ambitions.

Here's what he wrote in the ***Detroit Free Press*** *(April 5, 2015)* last Sunday. "…God was made human. Humans killed God. And God, in turn, rose from the dead and killed death to liberate us humans from the prison of our own making, from our own failings."

Killed death? Not that I've noticed. There's a life and death cycle everywhere, some of it natural, some of it inflicted. No one escapes it. The Archbishop stands with many, many creeds that will assert that life endures. But it's a life after our bodies age and die. Death remains. Religions like the Archbishop's tell us that we will never die. He also leaves open our possibly smoldering in a place of limitless pain. There's a persistent hope among believers however that that limitless expanse will be spent in happiness. Obey me, the Archbishop asserts, and you'll have a good chance at a limitless happy afterlife. He offers something like a guarantee or at least what's close to it.

Obey we do. Churches offer their service. To God, they say. That's easy to say but God isn't talking. We have ample evidence of one effect they offer. They appeal to our neurotic conclusions about what's within us. Generally it takes shape by offering weekly opportunities to huddle together, heads bowed, seeking forgiveness. For their congregations they give rules, the sorts of rules that yield comfort. A couple of men at a swim and racket club today talked about their Holy Week observances. One said he and his wife over many years have attended a local university's rendition of Handel's **Messiah**. The other spoke of his church's "Maundy Thursday" liturgy. It's good, one man said, I feel so peaceful. It's such feelings of peace that ex-Catholics no longer have readily at hand. They are on their own. Peace for them might be more like a certain satisfaction with where they've arrived in life. Peace implies a degree of passivity whereas satisfaction occurs from conclusions we can come to after a steady look at life. Practical realities elicit fresh interest like the growth-enhancing adjustments love prompts us to by way of marriage, the parent devotion that helps steer children around neurotic pitfalls, the respect we bring to the variables present among our fellowmen. Charting our own map amidst a complex world is the work of a lifetime.

Models Of Non-Oedipal

Lerner and Lowe's Broadway musical **Gigi** contrasts Gaston, who's become bored with the dull women he's been meeting, with his uncle who's ever energized by male-with-female dynamics.   Then he meets Gigi.   Her beauty exudes with her enthusiasm for life's challenges.   Gaston is challenged by Gigi, at first resistant, then thoughtful, gradually putting aside his cynicism and pride. During the play's "Soliloquy" he puts is all out there: "...she's just a girl, a little girl, and so backward for her years..." Then: "...and yet there's sweeter music when she speaks, isn't there?..."   And after that: "...when did your sparkle turn to fire, and your warmth become desire?..." And eventually: "...oh, what miracle has made you the way you are?..."

There are two things to note. Gaston puts aside his pride and independence.   We see joy in giving. Growth through humility.   Additionally we see a lover uninhibitedly embracing the worth of love-making. Orgasm is its blessing.   It's to be at lovers' service, meaning the Oedipal is denied entrance.

In this context you may wish to re-read Mary Carr's poem on page 75 where you'll find another model of the comfort we may wish we all had with sexual expression.   She uses a common female partnering in sexual intercourse to convey the exuding of beautiful music.

In the following subtler model find open-mindedness, a respect for when a person's doing as much as he can manage in life and the practice of setting aside one's prejudices in order to listen.   A glimpse at what such as that could achieve is provided in Leo Tolstoy's **War and Peace**; *Book IV, Part 3, Chapter 13.*   He fashions a self-reliant character admirable for a realistic stance he's arrived at that goes beyond what I feel are Oedipally-induced searchings for personal peace. It reads:

"There was a new feature in Pierre's relations with Willarski, with the princess, the doctor and all the people he met now, which gained for him universal goodwill. This was his acknowledgement of the freedom of everybody to think, feel and see things in his own way – his recognition of the impossibility of altering a man's convictions by words. This legitimate individuality of every man's views, which in the old days used to trouble and irritate Pierre, now formed the basis of the sympathy he felt for and the interest he took in other people. This diversity, sometimes the complete contradiction between men's opinions and their lives, and between one man and another, pleased Pierre and drew from him a gentle, satirical smile."

We want to get along with our fellows and need to. It could begin with recognizing the near impossibility of changing another's mind. Look how difficult it is to change your own! Acceptance of our fellows starts with getting along with, and maybe forgiving, ourselves. Humanity feels edgy about its goodness. Many feel better when they fast, kneel, humble themselves. Some feel it more than others. Words and rituals, relics, daily halts to normal commerce for prayer, fasting, reverent music, colors and sounds make a God who never shows up seem present. A religion's success rests in making God feel real.

For this the population will give money, lots of it. Churches do well everywhere among the poor as well as the rich. There's the universal feeling that worship might insure good fortune, maybe in this life, assuredly in the next. Churches assure us there's a "next". They can't do much about guaranteeing our good fortune now but the hereafter, that's where they can offer guarantees because that's what they "control."   People figure there's no harm in going along with religion's promises. After I'm dead maybe I can "cash in" on its claims. If nothing happens, at least I haven't invested too much. But if an eternity of happiness happens, I've done well.

Beyond such claims, assertions and promises is something else the Archbishop promulgates. He says we have made a prison for ourselves. Our "failings" built it.   God rose from death to "liberate us…" from the results of our failings.

What failings? When, where and by whom? The fellow who bought our car sent me a brochure with red-lettered quotes from St. Paul who told everyone who would listen to him that we were all sinners. Many did listen and still do. That's the approach the Archbishop takes in last Sunday's **Free Press**. He will find the same proportion of believers in our day as St. Paul found in his.

People find remedy in accepting the label of sinfulness because it fits a need.   Religious authority doubles down on that. God is peoples' design, not the other way around.   We expect him to be as big as daddy was felt to be when we first encountered "him" as infants. You may find insights you can rely on in the same kind of inner sense of wrong Sophocles detailed in **Oedipus Rex**. Plunging metal broaches into his eye sockets was Oedipus's desperate effort at atonement. He had had sex with his mother - the ultimate perversion.

Young lovers used to kneel before me at their wedding Masses. They felt better about sexual love expression when I blessed it first. I "blessed" them. Not

I surely, I was a human like they. Rather, garbed in "sacred" garments and touching gold-plated vessels in sacred rituals, I seemed close enough to the Eternal One to bring their self-doubting to quietude. If the only assurances they had before sharing love making were to get a marriage license and call in some friends and family to help them celebrate their commitment, they'd feel a bit uncomfortable. They wanted "permission", from God if they can get it. You've read these pages so you know why. What we repress into our unconsciousness continues to govern our choices.

F. Scott Fitzgerald had empathy for the weight humanity totes throughout life. This is how he chose to end his enduring work ***The Great Gatsby***: ***So we beat on, boats against the current, borne back ceaselessly into the past.***

Acknowledgements

Bringing a book to press involves many people I'll never see, referring to those who work with formatting, spelling and grammatical checking, and the art work and language placement on the front and back covers. But quite apart from the practicalities is the plain fact that the book has an author, a living and breathing person with his lifetime of widely varying relationships and experiences, all of which impact him feelingly – and so they endure. Somewhat diminished are my memory's images of people that go way back. The nature of this book's musings call upon influences from my earliest years that have as much impact as my earnest discussions with my wife.

Accordingly I remember Bill Keveney from early grade school. We surprised each other when we next met to take the entrance exam at the Sacred Heart Seminary. He would become a goad to "write fifteen minutes a day" to develop a writing skill. Dan Murphy and I were ordained on the same day and 61 years of friendship were to follow. In graduate school at the University of Detroit I met Dr. Mel Weinberg who became a mentor and friend. I had also entered into my personal analysis with Dr. Marvin Hyman to whom I am especially grateful. Over many years he kept a necessary distance in order to keep a lean focus on unraveling a tangle of defensiveness. The revivification he occasioned inevitably benefited my eventual wife and two kids. I'm deeply grateful to him.

It was our son to whom it occurred to say, You've had a varied life, you should write a book. Kate, our daughter, couldn't choose not to enlighten me, observing her wondrous formation into womanhood. She enjoys her peers, always has. By her sophomore year she had decided that Buddhism was gentler than Catholicism. Her modest manner inspires me to imitation; it's proving to be useful in today's contentious environment. My wife's (Pat) spontaneous interest in anything interpersonal, fused to her wish to share with me through vigorous conversation, was bound to burnish my bookish approach with a valuing of whatever warm-bloodedness I was finding inside my psyche. Besides she loves books and Beethoven – and me.

Without giving details, the loss of our family fortune some fifteen years ago had us seeking more modest housing in a condominium complex. Front doors empty into a terraced court so residents are always bumping into each other. When I mentioned filling a book with my thoughts about the current Church, some neighbors began a continuum of constant encouragement. They thought the book would do a lot of good. Other neighbors are ever contributing to our sunny milieu and they do my heart good. Until recently I'd meet with an ex-priest to drink coffee and sit together and talk. He's accomplished 30 years of sobriety with alcoholism. We'd talk of living with and without religion with his purview consistently that of the supernatural which confronted and deepened my thinking. Another soul-mate with a penetrating intellect and a generous heart is a solid friend. We meet bi-monthly. He's reviewed previous manuscripts of mine over the years and spent a lot of time to come up with well-balanced suggestions.

When it came down to setting up the manuscript's final drafts, Carol Masters was a sine-quo-non. She spent hours with formatting and coordinating data from our home computer to the PDF receiver that targets placements, dozens of them. I marvel at people like her. They give much and find delight in doing so.